The Miseducation of Women

THE MISEDUCATION
OF WOMEN

James Tooley

IVAN R. DEE
Chicago

To my sister, Rachel, with much love and some trepidation.

The publishers wish to thank the following for permission to quote from copyrighted materials: from *Bridget Jones's Diary* and *Bridget Jones: The Edge of Reason* by Helen Fielding, published by Macmillan, London, UK, reprinted by permission of Pan Macmillan; from *Alas, Poor Darwin* by Hilary and Steven Rose, published by Jonathan Cape, reprinted by permission of the Random House Group Ltd.; from *The Mating Mind* by Geoffrey Miller, published by William Heinemann, reprinted by permission of the Random House Group Ltd.; from *Misconceptions* by Naomi Wolf, published by Chatto & Windus, reprinted by permission of the Random House Group Ltd.; from *Answering Back: Girls, Boys and Feminism in Schools* by Jane Kenway and Sue Willis, published by Routledge.

Every effort has been made to locate owners of copyrighted material, but the author and the publishers will be pleased to hear from those not acknowledged here so that full acknowledgment may be made in future editions.

Library of Congress Cataloging-in-Publication Data:
Tooley, James.
    The miseducation of women / James Tooley.
      p. cm.
    Includes bibliographical references and index.
    ISBN 1-56663-544-6 (alk. paper)
    1. Feminism and education—Great Britain—History. 2. Feminism and education—United States—History. 3. Gender identity in education—Great Britain. 4. Gender identity in education—United States. 5. Education—Social aspects—Great Britain—History—20th century. 6. Education—Social aspects—United States—History—20th century. I. Title.
    LC197.T66 2003
    371.822—dc21   2003053208

Contents

Acknowledgements

I have been thinking about this book, on and off, since 1996, thanks to Michael Irwin who invited me on a study visit to New Zealand where I again started to think through feminist ideas in education. Thanks to all the academics who met me there and who gave willingly of their time and expertise in this area. Since then, of course, I have discussed these ideas with many women and men, most of whom I suspect would not wish to be mentioned here, but thanks to them all, particularly those with whom I have discussed these ideas at conferences and seminars in the United Kingdom, America, Canada, Japan and India. However, a few friends must be named: in Newcastle Upon Tyne, Christine Skelton, Carrie Sharman, Bruce Carrington, John Taylor, Matt Ridley and David Bell have all helped me formulate the ideas in this book. Bruce came up with a keen-witted title for the book which unfortunately was too clever by half. Above all, thanks to Pauline Dixon who read the whole manuscript and gave constructive advice and support, as always. Moving south, Richard Bailey has been a steady source of helpful comment and rigorous, critical debate. Sir Robert Balchin, Kenneth Minogue and Antony Flew have warmly encouraged me in this endeavour, as have Leon Louw from South Africa, and Terence Kealey and Charlie Brooker in Buckingham. Across the Atlantic, Lisa Oliphant helped inspire me early on with the book, and found numerous American sources. Katie McNinch read earlier drafts, and gave tips and enthusiasm for the project, as well as more American sources.

Anthony Haynes, my editor, I thank, as always, for his loyal support, direction and friendship. Finally, I wish to thank the three academic referees who gave so generously of their time and energy in reviewing this book. They provided a model of what it means to take part in academic debate, paying meticulous attention to detail, robustly critical but always in the most courteous fashion. I could not have asked for better help, and they renewed my faith in what we endeavour to do in the universities: if there are places where the argument is sound in this book, then it owes much to their insightful comments. I cannot name them; they were anonymous, but the sincerest thanks to them.

Introduction to the American Edition

I

When this book was first published in England last year, the London *Evening Standard* sent a very personable young woman, Alison Roberts, to interview me in a snug West End hotel. We took afternoon tea and chatted amiably about women and men and, at her gentle prompting, our relationships, past and present. The next day the two-page spread had a screaming four-inch headline: IS THIS THE MOST ABSURD MAN IN BRITAIN TODAY?

I'd become resigned to such things. Indeed, in the month surrounding the publication of *The Miseducation of Women* I had the uncomfortable satisfaction of appearing daily on some British or international television or radio program, or in the print media, castigated by feminist writers, young and old, for my "Neanderthal," "scurrilous," "envious" and "narcissistic" — to list a few of the more printable epithets — views.

But here's a conundrum. At the same time each of these feminists was telling me that I was completely out of touch with modern women, lost in some misguided fifties' romanticism, I was receiving literally hundreds of phone calls, letters, e-mails, cell-phone messages even, from women thanking me for writing the book. (I had one letter from a man too, from a maximum-security prison in Cambridgeshire, but his views are best left without comment.) Indeed, the article in the *Evening Standard*, circulated widely on American websites, prompted some of the most supportive correspondence: "Don't listen to what she's saying about you," the letters went. "Her overreaction only indicates the way in which you've touched feminism's raw nerve."

Full-time mothers thanked me for speaking out on their behalf, telling society that what they do is valuable and not to be despised. There were also young mothers impossibly trying to juggle careers and babies, feeling depressed in their new roles and relieved to hear of an alternative perspective on their situation. And, perhaps most poignantly of all, there were numerous letters from young women saying that I had described something they only dared think about in secret – that my book had empowered them to discuss this openly with their friends. Here's a twenty-two-year-old from Portland, Oregon (printed with her permission):

> I'm trying to get into graduate school, so that I can have a tremendous career. All of my young single female friends are in the same boat, but all of us secretly wish to be married with children. It's like we're not allowed to admit it because we've just spent all this time, money and energy at college. But how can I justify spending so much more time, money and energy on a grad degree I have no intention of using when I would much rather be making a loving home for my future husband and children?

Letters such as these made me wonder who was more out of touch with the concerns of modern women, me or the feminists.

II

This book was always intended for an American as well as a British audience, and throughout I refer to the situation in the United States and to its feminist literature. Indeed, it's clear that where American feminism has led, the rest of the world has followed. If we're to stand any chance of challenging where we've gotten to, we have to start by addressing American concerns. And where is it that we've gotten to? We have a problem at the heart of our schools. Current education policy, in the United States above all, religiously aped by other countries, is not in the interests of women. Many people talk about the injustice being committed against boys as they pass through schooling. But a much more serious injustice is being perpetrated against girls. It allows them to pass through schooling unscathed and with flying colors – unlike boys – but kicks in when they are older. The injustice against girls emerges when they reach Bridget Jones's age.

Visiting a high school in the United States to discuss my book, I talked to some wonderfully bright, articulate and sophisticated young women, sixteen, seventeen and eighteen years old. All had high-flying ambitions. They were going to be lawyers, doctors, CEOs, famous politicians. The one thing they may well not be is mothers. If present trends continue, perhaps two-thirds of these professional women will be childless by the time they reach their late thirties. And 90 per cent of them will profoundly regret it.

When they reach their late thirties, many may look back on the way they approached their most fertile and sexually powerful years and wonder why the only priority their education instilled in them was to rise to the top of their careers. They may wonder why their teachers thought the only appropriate life-plan for them was the one that clearly suits young men but may not have suited them at all. Perhaps they will say then, like the older woman (recorded by Betty Friedan) who had been at the forefront of the feminist revolution: "It was exciting at first, breaking in where women never were before. Now it's just a job. But it's the devastating loneliness that's the worst. There has to be some better way to live. A woman alone . . ."

And it's not just high-flying girls. Such attitudes have filtered down to the whole of womanhood, so that young women who previously may have been content to find fulfillment in family life are now forced to believe that the only way they will find satisfaction is in work. For young women today, absolutely nothing in their schooling, in the overt or the hidden curriculum, tells them that they may want to choose different priorities than boys do. From the role models held up on graduation day, to their career counseling, to the constant emphasis on achievement, everything tells them they can gain status and respect only by aping men – in work, business, politics or sports.

In America, just as in Britain, it is in fact illegal for a career counselor to suggest, however gently, to a young woman that she may want to choose motherhood or family life. Title IX of the 1972 Education Act enforces "gender equity" on all schools in receipt of federal funds – which in practice turns out to be the vast majority. And gender equity means, above all, that young women must become as hungry as men for careers, in order to steer them away from motherhood – to aim "higher than hairdressing," as one British minister for women put it. The only time the family and home receive mention in the British National Curriculum Aims is in the context of girls and boys challenging outmoded stereotypes. And in America, celebrating twenty-five years of Title IX, the secretary of education put it this way: "Somewhere in America today there are young women who are studying hard and achieving success on the athletic field who even now may be thinking hard about their careers as scientists, business owners, basketball players, or even the possibility of becoming president of the United States." Such women "can succeed and be part of the American Dream." And the American Dream, let us be clear, is about the achievement of women – the same as for men – in science, business, sports and politics. Family and home life are merely inconveniences, places that women must escape from in order to succeed.

For high school girls it is totally incomprehensible to hear someone like me pointing to statistics about women's potential lack of fulfillment later in life, asking if this isn't something they should be told about while still in school.

III

How did we come to arrive at such a sorry situation, where schooling pushes many women – certainly not all, but I'm not worried about those women who currently thrive – into a position where what they may prefer in their lives, motherhood and domesticity, are banished from their education?

There's nothing accidental about it, actually. The early feminists set out to denigrate domesticity, and boy, did they succeed. When I was discussing these issues on the BBC with Germaine Greer, our most famous adopted feminist, she was adamant that it was men who were to blame for trashing domesticity and motherhood. I couldn't believe what I was hearing from her! I'm sorry, Germaine, but the blame lies unequivocally with feminism here. In *The Feminine Mystique*, Betty Friedan described the housewife as a "parasite," her life akin to a prisoner in a Nazi concentration camp. She was only echoing Simone de Beauvoir, who in *The Second Sex* described married women as "leeches," "praying mantises" and "poisonous creatures." And, most gallingly of all, both admitted that women needed to be "forced to be free," because many – most? – women would not perceive themselves as being remotely oppressed in the roles that feminism has now succeeded in denigrating. As de Beauvoir put it in conversation with Betty Friedan in 1975: "No woman should be authorized to stay at home to raise her children. *Women should not have that choice, precisely because if there is such a choice, too many women will make that one.*" Or, as she put it thirty-six years earlier in *The Second Sex*: "What is extremely demoralizing for the woman who aims at self-sufficiency is the existence of other women of like social status . . . who live as parasites. . . . A comfortably married or supported friend *is a temptation in the way of one who is intending to make her own success.*"

Such sentiments were proudly taken up by education feminists, who even today write about the liberation of women from "domestic drudgery" and the "predicament" of motherhood, sentiments that pervade the schooling of all girls, working class and professional, in America and wherever American influence reaches. These early feminists believed that by denigrating domesticity and motherhood they would liberate women to something better. But their hopes have not been realized.

So what is to be done? In this book I don't spend much time on prescriptions – perhaps I should have, but I genuinely thought *that* would have been too galling for women to hear. I could set out what I saw as the problem. It surely was pushing my luck to tell women what to do next. I do have some tentative suggestions in the final chapter of the book, but I wanted to open the discussion, not to say that I have all the answers. My suggestions have to do with what I see as the crucial issue, that there must be no more sacred cows in education. If the educational system is not delivering what many women prefer in their lives, we must be honest about this. We must allow schools to be freed from the fetters of Title IX and the Sex Discrimination Act, able to take into account gender differences when it comes to career counseling, learning styles, grading and curriculum. Most critically, let's feel relaxed about the fact – for it is a fact – that girls and boys in general may prefer different pursuits later in their lives. And, most important, they may prefer to start planning for such differences even while they are still in school. Rather than juggling babies and careers, or missing out on babies altogether, perhaps young women might want to consider having their family first and their career later.

But, feminists have argued against me, women can't possibly do that, because families need two incomes in order to survive. This was a line of attack I hadn't really anticipated, or not realized that for some feminists it would be their strongest line of attack. It must be poppycock, though. How can it be that in the United States, the richest society this planet has ever known, families cannot afford the division of labor of home and working life that is simply taken for granted in even the poorest societies? Looking at the British statistics — and the American ones reveal the same — shows it is nonsense. Going back to the early 1970s when Germaine Greer was writing *The Female Eunuch*, official figures from the Household Expenditure Survey in Britain show something quite remarkable. When most families were headed by a single male breadwinner, average weekly household expenditure on the essentials — housing, fuel, food and clothing — was roughly the same as today (at constant prices, £148 then compared to £160 now, i.e., $92.50 compared to $100). Housing costs have risen, but the price of food and clothing has fallen. If a male breadwinner could provide the essentials of life thirty years ago, he could certainly easily provide the same today. What has changed is the extent of our spending on luxury goods, childcare, leisure and vacations abroad — expenditures on these categories have more than doubled during that period (from £55 to £117, i.e., $34.38 to $73.13). And automobile expenses too have nearly doubled during the same period. My secretary takes at least two foreign vacations a year, and her family has two cars, one for her and the children and one for her husband, and all the children have color televisions and computers in their bedrooms.

So there you have it. We've swapped a society where women could be full-time mothers — a role that many found fulfilling and satisfying — for one that fuels consumerism and clogs our roads with second cars on the drive to school, where spoiled children, buried under mountains of toys they can't be bothered to play with, watch suggestive TV shows in their lonely bedrooms. And we have this partly because the equality feminists forced us to believe that motherhood was parasitic, the housewife a leech.

IV

I worry about those high school girls I met in America. I feel guilty that an educational system of which I am a part will lead inexorably to a majority of them having lives that may not be fulfilling for them. It's time we said: Thus far and no further. That's why I wrote the book. And notwithstanding all the criticisms that have been thrown my way since it was first published, I'm prepared to stand by its central thesis. I'm looking forward to debating it in America.

Daisy Cottage
Northumberland, England
June 2003

The Miseducation of Women

1

The Bridget Jones Syndrome

I worry about Bridget Jones. I worry about my part in her downfall. Bridget Jones, heroine of *Bridget Jones's Diary*, the best-selling novel by Helen Fielding, started life in a weekly newspaper column in 1995. The popularity of the column led to the novel, which led to the sequel *Bridget Jones: The Edge of Reason* and then the film, which has become one of the most popular British movies ever.

Bridget Jones is intelligent, works first in publishing, then in television, is thirty-something, and – this is what defines her – is single and not happy with it. Like all her single friends, she is obsessed with finding a man, going into 'marriage frenzy' in her search for a husband and father of her children.

Bridget Jones has become an icon for young and not-so-young women everywhere, not only in Britain but across the world. The first novel has sold over four million copies in 30 countries. The rave reviews and massive sales indicate that she is describing something 'true to the marrow'[1] for women today.

Just over thirty years before Bridget Jones was conceived – or, to put it another way, around the time she would have been conceived, biologically speaking (if fictional characters can be thought of as being biologically conceived) – Betty Friedan, the 'founding mother of modern feminism',[2] finally faced up to the 'problem that has no name'. This is how she put it then:

> The problem lay buried, unspoken, for many years in the minds of American women. It was a strange stirring, a sense of

1

dissatisfaction, a yearning that women suffered in the middle of the twentieth century. . . . For over fifteen years there was no word of this yearning in the millions of words written about women, for women, in all the columns, books and articles by experts telling women their role was to seek fulfilment as wives and mothers. Over and over women heard . . . that they could desire no greater destiny than to glory in their own feminin-ity. . . . They learned that truly feminine women do not want careers, higher education, political rights – the independence and the opportunities that the old-fashioned feminists fought for.

The argument of this book is that there is a new 'problem that has no name' confronting women today. It too results in profound dissatisfac-tion and yearning. For the past 30 or 40 years there has been little written about this yearning. Women have been told that they must seek fulfilment in a career. They have been told over and over again that the greatest destiny is to glory in the marketplace and public space. Independence and opportunities are theirs in abundance in careers, higher education and politics. Today's problem that has no name is the fact that none of this has rid women of their dissatisfaction and yearning. It has made it far, far worse.

In the last chapter of her book, Betty Friedan revealed the 'final piece of the puzzle' as to what keeps women in their place, trapped in femininity rather than grasping the opportunities of the market: 'The key to the trap is, of course, education.' This is also the key to the problem that has no name today. It is through their schooling, at least in part, that girls grow into the women they are, learning the lessons of independence, equality with boys and the overriding import-ance of their careers. If the problem is to be addressed, then it must be to their education that the focus is turned.

Friedan coined the phrase 'the Feminine Mystique' to describe what she saw as the problem facing women back in the 1960s. The problem, as she saw it, was that women 'are kept from growing to their full human capacities', deprived of meaning, fulfilment and self-discovery by the beguiling mystique that surrounded femininity, motherhood and housewifery. To describe today's diametrically opposed problem, I've coined the phrase 'the Bridget Jones Syndrome'.

Women, said Betty Friedan, concluding her book in poetic optimism, confident that they alone had the world as their oyster,

> can stretch and stretch until their own efforts will tell them who they are. They will not need the regard of boy or man to feel alive. And when women do not need to live through their husbands and children . . . [w]ho knows what women can be when they are finally free to become themselves? Who knows what women's intelligence will contribute . . . ?[3]

Indeed, who knows? As it happens, Bridget Jones's creator, Helen Fielding, did write a book of which Betty Friedan would have approved, about a woman stretching and stretching to her limits, free to be herself. Fielding summed it up thus: 'Well, my first book was about a woman running a refugee camp in Africa. No one bought it.' *Bridget Jones's Diary* 'is about a woman struggling to lose weight, and four million women all over the world bought it'.[4]

Betty Friedan optimistically predicted that 'the time is at hand when the voices of the feminine mystique can no longer drown out the inner voice that is driving women on to become complete'. Forty years later, the symbol for young women encapsulating 'the search of women for themselves' is not Friedan's 'complete women'. Instead, it is a woman who is drowning her sorrows in glass after glass of Chardonnay, the feminine mystique now unobtainable but infinitely attractive, her inner voice crying out for relief from her independence.

Forty years after Friedan's optimism, young women, upon reaching thirty-something having pursued careers and 'liberated' sexual relations – that is, where men have commitment-free sex – are now more than ever obsessed with 'the regard of boy or man to feel alive'. Their icon is a young woman making New Year's resolutions that she will not go around sulking any more about not having a boyfriend, but will 'develop inner poise and authority and sense of self as woman of substance, complete *without* boyfriend – ' (Betty Friedan sighs with relief) ' – as best way to obtain boyfriend' (relief vanishes).

Far from being the liberating route to self-fulfilment, going to work 'has become like going to a party in order to get off with someone'. But work is full of 'single girls over thirty. Fine physical specimens. Can't get a chap.' The new icon for women today is obsessive about getting a man, yet 'the nation's young men have been proved by surveys to be *completely unmarriageable*'. And the sexual revolution has left her ill-equipped to deal with them. After a first date where she submits easily to his sexual desire, she sits waiting, agonisingly, by the phone: 'How can it be that the situation between the sexes after a first night remains so agonizingly imbalanced? Feel as if I have just sat an exam and must wait for my results.' And all the self-help books in the world, filtered through the minds of her supportive single friends, cannot stop her preventing the man from taking advantage of her.

Under the Bridget Jones Syndrome, life becomes an agonizing ordeal, every day 'constantly scanning face in mirror for wrinkles and frantically reading *Hello!*, checking out everyone's ages in desperate search for role models (Jane Seymour is forty-two!)'. She has reached the age when men of her own age 'no longer find their contemporaries attractive'. Life suddenly seems like 'a game of musical chairs where girls without a chair/man when the music stops/they pass thirty are "out"'. Being Bridget Jones is about looking back wistfully to the days when you could wear 'v. short coat and boots' and have 'lewd catcalls and embarrassing remarks' thrown your way; now dressed provocatively in the same attire, regretfully none come.

Her friends rave that 'too many women are wasting their young lives having children in their twenties, thirties and early forties when they should be concentrating on their careers', but once the Chardonnay has worn off, it all seems so empty. Who wants a career when you don't have the man, and cannot mother his child? For the Bridget Jones Syndrome is about wanting a baby more than anything – having a pregnancy 'scare', on the one hand she feels 'irrepressibly fecund!'. But because she has no security in relationships, and no chance of the man committing, this is all dampened with the terrible fear of turning into 'a hideous grow-bag-cum-milk-dispensing-machine which no one will fancy and which will not fit into any of my trousers, particularly my brand new acid-green Agnés B Jeans'. The confusion, she thinks, is the price she must pay for being 'a modern woman'. She tries to console herself with this thought, of being at the cutting edge of the 'modern woman' revolution, that she can just have fun, with her own income and home, and not 'need to wash anyone else's socks'. She can console herself that she is part of the 'pioneer generation daring to refuse to compromise in love and relying on our own economic power', mouthing words in the timeworn, now stale, style of Friedan, hoping that in 'twenty years' time' everything will be all right.[5]

This was what Betty Friedan thought in 1963, then again in 1981 at the time of her next major book, *The Second Stage*. I think it is time to put a stop to this and to say that in twenty years' time it won't all be fine. The new problem with no name – the Bridget Jones Syndrome – and its source in the education of girls and boys urgently needs to be addressed. That is the aim of this book. It sets the Syndrome in the context of feminist writings on education and, more broadly, in the context of reforms and a changing landscape that have altered schooling beyond recognition. It asks whether a terrible injustice is being committed against women because of feminism. Some are now worried about injustice being perpetrated against boys as they pass through schooling.[6] The novel argument of this book is that a much more serious injustice is being perpetrated against girls, that allows them to pass through schooling unscathed and with flying colours – unlike for boys – but which kicks in when they are older, when they reach Bridget Jones' certain age.

Some readers might think that I am getting rather carried away with this character, who, whatever her charms, is after all only a fictional creation. Perhaps I am taking her predicament too much to heart? But it turns out that four million women are not wrong. Survey after survey, not to mention anecdote after anecdote, all point in the same direction. Women's magazines are full of stories about women's current unhappiness and surveys to explore why. *Top Santé* – 'the UK's best-selling health and beauty magazine' – for instance, revealed in its summer 2001 survey that 'only nine per cent of working women (and four per cent of women with pre-school children) say they choose to work full-time'. In fact, if given the chance, '78 per cent of all working women' would quit their jobs tomorrow if they could. And a similar percentage think that their work is damaging their health, 'causing ailments such as headaches, constant exhaustion, backache, anxiety, forgetfulness, insomnia, irritable bowel syndrome and migraine'. 'Family life', says the report, 'is being driven to breaking point' by women's current lifestyles.[7]

It is not only women's magazines that support this claim. Germaine Greer, in her latest number one best-seller *The Whole Woman*, summarizes her review of all the evidence: in the 30 years since she wrote her own feminist classic *The Female Eunuch*, 'Women's lives have become more, not less, difficult.' She finds it deeply ironic that this should be the case. Because of the revolution she helped to inspire, 'Women no longer feel that they have to stay in unhappy relationships or that they have to bear children against their will'. So we should expect 'female malaise to diminish', as 'more and more women walk out of oppressive marriages' and claim their independence. Not so. 'The evidence', she says, shows 'that it is getting worse. Thirty years ago we heard nothing about panic attacks, or anorexia or self-mutilation. Now the ikons of female suffering are all around us . . .'[8]

Backing up Greer's position, endorsing the findings in the women's magazines, giving substance to Bridget Jones's angst, other research reveals the same increasing unhappiness. A survey of 1100 women conducted by the Policy Studies Institute, funded by a government research council, shows that 'the struggle to balance work and home life has become harder over the past decade'. Women who have children are working more hours than ever before. The report tries to put a positive gloss on this: the increase in working hours 'could be seen as part of an emancipation of women from the demands of childcare'. Emancipation? This is hard to square with the finding that the change has actually 'been accompanied by a sharp fall in the satisfaction of women'.[9]

Finally, perhaps the most comprehensive survey on the happiness and fulfilment of men and women was published recently. The survey examined well-being data on 100,000 randomly sampled Americans and Britons from the early 1970s to the late 1990s. It found that reported levels of happiness have declined overall in this period in the USA, while life satisfaction is about the same in Great Britain. But most interestingly, despite this overall decline, American men have grown happier. So what has caused the decline? It is women's well-being that has dramatically fallen during that period. Women in the late 1990s are very nearly 20 per cent less happy than they were in the early 1970s, and the British data give 'noticeably similar results'.

Bridget Jones in particular feels uncomfortable around the 'smug marrieds'. The statistics suggest why. For women, the research shows that a stable marriage is the single greatest predictor of happiness. In simple monetary terms, being married for Bridget Jones might be worth at least an additional $100,000 per year in terms of satisfaction, every year of her life. The key conclusion drawn by the British and American researchers is unequivocal: reforms for gender equity across society have 'not been successful in either country in creating rising well-being among women'.[10]

Bridget Jones' distress is based in reality. Bridget Jones is putting flesh on to the bare bones of recent statistics, and women recognize the flesh as their own. Forty years after Betty Friedan 'exploded the myth of the Feminine Mystique' (as the cover of the Penguin edition of her book puts it), 30 years after Germaine Greer incited women to their sexual liberation, women are far more unhappy then they ever were in the past.

BETTY FRIEDAN MEETS BRIDGET JONES

Perhaps this is all being a little unfair to Betty Friedan (and also to Germaine Greer, as we shall see below). For, although Bridget Jones would have been impossible to imagine as an outcome of her revolution back in 1963, by the time of *The Second Stage* Betty Friedan finds herself worrying about similar women.

Indeed, she herself notes similar disturbing statistics to those reviewed above, although she was still hopeful that these were only teething troubles, and young women were simply adjusting to their new found freedom. Studies, she says, conducted in 1954, 1959 to 1962 and repeated in the 1970s, reveal young women 'experiencing more signs of psychological stress than women in their twenties and thirties had in the 1950s and early 1960s, and were slightly more likely to feel on the edge of "nervous breakdown" than young men'. The effect kicked in most of all between the ages of 35 to 39, where 'nearly one out of three women in the 1970s reported an actual or impending "nervous breakdown" compared with only 23 per cent of women that age in the previous decade'. It does not seem much consolation to tell these young women, as she does, that these choices are 'in fact, improving lifelong psychological well-being for women', so they should just stick with them, and all will be well. But all is not well twenty years' later; the downward trend has continued. And the reasons for this are the same as those Friedan highlights in her interviews and anecdotes.

By the time of *The Second Stage*, Betty Friedan is having a stream of second thoughts about the process she has set in train. She admits that the whole thing has gone too far – and that there was now an equally as insidious '*feminist* mystique' to combat. It's odd; I don't see this book on gender education reading lists now, where *The Feminine Mystique* still has pride of place. To be fair, I don't see it mentioned much by anti-feminists either, where Betty Friedan is still vilified as the person who set it all going. Helen Fielding must have read *The Second Stage*, however, since her characters are all there in embryonic form.

In her book, Friedan is 'tired' of the concerns of the 'women's movement'; she is now 'nagged by a new, uneasy urgency' that won't leave her alone: something awfully wrong has been precipitated by women's liberation. For young women, even back in the early 1980s, have begun to flood her with 'undertones of pain and puzzlement, a queasiness, an uneasiness, almost a bitterness that they hardly dare admit'. The new problem that has no name, already revealed, even back in 1981. But they do admit their pain to her. These are young women who are suddenly realizing that they are *envying* the life Betty Friedan was living *before* feminism – and feel they have been sold a pass, discovering the fact too late.

There is the 'lovely' young woman in her late twenties in California, on a promotion path to vice-presidency in the television company, who wants to talk to Friedan alone before her boss arrives. She could almost have been the inspiration for Bridget Jones in her second job, apart, that is, from being '"dressed for success" like a model in the latest *Vogue*'. She talks to Friedan 'defensive' yet 'accusing': 'I know I'm lucky to have this job . . . but you people who fought for these things [already] had your families. You already had your men and children. What are we supposed to do?' Perhaps this young woman's angst would not have been mollified upon reading Friedan's glowing accounts of her own family life, even while she was writing her feminist tracts:

All the years I was working on *The Feminine Mystique*, I would blithely stop writing when my little daughter came home from school, or my boys were in a Little League or basketball game, or to make a martini when my husband got home, fix dinner, argue, go to the movies, make love, join an expedition to the supermarket or a country auction on Saturday, organize a clam-bake on the beach at Fire Island, take the kids over the battlefield at Gettysburg, or camping on Cape Hatteras – the stuff of family life. *We took all that for granted.*

Like Bridget Jones's 'smug married' friend Magda, who appears completely insensitive to the desperate effect the descriptions of her supposedly mundane married life have on her unhappy singleton sisters, it is almost as if Betty Friedan is deliberately rubbing it in for the poor lonely woman of today. It is these simple delights, as described by Friedan in apparently absorbingly tender detail, that the lonely young woman cannot now take for granted. She cannot take them for granted because Friedan changed the rules.

The stories of pain go on and on. A trial lawyer tells her: 'When I got pregnant, my husband and I both got depressed; it would interfere with our careers. I had an abortion. Today, it's not so exciting, just being a cog in the corporate machine. I envy my sister with the three-year-old child and her boy going on six.' Then there's the New York woman 'in her thirties' who has just been promoted, who tells her: 'I'm up against the clock, you might say. If I don't have a child now, it will be too late. But it's an agonizing choice. . . . If I don't have a baby, will I miss out on life somehow? Will I really be fulfilled as a woman?'

Here's a producer of a news show, a 'competent, seasoned professional in her late thirties', who had been told by her mother, 'Don't do what I did. Have a career, *do* something with your life. Don't depend on anyone else.' And she was scared of giving up her independence. But then,

I began to be obsessed about having children. Every woman my age is agonizing about that, whether they admit it or not. After all those years of proving I could do these jobs as well as any man, I began to feel something very strong about being a woman. I realized that I did want to have a child.

Finally, one's heart goes out to an 'older woman in Ohio', who says:

> I was the first woman in management here. I gave everything to the job. It was exciting at first, breaking in where women never were before. Now it's just a job. But it's the devastating loneliness that's the worst. I can't stand coming back to this apartment alone every night. I'd like a house, maybe a garden. Maybe I should have a kid, even without a father. At least then I'd have a family. There has to be some better way to live. A woman alone. . . .'

Friedan hears all these stories. She hears, too, the criticisms that the women's movement is being blamed for the growing insecurity of 'housewives who can no longer count on husbands for lifelong support'. Feminism is being blamed for 'the destruction of the family', the 'rising divorce rate' and the 'apathy and moral delinquency' of young people. She believes that these criticisms cannot simply be shrugged off as part of 'enemy propaganda',[11] what Susan Faludi was later to call the 'backlash'.[12] No, she says, there may be something in it all: 'I think we must at least admit and begin openly to discuss feminist denial of the importance of family, of women's own needs to give and get love and nurture, tender loving care.' she continues: 'What worries me today is the agonizing conflicts young and not-so-young women are facing – or denying – as they come up against the biological clock, at thirty-five, thirty-six, thirty-nine, forty, and cannot "choose" to have a child.'

In 1981, Betty Friedan knows that a rethink of feminism is desperately needed. With admirable candour, she wrote:

> I and other feminists dread to admit or discuss out loud these troubling symptoms because the women's movement has, in fact, been the source and focus of so much of our own energy and strength and security, its root and support, for so many years. . . . But we can't go on denying these puzzling symptoms of distress. If they mean something is seriously wrong, we had better find out and change direction yet again – *as much as we ourselves resist such change now* – before it is too late.

But change is hard. Because many women have 'almost a religious feeling . . . about the women's movement', a 'sacredness, a reverence, an awe'; it *keeps us from asking those questions* about what really matters to women now. And so inconsistencies appear. She notes young women's angst, but then seems compelled to perpetuate it: she tells the story of a young woman in Florida who had invited her to speak at a feminist week at her university: 'slim, dark, assured, a sorority girl, and very ambitious . . . she confessed, she'd already been offered a job when she graduated'. The job was in Boston, 'but her boyfriend was at law school in Miami'. Not so much Bridget Jones, more Ally McBeal this time.

Betty probes her and asks her about her commitment to equal opportunities. The young woman retorts, 'I've never been discriminated against'. Betty is 'appalled', incensed. Slipping quickly back into feminist dogma, she tells her that she could never have gone to college or got the easy job offer if it hadn't been for feminism: 'I don't care how smart you are', she lectures her prissily, 'a Florida sorority girl twenty years ago, even ten years ago, wouldn't have even thought of trying to get a job like that, much less have the offers you're mulling over now.' This young 'eager-beaver hotshot' retaliates by telling Friedan 'defiantly' that she had taken part in the university beauty contest. Anyway, the long and the short of it is that the young woman hears her speak, and is persuaded that Friedan is right. Driving Friedan to the airport the following morning, she says, 'You know, you kind of shifted my brains last night.' The problem she says is that she is torn: 'I really do love my [boy]friend in Miami. And I want a job like the one I've been offered in Boston, and every time I try to think of how I can do both, I feel sick in my stomach.'[13]

And so: is another Bridget Jones created? Is this another young woman, under Friedan's persuasion, setting off to pursue her career at the expense of her man and future family? And does Betty Friedan sit by guiltily, but not quite able yet to withdraw her feminist prescriptions, even though she knows they are likely to lead to unhappiness?

BRIDGET JONES: MY PART IN HER DOWNFALL

It would probably have been better if a woman had written this book. Women's voices channelled through a Betty Friedan, Germaine Greer or Helen Fielding are much more likely to be heard and appreciated. Men may write about 'the crisis of masculinity', as Anthony Clare has done, but must not overstep the mark to write about women. Women, of course, can be more flexible – they can write about their own problems, but also about problems of boys and men too – Susan Faludi has written *Stiffed* about the problems of masculinity as she sees them, and no-one worries about that. Christine Skelton has written *Schooling the Boys* and no one thinks this the least bit strange.[14] But a man writing about the problems of women seems to be violating unwritten rules. Some have told me that a man writing about these problems might even rock the boat. Women know what you're saying is true, I've been told, but if you write these thoughts they will react against them, and the whole cause will be put back several years. Why, as one American critical friend put it, be the skunk at the dinner party?

I am not convinced that it is better to remain silent. For although I see much confusion and disappointment, unhappiness and lack of fulfilment in women, I don't see anyone actually running with this particular idea, not yet anyway. The problem is that one kind of feminism is ruling the education roost. It may be because these feminists have been successful in wresting control, or it may simply be that this kind of feminism is very convenient for men in power – certainly male leaders seem to embrace current feminist-oriented education policy with enthusiasm. I am not in a position to adjudicate on this here. But for whatever reason, it is clear that many women's voices are not being heard – and these voices cover a whole range of women, from those who would describe themselves as anti-feminists to those who describe themselves very much as feminists, as well as ordinary women who have not time to decide under which of these headings they may fall. Although I do see the logic of the idea, in embryonic form at least, in a multitude of writings – feminist and anti-feminist – no one seems to be spelling it out explicitly. No one

12

seems to be spelling out explicitly that current education policy is not in the interests of most women, although it may be in the interests of a few. So perhaps I must write the book while reliving a particularly masculine tradition, that of chivalry. I worry about Bridget Jones. As a chivalrous act, I will write this book. Just as I would open the door for her, or help her up the stairs with her suitcase: I hope she will understand the act for what it is.

But the deeper truth is, I feel implicated in the problem. On the simplest level I feel implicated simply by virtue of my position as a professor of education at a prestigious Russell Group university. If I keep quiet about my disquiet about the current educational landscape, I will be guilty of a sin of omission. But I feel implicated in further ways too. Many feminist books begin with personal stories; how the author got to this position, their personal confessions and reflections. These often touch upon an unsuccessful relationship, how an epiphany followed, through which the women arrived at their moment of unadulterated self-realization. Women seem to like this approach. Part of me hankers after it too. Perhaps I may be permitted similar catharsis during this first chapter, before I am let loose on some of the evidence and arguments in later chapters? But for those readers who do not believe that writing this book needs any further justification, or who would feel uncomfortable with any personal revelations, nothing substantial will be lost to the argument by jumping straight to Chapter 2. Still on board? In what ways, then, do I feel implicated in the Bridget Jones Syndrome?

First, as a man. Second, as an educator. Third, as a feminist during those crucial years of the 1970s and 1980s. I find it hardest to do the 'man' bit first, so let us deal with them in reverse order. First, what part did my feminism play in the downfall of Bridget Jones?

I became a feminist when I was in my teens. It was through talking to the French assistante at school, herself a liberated young woman from Guadeloupe, full of the problems that women like herself encountered, racism exacerbating the sexism she experienced. She opened my eyes, showed me the oppression under which my mother lived, day in, day out, showed me the hidden curriculum forcing my sister to develop in ways different from me; undesirable ways. She showed me the truth, first in our snatched after-lesson chats at school in Bristol, and later when I visited her in Paris, walking the banks of the Seine, sipping coffee in the Quartier Latin, listening to her accounts of feminist grievances. It was heady, romantic stuff.

It all seemed so obvious. Her analysis fitted perfectly with my own rationalist perspective. I absorbed all the feminist literature she guided me to, from Betty Friedan to Germaine Greer, and, of course, to Simone de Beauvoir. I lapped up all the feminist novels too, especially Marilyn French's *The Women's Room*. And I in turn passed on these lessons to my younger sister, lecturing her into the night on her oppression, taking her on pro-abortion marches, inciting her to her feminist liberation.

I was a young feminist – as we men were permitted to call ourselves then, although I understand that fashions have changed and 'pro-feminist' would be the acceptable term today. As a feminist I believed in *equality* and, in particular, equal relationships. To a young man, this meant – an approach supported by all the feminist literature of that time and much of it now – that women should be liberated *to be like me*. Women wanted independence as much as I did. If they did not, I was entitled to point out to them, kindly but firmly, as did the feminist authors I so admired, their own false consciousness. A girl had to understand that I was a man who 'must be free', as the Hart and Rodgers' song 'Have You Met Miss Jones?' put it – a cover version of which was included in the film version of *Bridget Jones's Diary*. And, most importantly, she had to be free too. If women did not grasp their independence, this was because they were caught up in the romantic nonsense of the feminine mystique. If necessary, they must be forced to be free.

One incident from my student career illustrates my approach at the time. We were having tea with a mutual friend, my girlfriend and I. He asked her what she was going to do when she graduated. She said: 'Well, we're either going to go to Zimbabwe to teach, or to Manchester to do a Masters, or perhaps the LSE.' I was stopped short in my tracks. For those were *my* choices, the things we had been talking about that *I* would do. It had not occurred to me that she was assuming she was coming along too. It had not occurred to me that she didn't also have her own ambitions (which presumably we had not yet got around to discussing). I said as much in front of our friend, and he duly admonished her; she took it in good grace, accepting that she had been caught out here. Yes, she should have her own ambitions, yes, she should not want simply to follow me. After all, was that not the lesson we had learned from *The Women's Room*, where the woman, Mira, realizes she does not have to follow her man to Africa, that she has her own independent life to lead? Indeed, the man's – Ben's – assumption that she would follow him was precisely part of the oppression we were fighting against. I was better than Ben, more self-aware. I was not assuming she should come with me at all.

How convenient it all was for me, not to have to consider her well-being. That was our feminism. It relieved me of any responsibility for thinking of her as a women with different needs and desires to mine.

After university, I opted for the 'teacher in Zimbabwe' choice, and she did accompany me a few months later, although, perhaps not surprisingly given my attitude, the relationship did not last. This brings me to the second level in which I am implicated in the Bridget Jones Syndrome: as educator. I began my teaching career in an all-girls' school. It was wonderful, I could tell others in all seriousness, because I could be a part of helping the girls to discover their oppression. Looking back on it now, we were all imperialists, us expatriate teachers. We really believed that the people were backward, but not in any conventional sense of imperialist backwardness, of course: the people were backward in their attitude to women, in their ignorance of the major tenets of feminism. In the all-girls' school, time and time again, I came up against women's false consciousness, and tried to tackle it whenever it reared its ugly head. My endeavours must surely have borne some fruit?

First, it was in mathematics. In my maths class I was very conscientious in always changing the examples in the dated textbook from 'boys' to 'girls', or from 'men' to 'women'. I ignored the questions about cricket and football scores, and tried to conjure up more relevant examples, about child poverty in the communal lands, or food production on cooperative farms. One evening I sat down and did a count of questions in the textbooks, and found that it was much worse than even I had thought. In *Common Core Arithmetic Book 1*, for instance, out of the 50 questions that mentioned either boys, girls, men or women explicitly (and this was not counting everyday usage where it was implicit that male jobs or games were being referred to),

40 referred to men and boys, and only ten to women or girls. Of these ten, *all the girls were either nurses or housewives*! I felt indignant on behalf of my girls. No wonder they were unmotivated by this sort of stuff, no wonder they were constrained in the choices they made later in life!

Determined to do something about it, I raised the subject with them. It is in my diary, a moment that could have been an epiphany to me, but wasn't: 7 February 1984. We would not do any maths today, I told the class, there was something far more important to engage with. They looked pleased, and gathered around. I told them of my findings. I showed them the examples, gave them the theory I had absorbed from various feminist texts, then handed it over to them. What did they think?

They were not at all slow in coming forward. There was not a dissenting voice. The facts were not disputed. Yes, their texts were biased with examples of boys and men, and manly pursuits. But no, of course this did not make mathematics uninteresting! Boys would not want to hear about girls and girlie pursuits, young boys simply weren't interested. But girls *did* want to hear about boys. They matured sooner, so wanted as much information about boys as possible. In fact, much to young feminist Tooley's horror, a majority of the girls said that having this male bias made the textbooks *more* interesting to them.

They would brook no alternative. I coaxed them with the fact that having more examples about girls, especially in alternative occupations, would be much better, would make them feel more valued. Of course it wouldn't, they said, and besides, they already felt valued. I tried the line that, at our school, the only male teachers were mathematics teachers, and this was bound to put them off the subject. This was not a clever line to take. 'Are you fishing, sir?', said one, 'having a male mathematics' teacher makes the subject *much* more interesting to some of us', and they all giggled. Recovering, but blushing deeply, I said that their self-image must suffer as a result, trying to remember all the things I had picked up in the feminist texts. Would they not agree that the mathematics textbooks were reinforcing this image of themselves as passive, as outsiders? They would not. Some did agree about the passivity, but could find nothing wrong with it. 'Women have different ways of being strong and being noticed', said one, sitting there in her blue summer skirt and white ankle socks.

As an extra-curricular activity I ran the senior debating class, and here I had more success. All of us expatriate teachers found the way women were treated in the rural areas disgusting. They were treated almost as beasts of burden. Travelling through the countryside, we would see women carrying heavy loads of wood – huge branches on their heads, a man and a woman walking together, the woman carrying huge burdens, plus a child, while the man, carrying a small bag, strode ahead. Or, more often, the men would be taking no part at all, drinking away their earnings on *chibuku* in the local beer hall and chasing prostitutes, while their womenfolk worked hard at childrearing and growing the rural economy. Although my girls in the senior debating class agreed with the problem, my proposed solution was anathema to some of them. The women need feminism, I told them. That was so obvious and logical. There is a problem with how women are treated; the answer must be feminism, the answer we were accustomed to think of back home.

Some of the girls – and here is my guilt again – went along with these ideas, perhaps for their own purposes, and I fed them feminist texts to help them along their path, as I had earlier fed my sister. But some of the bright sixth-form girls would not buy this at all. One eloquent girl spoke out. She said that the problem in Africa is that women are not respected enough, the problem is *a lack of chauvinism*, not too much of it. What she valued about the Christian West, she said, was that women were revered. Chauvinism was about men recognizing their duty to serve women, to carry their heavy burdens, to refrain from drinking in the beer hall, and to refrain from chasing other women. The last thing they wanted, she said, was more independence from men – men were already far too independent. No, what she wanted was what she saw in the traditional images of white society in Zimbabwe, where women had succeeded in pulling men close to the home and hearth, where the women were in charge of the family budgets, where men went out to work but returned home early every evening, and stayed there all night, where the men did the heavy work, and women could be *free* to love and care for their children, not to do all the hard labour that I saw women doing in the rural areas. What women wanted, she said, was for men to recognize their dependence, not for women to be more independent, which would only complete the liberation of men from the responsibilities of family life.

Of course I disputed all of this. Gently but firmly I put this young woman down. Her voice was not one that should be heard. It was retrograde stuff. Instead I supported and reinforced the students who were minded to side with me. I must have influenced some of them. I must have changed some of their lives. Some of them would have done anything to please me, their mathematics teacher, and even become feminists. And of course I was on the winning side, as feminist ideas swept across the world, finding root in places even as distant as Zimbabwe.

Later, on my return to England I became a researcher at the National Foundation for Educational Research (NFER), working on assessment for National Curriculum mathematics. Our team was explicitly told that we must avoid writing questions that brought in any areas of interest which might be favoured by boys; thus questions on football, cricket, velocity of cars and motorcycles were all outlawed. I suppose I was still a feminist then. But most of all, I think by this time, I was simply afraid of the women who told me what I had to do. There seemed to be a lot of very powerful, intimidating women in education, and in mathematics education in particular at the time. A new researcher still wet behind his ears had to toe the line, or risk not getting on in this line of business. So I developed 'gender-neutral' questions, as we male researchers chivalrously called them; that is, questions which would favour girls and penalize boys. Implicated again, in a minor way, true, in the gender reforms sweeping the country. It was my own small contribution to creating the educational landscape of today, the landscape of Bridget Jones's school-days.

What is it exactly about this landscape that I think may be bad for women, in which I am implicated as educator? What exactly was I guilty of perpetrating in Zimbabwe? The girls there, and the girls brought up in the educational landscape I was helping, in my own little way, to create at the NFER, would all be immersed in the idea that their careers were the most important thing for them to develop during their teens and twenties. It was an explicit part of what we taught, and heavily there in the hidden curriculum. Over the years I have watched students, and friends and acquaintances, growing up in this milieu. There follows a composite story, based in part on the interviews conducted for the study of courtship patterns of young adults for the National Marriage Project at Rutgers University,[15] to convey something of the problem that makes up part of the Bridget Jones Syndrome.

She was training for some profession, say, in law, medicine or architecture; he was in the same field, but a few years ahead of her. They were very serious about each other, but there was always some reason why they could not get married this year – initially because she was so busy with her training, not because of any of his misgivings. But then he did start to have misgivings, and these grew steadily stronger as each year of her training continued. Then, when she was 29, within a year of her long years of training coming to an end, he made life so unbearable for her that she ended the relationship. (Bridget Jones will surely recognize this as his way of ending the relationship, namely getting her to do it for him.)

Of course he was heart-broken when the situation he had finally contrived came to pass, and he was on his own again. He certainly could not have admitted his reasons for wanting to end his relationship with her, or to anyone else for that matter. But he had found the notion that she wanted to work so that she could be independent of him – something she explicitly told him – increasingly insulting. He was struggling to be like his own father, faithful and committed, against all the odds in society, against all the pressures that said it did not matter one jot if he was unfaithful and uncommitted. He knew that he would never leave her, or their children when these arrived. And, if a terrible thing should happen to him, he would have been sensible with life assurance and pensions in order to make them as financially comfortable as if he were still there. Everything she did undermined the romance of being a provider, made him feel less masculine, and her less feminine in his eyes. The more she put into her high-powered training, the less he felt like being committed to her. The more she trained, the less he felt like having a career wife. If she was like this then, why would she not carry on being like this throughout their married life, always having something that was more important than him and the children?

Once or twice they had conversations about what would happen when they had children, and these discussions left him feeling even more cold towards her. He was being sexist, she said. Did he not think that she was as entitled to a fulfilling career as he was? He wanted her to be chained to the kitchen sink! No, of course he didn't, dear. And what would happen if he left her? She had to be independent, because men could not be trusted. Of course she was right, dear. And so it went on. He became more and more fed up with it, and eventually he could stand it no more. He wanted to be a provider. He wanted someone to value what made him valuable in his own eyes, his career and his aspirations. So he got her to dump him.

But the odd thing was that the story had a happy ending for him. He had been heart-broken, and very fearful about being back in the dating market. When he first met her he had been a humble graduate student, with few resources and finding it very difficult to attract a woman. To be honest, this was one of the reasons why he had stuck it out for so long; he had only memories of that desperate loneliness, that desperate longing for a cuddle, for loving sex, and no takers. Although he was a few years older than she, and had spent quite a while with her, he found, much to his surprise, that his ageing had apparently only increased his attractiveness to the opposite sex. Now he was back in the dating game he was established with a promising career, house and car, and his few grey hairs, far from ruining his chances, seemed to make him even more attractive – and to younger and younger women. It was all most perplexing, but he entered into it all with enthusiasm.

Apart, that is, from his concern about her. For it wasn't the same for her. He had monopolized her when she was in her twenties, and now, turning thirty, her prospects seemed to be completely different to his. Her memories of the dating game had been different too. When she had started going out with him he had been one of many admirers, fellow students and older, more established men. She was much in demand wherever she went. She was always turning down dates, always hassled by men wanting her. She had not expected this situation to change when she ended her relationship with him. She had expected to be snapped up immediately, or as soon as she was ready. But for her now, it wasn't like that at all. To be honest, in part, this was through her own choice – she seemed to be pricing herself out of the market, as it were. There were quite a few men, who did want to date her, but they just weren't good enough. She was now a high-status woman. However, instead of her economic independence enabling her to eschew the need for a man to support her, the opposite seemed to be true. She was no longer happy with lower status men; she wanted only a man to look up to. But the problem was that these higher status men were either already taken, or, curiously, more enamoured with younger para-professionals, who seemed only too keen to give up their work (and their independence) to marry and have his children.

Suddenly it all seemed so unfair to her. Her ex-boyfriend had picked up the pieces very easily. Now it seemed he had been able to pursue his career single-mindedly throughout his twenties right up to his mid-thirties, apparently without compromising any of his opportunities to find a mate and settle down. But just at the moment when she was ready, when she was about to finish her long training and was finally prepared to have children, she found it was far more difficult than she could possibly have imagined. Horribly, the challenges and pleasures of her professional work seemed in her worst moments to pall into insignificance when seen in the context of a terrible future loneliness. Like Bridget Jones she feared dying alone, to be found weeks later 'half-eaten by an Alsatian'.[16]

This couple were influenced by the norms in society in general, and, of course, a whole range of influences had come their way; but much of what they had learned had been in school. The lessons from her schooling were clear. As a bright, capable young woman, her career was the most important thing to her. Everything in her schooling was geared to that. If you *could* do it, you *must* do it. If you were good at science, you must devote yourself to it. If you feel that you would rather not succeed in these areas, these are misguided feelings. Certainly if you hesitate not to succeed because it might alienate boys, then that is a *very* retrograde thought. You, as much as him, must be independent; there is no question about that. And you are the same as he is in terms of your sexual needs too – the only difference being that you can get pregnant, so make sure you go into the fray prepared (Here's how . . .). Throughout their schooling, the message was loud and clear: girls are identical to boys, and have identical career and lifestyle interests. Both were imbued with this spirit, so much so that they took it for granted. Nothing in their schooling had prepared them for the situation that did arise.

All this makes me believe an injustice is being perpetrated. As an educator I am implicated in all of this, which is one reason why I have to write this book.

Finally, what about being implicated as a man? As I write this, Jane Andrews, the Duchess of York's former dresser, was jailed for life 'for murdering her boyfriend after he told her that he no longer loved her and did not want to marry her'.[17] My heart goes out to her. She was 34, he 39. They had been going out for two years or so. She knew that once it was over, she might be out of dating for a while; it might take a couple of years for her to get over this serious relationship. And then, at 36 or so, she'd be back in the mating game. It had been bad enough when she was 32. She knew that the mating game would not be kinder to her later on. How dare he not want to marry her! Perhaps it was true that he did want to marry and have a family, but she just turned out to be the wrong person. Perhaps he really did know this after six months, but 'let her down slowly' over eighteen months to avoid hurting her, as his mother reported in court. Whatever the rights and the wrongs of *his* case, however, there are plenty of thirty-something men out there who are not looking for marriage, and who are leading younger women up the garden path – to be fair to them, the norms and rules have changed so much that they are not deliberately doing anything they believe is wrong. But it is, and they should know it.

For all the talk of masculinity in crisis, young men really can 'have it all'. In particular, they can have marriage-like benefits without commitment; a jolly combination of sex, companionship and economy-of-scale convenience is theirs for the taking, without anyone raising an eyebrow. It would be fine if women were happy with this too – as us erstwhile feminists believed they would be in the 1980s, that our ways were what women also wanted. But it now seems much clearer that they are not.

Jane Andrews had every right to be severely upset. The dice were all loaded against her, as against Bridget Jones. Resorting to murder was somewhat extreme, however. What she really needed was for the norms in society to support her, to defend her interests against cavalier young men. If only society would call us cads and bounders again, as they did in my father's generation, and shun us socially, then young women could be allowed the dignity of being able to pursue their own interests rather than ours. As a man, I am implicated in all of this. I feel guilty and need to stand up to protect women. Perhaps I can appease some of this guilt by writing this book.

THE SKUNK AT THE DINNER PARTY

Guilt is a powerful emotion, but so is fear. One reason why it would have been better for a woman, any woman, to write this book is because it would let *me* off the hook. And that would be very convenient, because it might be dangerous for me to write this book. When I was going through the motions of trying to decide whether or not to complete the manuscript, Neil Lyndon was writing long articles in *The Sunday Times* about the way his career nose-dived after writing *No More Sex Wars* back in the early 1990s. He was recently on the radio with John Humphreys[18] repeating the same, how it made him lose his wife, family and career and made him bankrupt. Feminists converged on him in an aim to get rid of this dissenter, he claimed. This was something that I don't relish happening to me in academia.

But then a catalogue of events made me determined to write this book, whatever its consequences. Here are two. First, one feminist colleague who genuinely does believe in debate on these issues asked me to give my emerging perspective into her undergraduate gender and education course. It was at the stage that I was losing interest in writing the book, fearful of how it might jeopardize other work I valued.

The session was eye-opening. I asked students for their views on the desirability of an equal education system. The young women (for there were only young women on this course) said that, yes, equal outcomes for men and women were necessary. If not, women would suffer in terms of not getting the best jobs and the highest wages. And why would they need these equal outcomes? Stupid boy! Because women need independence and freedom. They need to be out there in the world of work, the public space, not confined to the private space of home and family. I outlined some of the ideas presented in

Chapters 3 and 4 below, which explore whether women really do need and value independence and success in the public area, or whether the 'degradation of domesticity' that feminism has promoted was such a good thing after all for women. Perhaps what women wanted most of all, I suggested, as I do in this book, was to prioritize family life, and this was not now possible for them. They argued with me at length. Even if women wanted these things, they said, you cannot trust a man now, we all know that 'four out of ten' marriages fail: even if you want a family you have to be independent. That is now the way of the world; you cannot go back even if you would want to. I questioned why, as idealistic young women, they were simply acquiescing in the way things are in the world rather than trying to change things in ways to suit them better: they did not react the same way about the problems of the environment, for instance, or animal rights. Some nodded, realizing the inconsistency.

Finally, I asked them about gender differences, and whether any of these might be biologically based. They all said they did not believe there were: all our gender differences are social-cultural in origin. There are very few differences in any case, and those that are there are all the result of socialization under patriarchy. I briefly outlined some of the ideas that I present in the second half of this book – in Chapters 5 and 6 – about the magnitude of some gender differences, and how evolutionary psychology strongly suggests a biological component to some of these factors that may be educationally relevant. They listened and argued.

At the end of the session, two of the women approached me, and said I had raised questions which they had never thought about, and brought ideas to them that had never come their way before. They felt challenged and keen to know more. One said it had helped her to realize that the things she thought about in secret were not really so beyond the pale. Was there anything else she could read?

Those two young women are the main reason why I decided to finish the book, why I decided to put my head above the parapet. If they are taking courses in gender studies and have never come across any of these alternative ideas, then something is seriously wrong. If they are at all representative of young women undergraduates in our universities – and I have no reason to believe that they are not – then some part of their education is seriously missing.

these worked with teachers 'to reduce sex-stereotyping on the part of both pupils and teachers', and each set out to promote ' "gender-fair" interaction in classrooms, so that girls would feel encouraged to study scientific subjects'.

There were also numerous projects that challenged male-domi-nated subjects, and 'the masculine content and orientation' of 'most textbooks, topics and tests'. There were initiatives, too, that 'concen-trated on reducing the impact of sexism on girls', including projects that raised teachers' awareness of 'detrimental sexist language'. Male teachers' bonding with boys 'through humour and shared male refer-ences (such as to football)' was also the subject of disapproval and re-education. Feminists also addressed boys' dominance of 'classroom discussions, control over playground space and sporting fixtures in schools'.[2]

Throughout this period, the Equal Opportunities Commission (EOC), the pre-eminent statutory body in Britain concerned with gender issues, was leading the way. Its 1985 publication *Do You Provide Equal Educational Opportunities?* provided numerous handy tips to smooth the progress of schools towards compliance with the 1975 Sex Discrimination Act that had outlawed gender stereotyping. Schools were encouraged to use 'non-sexist reading books and materials'. They were strongly advised to incorporate 'reversals of traditional sex roles into drama activities'; mathematics work-cards should be rewrit-ten to feature 'men going shopping' and 'women using bank accounts and driving cars'. And adventure stories should be rewritten too, to make 'girls and women the central characters'.[3] It was on the crest of such reforms that I was working at the NFER, as I noted in Chapter 1, eliminating any examples in my mathematics questions that would be of interest to boys.

The chief concern in all of this, of course, was the problem of gender stereotyping. Boys tended, in general, to opt for subjects in schools such as mathematics, science and technology, while girls tended to prefer languages, humanities and domestic science. The authors of *Closing the Gender Gap* point to the extent of this problem in the early 1980s, when girls made up the great majority of pupils in 'the humanities and domestic subjects' in school leaving exams. Only 1 per cent of girls took woodwork and metalwork, and only 3 per cent technical drawing and 4 per cent design and technology. On the other hand, 'there was 100 per cent female take-up of needlework and 97 per cent take-up of cookery'.[4]

The culmination of all these 'girl-friendly' reforms in Britain was the National Curriculum, as well as the new school-leaving examination, the General Certificate of Secondary Education (GCSE), introduced in 1988 and 1987 respectively. These reforms deftly eliminated the problem of gender stereotyping in schools altogether, by statute. The reforms made it illegal for girls to opt for different subjects from boys. There was a compulsory core curriculum that permitted no choices, initially up to the age of 16. Boys and girls must take exactly the same subjects, domestic and technical, scientific and humanities. The law is quite clear on this, as indeed are the updated National Curriculum documents: the recently published guidance specifies that boys and girls must be given access to 'the *same* curriculum, particularly in science, design and technology and physical education' and that schools must avoid 'gender stereotyping . . . particularly in science, design and technology, ICT, music and physical education'. As one of its four 'main purposes', the National Curriculum 'secures for all pupils, *irrespective of . . . gender*', an entitlement to the same areas of learning.[5] Teachers, the statutory guidance says, need to be aware of equal opportunities legislation, especially the Sex Discrimination Act (SDA) of 1975, which is interpreted as outlawing, amongst other felonies, the use of separate tests for boys and girls (indeed, on the reporting of these tests, 'boys and girls should not be listed separately'); the exclusion of pupils from courses of study solely on the ground of sex; and, perhaps most significantly, any sex discrimination in careers guidance.[6]

It is not just in Britain, of course, that such legislation has been enacted. More or less the same situation pertains in the USA, where the parallel legislation is Title IX of the Education Amendments of 1972. This prohibits any educational institution that receives federal funding from practising any discrimination on grounds of gender, including in terms of curriculum, assessment and careers guidance. Almost all schools receive some federal funds, so Title IX applies to nearly everyone.[7]

So are feminists content now that gender stereotyping of subject choices has been made illegal in schools? Unfortunately not. Restless and questing, the focus of their gaze has shifted, for, having clamped down on subject choice in schools, the problem has not gone away. Far from eliminating the problem of gender stereotyping, this carefully crafted equality has merely shifted the problem along a little. For *as soon as girls (and boys) are given any choice*, they select the traditionally feminine (and masculine) subject with renewed gusto. As the authors of *Closing the Gender Gap* put it, the 'historical legacy' still 'maintains its grip' on educational choice whenever girls and boys are given freedom to choose.[8] Or, as the Equal Opportunities Commission Annual Report puts it, 'At all qualification levels, gender stereotyping of subjects is prevalent *wherever choice is allowed*'.

Let us be clear: the problem at these levels has nothing to do with the numbers game. At A level, the school-leaving examinations at age 18, men and women's grade performance is roughly equal. In university higher education, there are now *more* women undergraduates than men. In addition, women do better than their male counterparts, with considerably more women than men gaining an upper second-class honours degree. Although men gain marginally more first-class honours than women, they are almost twice as likely to gain a third-class honours or pass degree than women, which surely evens things up here too. However, these statistics simply conceal the major and worrying problem for feminists today, for, if the number of young women continuing in further and higher education is equal to the number of men, the subjects they take are markedly different.

The Equal Opportunities Commission warns us against being lulled into any false sense of complacency by the statistics. It now sees not success for women, but only the major problem of gender stereotyping that raises its ugly head whenever choice is allowed. For at A level, all the sciences apart from biology are male-dominated; in contrast, *all* Arts subjects are dominated by young women. At university, men "are *over-represented* in Engineering and Technology whereas women are *over-represented* in Education and the Humanities'. Further education (vocational education at below degree level) is also heavily gender stereotyped, with young women much more likely to study subjects 'allied to medicine, the social sciences or creative arts', and young men more likely to study 'mathematical sciences, agriculture, engineering or technology'.[9] And young men make up 96 per cent of all engineering and nearly 70 per cent of information technology (IT) starters. By contrast, 80 per cent of business administration starters and 92 per cent of hairdressing starters are young women.

It is not just the Equal Opportunities Commission that is worried by this problem. Other government bodies in Britain and in the USA are just as concerned. Even Chris Woodhead, until recently Her Majesty's Chief Inspector and regarded by many as beyond the pale for his entrenched conservative values, commissioned studies for the Office for Standards in Education that reported on gender issues in education. Its two most recent reports on this issue, *Recent Research on Gender and Educational Performance*, written by top academics at the University of Cambridge (including Madeleine Arnot, one of the authors of *Closing the Gender Gap*), and *The Gender Divide*, published in association with the Equal Opportunities Commission, share the same concern with gender stereotyping.[10]

The Gender Divide notes that the '*most troubling aspect* of the gender pattern of sixth form study is that, despite their success in these subjects at GCSE, relatively few young women are taking A-level courses which are wholly mathematical, scientific or technological'. Indeed, the only major A-level subject that was entered by equal proportions of girls and boys was history. No other subjects had entry gaps that could even be described as small.[11] And *Recent Research* notes the disturbing fact that, when boys and girls are asked to rank subjects, studies consistently show that they *still* rate science, mathematics and technology as 'masculine' – and these subjects are still preferred by boys – while the subjects preferred by girls and rated as 'feminine' include English, the humanities, music, and personal and social education.[12]

Exactly the same problems are found in America, too. The seminal feminist education work from the American Association of University Women (AAUW), *How Schools Shortchange Girls*, shows that boys take more mathematics and science credits than do girls at high school, and, to boot, girls opt primarily for biology and chemistry, while boys opt for physics. One study found that nearly four times as many male as female students who had taken physics and calculus were going on to study science or engineering in college. Their recommendations could not be clearer: 'Young women in the United States today are still not participating equally in our educational system . . . they often are not expected or encouraged to pursue higher-level mathematics and science courses. The implications are clear: the system must change.'[13]

The influential book *See Jane Win*, by Dr Sylvia Rimm, reporting the findings of The Rimm Report on 'How 1,000 Girls Became SUCCESSFUL Women', again points to the problem of gender stereotyping, and how this – especially with regard to mathematics – prevents girls from achieving their full potential.[14]

FEMINISM'S FAULT LINE

If gender stereotyping is a major preoccupation of feminists in education, this is not to say that they uniformly see the problem in the same way. In fact, *two* dramatically divergent feminist positions emerge on this issue, and these two positions reveal the fault line that runs throughout feminist thought. The two positions provide a spring-board to examine profound differences in the way feminists view potential education reform, two approaches that will be fundamental to the argument throughout this book.

The *first* approach says that gender stereotyping is bad because it restricts girls' choices in their future careers. Through gender stereotyping, girls are excluded from the more prestigious career paths. Worryingly for the government, this has a negative impact on the economy. The *second* approach is more nuanced and complex. Yes, gender stereotyping exists; but perhaps this reveals significant differences between boys and girls that might not always be bad. Indeed, if we try to eliminate these differences, perhaps this will lead to significant loss.

Higher than hairdressing

'Girls will be helped to aim "higher than hairdressing"', ran a recent headline.[15] Tessa Jowell, then Minister for Women (now Secretary of State for Culture, Media and Sport), was worried that 'too many young women . . . are joining the beauty and child care industries instead of engineering and other skilled work'. She therefore

31

recommended that teenage girls be given assertiveness training at school, 'to help them resist pressure to go into "female" jobs such as hairdressing, care work and health care'. Girls do exceedingly well at school, she says, but then, disappointingly, they 'quickly lose their ambition and drop out of education or a career'. Tessa Jowell to the rescue: girls must be given 'personal advisers', organized through the employment service, to 'help them pursue traditional male careers in construction, physics or chemistry'. She warns, if girls do not take to this, it will 'have a significant impact' on their 'lifetime earnings'.

Tessa Jowell's concerns typify the first approach; the authors of *Closing the Gender Gap* share the same sentiments. They bemoan the fact that, even today, there is a *'curious contradiction'* in young women's behaviour: 'young women, no longer unaware of sex segregation and the lack of female bargaining power', still choose 'women's work'. And young women still 'continue to choose traditionally feminine routes and occupations', they still want 'people jobs' and avoid 'work contexts that might cause extra stress'.[16]

All the official voices in Britain and the USA share the same general concern. Chris Woodhead's old department, the Office for Standards in Education (Ofsted), stresses that girls' choices deny to women 'career opportunities in science, engineering and technology'. Female students are denied 'access to further training in scientific and technological areas', leading to a curtailing of their future career prospects. Gender stereotyping is bad for girls; as importantly, it is bad for the economy, not allowing the country to lay its hands on all available technological talent. This is one of the reasons why the Sex Discrimination Act allows 'positive action in vocational education and training', aimed at encouraging young women into 'non-traditional types of work, such as the establishment of girls-only computer clubs and events to encourage girls contemplating careers in science and engineering'.[17]

There is exactly the same concern in the USA. *How Schools Shortchange Girls* regrets that high-school girls, 'even those with exceptional academic preparation in math and science', choose mathematics and science *careers* 'in disproportionately low numbers'. For the feminists, an 'important area of concern' is 'the distribution of young women among sex-stereotyped occupational fields'. What is needed is a 'policy change' to 'provide these young women with the skills needed *to obtain higher-paying jobs'*. What is required, they say, is encouragement for girls and young women 'to take nontraditional courses and help place them in jobs or post-secondary institutions requiring the skills learned'.[18]

In 1998, the AAUW published a follow-up report, *Gender Gaps: Where Schools Still Fail Our Children*. Things were still bad; not much had improved since they had published *How Schools Shortchange Girls*. Further reforms and vigilance were still required. The gender gaps in science and technology – reflecting freely chosen paths of young women – 'threaten to disadvantage girls as they confront 21st century demands'.[19] And the Department of Education's Women's Equity Educational Act Program (WEEA) posts similar concerns. Despite the successes of Title IX, 'males and females are still limited in their educational choices by their gender,' they say. 'Boys are much more likely to be awarded national, state and college scholarships, while girls are still severely under-represented in most scientific and technical fields.'[20] They note the pressing problem that in college, 'young men go on to major in math and the sciences in rates that exceed those of young women, *many of whom are shut out of the career opportunities these fields can provide*'.[21] Success in the fields of mathematics and science are 'critical to . . . success in an increasingly technological world'. Girls' choices have serious and undesirable 'labor market consequences'.[22]

The issue of gender stereotyping as described here is relatively unproblematic. Whether or not we agree with it, we can easily understand what is meant by it, and we can easily see its ramifications for career choice and success in the marketplace. However, not all feminists offer such a simple diagnosis. The second approach reveals new complexities about feminism and education.

Same difference

In *The Whole Woman*, Germaine Greer points to the 'essentialist feminist paradox'. The tensions here are 'not merely academic', she says, but deeply affect the realities for all women: 'The contradictions women face have never been more bruising than they are now. The career woman does not know if she is to do her job like a man or like herself. . . . Is motherhood a privilege or a punishment?'[23] These tensions provide the backdrop to the second approach to gender stereotyping in schools. Far from simply assuming, as the feminists do in the first approach, that girls not taking maths, science and technology is a problem for girls, they instead turn their gaze back to the subjects themselves. What is wrong with girls' refusal to engage whole-heartedly with these subjects? Perhaps there is nothing wrong with them at all, perhaps there is something wrong with the subjects themselves? Perhaps girls are right to be wary in their preferences, after all?

To access this contrasting approach, we will focus on two recent and important books by feminist educators who are inclined towards the second approach. The first is Carrie Paechter's latest book, *Educating the Other*.[24] The second is a distinctive contribution from Greer's Australian countrywomen – *Answering Back*, by Jane Kenway and Sue Willis.[25]

In keeping with Germaine Greer's sentiments, *Answering Back* exhibits a weariness with feminist attempts to challenge gender stereotyping. Throughout the ten-year period of their research, the 'most pervasive and persuasive gender reform story' was that girls and young women should overcome gender stereotyping. To do this, girls had to succeed in male-dominated school subjects and must overcome stereotyping in career choice. The authors have been doing this work in 30 schools in Victoria and Western Australia, and frankly they seem a little tired of it all: they describe the changing 'fashions' of gender reform, outlining their scepticism of the process.

Pointing to current concerns about boys' underachievement, they say that the proposed solutions remind them of earlier gender reform discourse being 'naive and simplistic'. They list at length the types of gender reforms they have seen come and go, from single-sex maths classes; self-defence for girls; gender and personal development classes; a project for girls in technology studies; an action plan to produce a gender-inclusive commerce curriculum to encourage more boys to do keyboarding; a girls and middle school physics curriculum project; a gender-awareness staff development programme for maths, science and technology teachers; more attempts to encourage girls in maths and science, the trades and physical education; encouraging girls to use more linguistic and playground space, and so on. And they point to one reason why these reform programmes fizzled out: 'We all just got sick of it', as one teacher summed it all up.

One of the major 'sub-plots' in the project to overcome gender stereotyping concerned mathematics. 'Mathematics is imbued with an almost mystical power to make and remake futures', they note. This led to 'perhaps the most expensive single educational intervention strategy ever mounted in Australia', the 1991 multimedia campaign *Maths Multiplies your Choices*. Advertisements exhorted parents to encourage their daughters in mathematics, telling them that '80 per cent of all jobs require mathematics', so this would lead to '400 per cent more choices' for their girls.[26]

However, the authors of *Answering Back* note – sympathizing with those on the receiving end of all this gender agitprop – that girls resisted being told what they had to do. As one Year 10 girl put it: 'Before we were told not to do [mathematics], now we're told we have to do it . . .' They note that for such girls, 'the voice of feminism . . . is authoritarian and insensitive'.

All this seems clear: the authors are not at all sure that trying to force girls into mathematics, science and technology is necessarily a good idea. The major problem, they say, the 'inescapable, undeniable and unfortunate truth', is that 'some forms and fields of knowledge are more valued and powerful than others', and mathematics is the chief offender here. Knowledge in the school curriculum, they argue, 'has been shaped by powerful, white Western men in their own image and interests'. They write that the 'almost exclusive promotion' of maths, science and technology 'accepts the dominance of masculine values and knowledge'. This reinforces 'what many students already know, that those subject areas most associated with the masculine are to be valued over those most associated with the feminine'.[27]

Parallel arguments are presented by Carrie Paechter in *Educating the Other*. One of the most important distinctions in Western philosophical thought, Paechter argues, is between man and woman. To be male is 'to be rational, concerned with the mind and active in civil society'; to be female, on the other hand, 'is to be emotional, concerned with the body and passively waiting at home'. And society places greater value on the masculine ways of knowing rather than feminine. Schooling, she says, becomes more 'masculine' the older the

child gets: 'The curriculum, particularly at secondary level, is dominated by reason and rationality, with the more highly valued subjects
being the "detached", supposedly emotion-free areas of mathematics
and science'. There are 'male-identified attributes' such as 'reason and
logic' which 'are seen as being more important for all students'.

The dominance of masculine forms of knowledge puts women in
a subordinate position to men, she argues, placing girls and women in
the position of the 'Other' of her book title. The dominance of
masculine forms of knowledge leads to the oppression of women.[28]
But – and here is the crux of her argument – there are feminine forms
of knowledge that are as valuable, if not more so, than these masculine
forms. This step in her argument is spelled out by looking at Carol
Gilligan's work on alternative moral voices.

Carol Gilligan was the first Professor of Gender Studies at Harvard
University, who in 1982 published a now celebrated work, *In a
Different Voice*. In this book, she challenged the 'masculinist' theories
in moral psychology that prevailed at the time, suggesting that current
research was based largely on boys and men, and hence could at best
only lead to an understanding of *male* moral reasoning; when women
were measured against these standards they seemed deficient, stuck in
a lower stage. However, Gilligan suggested that masculine and feminine ways of moral reasoning were *different*. Women approach moral
questions applying an 'ethic of care', a less abstract and competitive
model; men, on the other hand, approach moral issues through an
'ethic of justice', applying rules and abstract principles.

Leaving aside for now whether Gilligan's original research was
thorough enough to support such claims,[29] Paechter draws out the
implications for education, focusing on gender differences in problem-
solving. Women and girls, she says, use 'troubles talk',[30] in which
'problems are shared and discussed, often at length, as a way of
reinforcing interpersonal connection; the conversation, as an
expression of solidarity in adversity, is more important than solving
the problem'. On the other hand, men and boys 'prioritize coming to
a solution', finding it 'puzzling that when a woman says she is troubled
by something she does not necessarily want to be told what to do
about it'.

All this leads Paechter to conclude that her preferred route would be for girls to be free to pursue their interests in these 'feminine ways of knowing' in the school curriculum, as well as outside. Paechter is clear: there is something about girls and women, in general, that makes them prefer these 'feminine' ways over 'masculine' ones. It is these preferences that make them, in general, prefer 'the more discursive humanities' over the 'solution-focused mathematics and science'. The preferences of girls in this way should not be dismissed; we should, as the title to one of her chapters puts it, 'revalue female voices'. There are alternative ways of knowing: Gilligan's challenge to the 'dominance of reason in models of moral development' may be used to create a parallel argument to challenge the dominance of logic and reason in the school curriculum. The arguments show that 'by hearing only the dominant male voice Western thought has closed off potentially fertile avenues of investigation'.

In short, we would create a better, more just society if we could promote these feminine ways of knowing and approaches in schools and society at large, and if we could recognize 'connectedness, as much as independence', feminine ways as much as masculine ways. It would be more just for girls if these alternative ways of knowing were made available and more valued in the school curriculum.[31]

In other words, in both *Educating the Other* and *Answering Back*, the conclusion is reached – although they do not put it in precisely these terms – that there may be nothing wrong with gender stereotyping *per se*, providing that the female voice is as valued, or more valued, than the masculine one.

It may be, too, that neither book is totally comfortable with this outcome. As the authors of *Answering Back* candidly put it in describing a male physics teacher who did not know what to do to get the best out of his girls: 'The problem for Jim is that he isn't sure whether he should be treating girls and boys the same or treating them differently. This, of course, is a problem he shares with many feminists.'[32]

But if I have got their arguments right, what then is the curriculum alternative that would satisfy these authors? If this 'exclusive pro-motion' of maths and science as worthy subjects for girls is wrong, if the exclusive engagement with reason and logic is masculinist, what would they want in terms of the curriculum? This is one of the key questions that I hope to clarify throughout the course of this book.

For instance, I have been reading some older curriculum ideas, guided to these by feminists who are strongly critical of them. What would the current authors make of these ideas?

Harriet Harman, now Solicitor General in the Labour government, wrote a feminist tract back in 1978, in which she heaps condemnation on the curriculum reform proposed in a post-war government report, with its line that the direct interests of girls in 'the problems of human relationships should be given a central part in her education' – based on the assumption that 'it is sound educational policy to take account of natural interests'.[33] Harman does not like this at all. No, she says, girls should be helped into mathematics and science, not led astray by this sort of chauvinist thinking. Harriet Harman would seem to be exactly the sort of person that the current authors would be criticizing. However, if they were to criticize Harman's approach, that girls must be encouraged into masculine areas rather than where their own concerns would lead them, would they then endorse these old-fashioned curriculum ideas?

Similarly, Gaby Weiner, one of the authors of *Closing The Gender Gap*, cannot abide by the arguments in a government report of the inter-war years, with its endorsement of a 'system of differentiation under which either sex seeks to multiply at a rich interest its own peculiar talents'. Weiner thinks the report is completely off-beam when it argues that 'Dissimilars are not necessarily unequals; and it is possible to conceive an equality of the sexes which is all the truer and richer because it is founded on mutual recognition of differences and equal cultivation of different capacities'.[34]

Clearly these erstwhile curriculum reformers do not want to force girls into studying 'masculine values and knowledge'; they would have no truck with 'exclusive promotion' of knowledge 'shaped by power-ful, white Western men in their own image and interests'. So would this approach, at least potentially, fit in with these feminists' preferred approach of seeking to 'revalue feminine forms of knowledge', on the way challenging 'dominant conceptions of important knowledge as ultimately diminishing girls' and women's power'?

The key question is: would these feminists approve of these old-fashioned curriculum ideas, and if not, why not? This is a question that will inform the discussion throughout this book, and which will be taken up again explicitly in Chapter 7. If gender stereotyping is not necessarily a bad thing, what does this imply in terms of curriculum choice?

THE FEMINIST PARADOX:
TWO FORMS OF FEMINISM

Let us sum up. For some feminists, the answer as to whether or not gender stereotyping is bad is an unequivocal 'yes': 'Yes, it's bad because it constrains women's choices. It's bad and must be combated.' Governments and their agents in the UK and USA, together with feminist writers such as those in *Closing the Gender Gap*, *See Jane Win* and *How Schools Shortchange Girls* appear to fit squarely into that camp.

For other feminists, however (those in *Answering Back* and *Educating the Other*, for instance), the issue is far more complex and perplexing. Yes, it is bad and must be combated . . . but, wait, there are different ways of knowing. If we throw in our lot with those who want to eliminate gender stereotyping, are we not also throwing in the towel as regards promoting valuable feminine virtues and knowledge? But the evidence shows that girls and women *do* (in general) value different ways of knowing and being — for heaven's sake, we as women know this to be true, and prefer our own ways and values. Anyone brought up in the era of *Men Are from Mars, Women Are from Venus* knows it. So perhaps we should not throw out the baby with the bathwater. Perhaps our baby — the feminine ways of knowing — should be allowed to be reborn as something valuable, celebrated even. And then, would it matter if there was gender stereotyping in schools and career choices, provided that the feminine forms are valued, and provided that no-one is forced into ways that they don't want to go?

Anyone familiar with feminist writings will recognize that there is nothing original about noting this dilemma. The feminist philosopher Anne Phillips, for instance, sums it up neatly. She points to the 'ever-present tension in feminist thinking' between 'the plea for equality and the assertion of sexual difference'. 'When people first hear of feminism', she continues, 'they often assume it denies sexual difference: "anything he can do I can do too." Yet as long as women bear children there is at least one inescapable difference between the sexes.'

Indeed, the argument has been made that feminism developed over the years, moving away from the aspiration of the 1970s to be treated as an equal 'person' rather than 'woman', to asserting women's 'experience and values over and against the different values of men'. But this led to the feminist paradox: the 'essentially 'female' qualities' that women bear 'sometimes replicate too closely for comfort the very stereotypes feminists once tried to avoid: emotional rather than rational; peace-loving rather than destructive; caring about people rather than things'.[35]

However, as we have seen, far from one leading to the other, these two feminist 'projects' sit uncomfortably alongside each other in the same time period (witness *Closing the Gender Gap* alongside *Answering Back*). One of the aims of this book is to try to unpick these two positions, to see which is more plausible, and to explore the ensuing policy prescriptions.

Given the importance of these two positions, we need some way of identifying them. Usefully, Germaine Greer provides two constructive labels. In *The Whole Woman*, she distinguishes between feminists who are concerned with 'equality' and those concerned with 'liberation': 'Seekers after equality', she says, 'clamoured to be admitted to smoke-filled male haunts.' 'Liberationists', on the other hand, 'sought the world over for clues to what women's lives could be like if they were free to define their own values, order their own priorities and decide their own fate.' Liberationism, she says, is about being at 'ease in my woman's body'.

Equality feminists would support the statement that 'We all agree that women should have equal pay for equal work, be equal before the law, do no more housework than men do, spend no more time with children than men do'. But liberationists argue that, in a 'world unchanged', this is all 'a nightmare'.[36]

In other words — and in other feminists' language — equality feminists would be those who want 'positive steps to be taken to encourage females into non-traditional options, jobs and levels of seniority'. The liberationist feminists, however, would reject this striving after equality with men. Instead, they would 'value women's perspectives, accepting that many women learn and administer differently from many men'. Emulating men will 'not liberate women'. Instead, 'women should reclaim their history and culture'.[37]

This important distinction between *equality* and *liberation* feminists will be used for the rest of the book. Greer is saying – and I concur – that whatever other brand of feminism someone is loyal to – whether it be old feminism, new feminism, radical feminism, cultural feminism, post-modern feminism, post-structuralist feminism, gender feminism or lesbian feminism, to name but a few[38] – one's feminist ideas may be usefully characterized as falling under one of these two categories. Throughout the book too, I will be returning to these categories to attempt to adjudicate between them. Importantly, as a shorthand however, I will be following what I take to be standard usage and sometimes simply refer to equality feminists as 'feminists'. I am sure this is the way the term is used by most people outside of academia. Liberation feminism is the more subtle version that some-times gets lost in debate. For instance, the editor of *The Spectator*, Boris Johnson, refers to Germaine Greer as an '*ex*-feminist' now that she no longer seems to embrace *equality* feminist ideas.[39] Thus if ever the term is left unqualified in what follows, it is the equality feminists to whom I will be referring.

When I was writing an earlier draft of this book, before I had read Germaine Greer's latest, I coined the terms 'rationalist' and 'celebra-tory' feminist to describe what seem to be the same two categories. For 'equality' feminists, it seemed to me, have a 'rationalist' dimen-sion. An equality feminist will protest about the irrationality of much of our gendered divisions in society. Why should girls not be as good at higher mathematics as boys, given that there are well-paid jobs at the end of it? Why should young women not pursue careers as whole-heartedly as men, given the financial and status rewards that will accrue to them? On a prima facie level it seems irrational that they should not do so, and this is one of the motivating forces for the equality feminist reform programme. Meanwhile, liberation feminism is above all about *celebrating* gender differences – or, at the very least, celebrating the qualities that women have. Rather than assume that the male devil has all the best tunes, the celebratory feminist will argue that females are also worth listening to, sometimes to the extent of excluding any other voices.

Whatever the virtues of either equality or liberation feminists, we see how the two approaches to gender stereotyping fit neatly into these categories. The first approach – that there was something very wrong with gender stereotyping because it led to negative career choices for girls and women – clearly fits into the equality feminist line. The second approach – that there may not be anything wrong at all with gender stereotyping, that it may point to something to be celebrated – fits squarely into the liberation feminist line.

Most significantly, as we have begun to note in this chapter and will continue to observe in subsequent chapters, it is the ideas of the equality feminists that hold sway over government and education reform, in America, Australia and Britain as well as elsewhere. It is not particularly important for this book whether they hold sway because the feminists themselves have succeeded in wresting power, or because it is in men's interests to have these ideas enshrined in law, or perhaps a combination of both. The important point is that reforms for 'gender-neutral' curricula and school organization fit in with the ideas of the equality feminists. And it is the equality feminists who dominate the debates about overcoming gender stereotyping, who argue for vigilance and struggle in order to climb to the lofty heights of gender equity.

DÉJÀ VU

We introduced the issue of gender stereotyping by looking at what the Equal Opportunities Council (EOC) currently had to say about this issue, and the EOC has recently published a huge list of prescriptions for combating the problem now. These include pupils being 'positively encouraged beyond conventional choices', with 'positive images' of 'girls in technology' used to encourage women; similarly, 'boys that (sic) choose modern languages, home economics or secretarial studies' must not be 'deflected by sexist assumptions'. Very importantly, 'Careers guidance and counselling must not be discriminatory'. To further stop the rot, they give a list of guidelines with which *parents* should comply within their own homes:

- In two-parent households, try to divide parental responsibilities and household chores so that it is apparent to children that both mothers and fathers can cook, garden, repair plugs, look after children and use tools.

- From the earliest possible age, ensure that both girls and boys have access to a wide range of toys, for example, those of a constructional or mechanical nature, dolls, cookery and chemistry sets.
- Encourage girls and boys to take part in a range of games, sporting and artistic activities, and role-playing which avoids stereotypes.
- Give equally of your time and attention to girls and boys to help them grow up with a sense of equal entitlement.
- Support and encourage the participation of your child in initiatives such as 'Take your Daughter to Work' days, and 'Women into Science and Engineering'.
- Boost self-esteem and a sense of self-worth by giving praise, especially for achievements in areas traditionally seen as the realm of the opposite sex.[40]

Similar prescriptions for change are to be found in current feminist agendas in the USA. *How Schools Shortchange Girls* offers a manifesto for change to move forward the gender equity agenda:

- TEACHERS, ADMINISTRATORS, AND COUNSELORS MUST BE PREPARED AND ENCOURAGED TO BRING GENDER EQUITY AND AWARENESS TO EVERY ASPECT OF SCHOOLING.
- State certification standards for teachers and administrators should require course work on gender issues, including new research on women, bias in classroom-interaction patterns, and the ways in which schools can develop and implement gender-fair . . . curricula.
- Teacher-training courses must not perpetuate assumptions about the superiority of traits and activities traditionally ascribed to males in our society. Assertive and affiliated skills as well as verbal and mathematical skills must be fostered in both girls and boys.
- Teachers must help girls develop positive views of themselves and their futures, as well as an understanding of the obstacles women must overcome in a society where their options and opportunities are still limited by gender stereotypes and assumptions.

- Curricula for young children must not perpetuate gender stereo-
types and should reflect sensitivity to different learning styles.
GIRLS MUST BE EDUCATED AND ENCOURAGED TO UNDER-
STAND THAT MATHEMATICS AND THE SCIENCES ARE IMPORT-
ANT AND RELEVANT TO THEIR LIVES. GIRLS MUST BE
ACTIVELY SUPPORTED IN PURSUING EDUCATION AND
EMPLOYMENT IN THESE AREAS.

And so on. And to make sure that all educators comply with their directions, teachers, administrators and counsellors 'should be evaluated on the degree to which they promote and encourage gender-equitable . . . education'.[41]

However, as Yogi Berra might have said, this feels like *déjà vu* all over again, since such measures have been common on both sides of the Atlantic for decades. We have already seen how, in Britain, the EOC was part of the influential movement in the 1970s and 1980s to ensure that there were legal changes to enforce the equal curriculum for boys and girls. Their 1985 *Do You Provide Equal Educational Opportunities?* is in many ways a quaint reminder of this earlier time, making us realize how much has changed in so short a span. The booklet is full of photos of the brave new world they saw just over the horizon, of girls doing woodwork, metalwork and painting, and boys doing cookery and sewing. In primary schools, we are told, teachers must make sure that children's games 'avoid reinforcing traditional sex roles', so that nurses must not always be girls, or doctors boys. And we are sternly asked: 'Do all the parenting and family pictures used in school always show the women washing up, feeding the baby, making the beds, clearing up, and so on, while the man is always shown repairing the car, painting the house, reading the newspaper, going out to work?'

Little chance of that in schools today, it would seem, but the *déjà vu* is most obvious in the discussion on careers guidance – the 2000 guide for parents is almost identical in wording to the 1985 piece! Careers guidance must be 'non-discriminatory', it said fifteen years before:

All teachers should ensure that they do not discourage pupils from considering non-traditional careers, either by ridicule or by over-stressing the difficulties which the pupil might have to face. All careers literature should be free from sex discrimination which can occur not only in the text but also in the illustrations, with people shown only in traditional roles.

Moreover, it is 'particularly important that girls who are thinking of dropping science and mathematics as examination subjects are made aware of the limitations which this will place upon their career and further education choices'.[42]

All of this must make rather disappointing reading for the EOC today, should they ever go back to their archives and see their faded hopes of the past. As we have already noted, their ambitions were largely realized in Britain with the 1988 National Curriculum and revised school-leaving examination. Girls and boys were not allowed to make choices about the subjects they were able to take in primary and secondary school. Many of the approaches they recommend as best practice were introduced in all schools. It would be very hard to find examples of the 'hidden curriculum' to which they so objected in terms of curriculum materials and practices in primary or secondary schools now. Yet, as soon as they are allowed to choose, girls and boys revert to type in the sixth form, and in further and higher education.

If a week is a long time in politics, 30 years of gender reform may not be long enough to change human predilections. But the fact that so little has changed when young men and women are given choices, even though so much *has* changed in the legal framework and the educational landscape more broadly, is at least one reason why it is perhaps time to review the major assumption behind the EOC's optimistic predictions. The major assumption is that *socialization*, more or less on its own, is the reason why women and men make gender-stereotyped choices.

Feminists and government agencies are entirely open about this assumption. In 1985, the EOC proclaimed that the reason why fewer girls than boys pursue science and technology subjects is simply and only 'the obvious sex-differentiation which is found in the school curriculum'.[43] When such socialization is removed, when there was no 'sex-differentiation' in the curriculum, then the problem of boys' and girls' different career choices would disappear later on. Once the curriculum, hidden and overt, is tackled, girls can take up their rightful place in high-tech society.

However, *déjà vu* again, such an assumption is clearly there fifteen years later. In the foreword to *An Equal Opportunities Guide for Parents*, Sam Galbraith, Minister for Children and Education at the new Scottish Parliament, rehearses common themes about how socialization leads to gender differences: 'It is easy to unwittingly treat children in a limiting way', he writes. Boys and girls 'are often not given the same range of toys', and 'girls can be supervised more closely than boys'; even 'the language used when talking to them can be more protective'. Such differences are present throughout childhood: 'girls are less likely to be asked to help with hobbies of a technical nature, or DIY at home, but they will be expected to help with domestic chores'. It is parents who are able to 'engender the belief that, given the necessary aptitude, any pursuit, any job, any ambition can be achieved, regardless of gender'.[44]

A similar assumption is found in American feminist literature. *How Schools Shortchange Girls* is very clear on the origins of gender differences: 'From pink and blue tags in hospital nurseries, to Barbie dolls and G.I. Joes, and on to cheerleaders and football players, our society holds different expectations for girls and boys. These expectations in turn generate different patterns of behavior towards children depending on their sex.' The report approvingly quotes research which shows that sex differences 'consistently seem to be the result of social factors'. Such factors include 'both the different socialization experiences that males and females have and the socially determined assumptions and viewpoints of researchers studying the area'. Finally, in their discussion of mathematics and science, they firmly state that 'There is no Math Gene',[45] contradicting the recent press speculation that boys' superior mathematical performance has anything to do with genes rather than socialization.

Most recently, Naomi Wolf in her new book, *Misconceptions*, notes how children grow up to be boys or girls through socialization:

The most common thing I heard grown-ups say to little girls was, in a goony, Mickey-Mouse hyper-admiring voice: 'I like your *shoes!*' At first the two-year-olds would look down at their feet, bemused: What's that about? But by three, they have accepted that a normative social greeting involves some adult admiring their footwear. By three-and-a-half, they refuse to wear anything but Mary Janes. Then we say, 'What a girl!'.

Boys are ignored or discouraged if they carry their mother's handbag or play with her necklace, but encouraged if they engage in combat behaviour. Girls are encouraged when they preen and flirt. She writes: 'You don't have to be a genius, at the age of three, to figure out that if you're a girl, you'd better act in ways that the grownups identify as girl-like, and vice versa.'[46]

The assumption in all of this feminist writing is clear. Just as the Jesuits could take any child at age 7 and make of him what they wanted, so it is believed that any girl can be made into anything, provided that she is correctly and appropriately socialized.

On its own, the fact that so much has changed in schools, yet gender stereotyping stubbornly persists, suggests that this assumption is at least worth examining, even out of purely academic interest. But the Bridget Jones Syndrome makes it much, much more important to question than that. Women are becoming increasingly unhappy. Betty Friedan noticed it, after less than two decades of modern feminism. What she worried over back in 1981 was that, following modern feminism, *many* young women were breaking through the gender stereotypes of what was expected of them. They were not going straight on to have families, husbands and children, they were pursuing high-powered careers as her movement willed them to do. Yet it seemed to be making them increasingly unhappy. *Going against their gendered stereotypes*, that is, seemed to be making them feel increasingly unfulfilled.

Friedan hoped it was all a teething problem, gritting her teeth as she heard sad story after sad story recounted to her: we must stick at it, girls, and all will be well. Recent evidence – and the monumental success of Bridget Jones and all its imitation read-a-likes – suggests that this dogged determination has not made it any better. When women fight against gendered stereotypes of family and home, it does not seem to make them any happier.

Interestingly, in several places in *The Second Stage*, Betty Friedan herself seems to be *hinting* at a possible reason. Describing motherhood, she notes '*the profound human impulse* to have children'. She points to the *'compelling life urge'* that makes itself heard, drowning out these worrisome questions, as women hit thirty, thirty-five: 'Will I miss out in life if I do not have children?' And she puzzles that:

> I hear such sullenness from some younger women who now are living *their personhood as women* as if this somehow excludes all those emotions, capacities, needs that have to do with having babies, mothering children, making a home, loving and being loved, dependence and independence, softness and hardness, strength and weakness, in the family.

She continues: 'To deny *the part of one's being as woman* that has, through the ages, been expressed in motherhood – nurturing, loving softness, and tiger strength – is to deny part of one's *personhood as woman.'* And finally,

> Our daughters, in the compulsion and challenge of their new career choices, are *surprised* when the power of that other choice now – the to-be-or-not-to-be of motherhood – *hits them* with an agonizing indecision. *They discover it as some blessed possibility we kept from them* or were too blighted, perverted to appreciate.[47]

Writing about 'profound human impulses', 'compelling life urges' and the 'personhood of woman' expressed in terms of having a family all suggest that Friedan is here apprehending something far deeper and more valuable than a mirage brought on by patriarchal socialization. Writing about 'the power of the impulse to love', the 'surprise' with which this 'hits women', as they 'discover' this 'blessed possibility we kept from them', does not sound like a description of socialization practices at all. Surely she is hinting at something more profoundly connected with being female than that?

Thus we arrive at a pivotally important question for this book: are the gender stereotypes we have explored in this chapter all about socialization, or could there be another explanation? Perhaps there really is something in *the nature of woman*, as Friedan is hinting, that leads to her happiness lying in the family and home, and results in unhappiness when these are eschewed? If that is the case, perhaps there is something in the nature of women that also leads them to make stereotyped choices of subjects and careers? And perhaps this will have very little to do with socialization? Whisper this quietly, but in Chapter 6 we will ask whether or not *biology* might have something to do with it. If it does, does anything follow for education policy and our tackling of the Bridget Jones Syndrome?

3

Romantic Illusions

Bridget Jones wants a boyfriend more than anything, as a path to having what she knows will lead to her fulfilment: a family – a baby, children and a home. In the film version of *Bridget Jones's Diary*, from almost the first moment she gets any romantic interest from her boss Daniel, she fantasizes about walking down the aisle with him. Soon she is playing with her name and her boyfriend's, matching them together in matrimonial order. Later, she believes she is pregnant with his child, and feels 'all nesty and gooey . . . smug about being a real woman – so irrepressibly fecund! – and imagining fluffy pink baby skin, a tiny creature to love, and darling little Ralph Lauren baby outfits'. It changes her whole approach to life. Instead of wanting to throttle her female line manager for her perpetual demands, she smiles 'in a beatific sort of way, thinking how soon all these things were to be immaterial to me, alongside caring for another tiny human being'. And then: 'Next I discovered a whole new world of Daniel fantasies: Daniel carrying the baby in a sling, Daniel rushing home from work, thrilled to find the two of us pink and glowing in the bath, and, in years to come, being incredibly impressive at parent/teacher evenings.' Even though the pregnancy turns out to be a 'scare', her thoughts continually return to these themes: 'Head is full of moony fantasies about living in flats with him and running along beaches together with tiny offspring in manner of Calvin Klein advert, being trendy Smug Married instead of sheepish Singleton.' The Smug Married, like Magda, who gets to live 'in a big house with eight different kinds of pasta in jars, and gets to go shopping all day'. The

Smug Married who can delight in 'Tiny fluffy children in pyjamas with pink cheeks looking at the Christmas tree excitedly'.[1]

I am told by female friends that many of these themes and fantasies will not be remotely unfamiliar to a great many young women. Indeed, it seems they would not be remotely unfamiliar to some familiar household names either. Who is the subject of this tabloid headline? 'I WAS DESPERATE FOR A BABY AND HAVE THE MEDICAL BILLS TO PROVE IT!' Some smitten soap star? No, it is Germaine Greer, one of the great icons of modern feminism. Greer wrote *The Female Eunuch* back in 1971, its groaning page-long paragraphs uncompromising with notions of childbearing as 'constricting, suffocating, an enemy of a liberated woman's larger hopes'.[2] Germaine Greer was the feminist icon who inspired a generation of women *not* to want motherhood: 'Greer helped cut the umbilical cord of motherhood as a biological imperative', writes one, now infuriated feminist: 'It was okay not to have kids, not to want kids.' Indeed, while it seemed natural to describe Betty Friedan as the 'mother' of modern feminism, the very description would have seemed incongruous if applied to Greer then: 'She was anti-maternalism as fiercely as she railed against paternalism and patriarchy; an exemplar of body politic independence, rabidly sexual, deliberately promiscuous . . . and at heart, anti-authority. All this in a physically attractive (it helped), leggy, academic package.' The disappointed feminist continues, 'A lot of women believed in her', and 'put off children until they'd achieved other goals, pro- fessional goals usually.' And now these women feel betrayed by her '*mea uterus*': 'Her lament over motherhood deferred and then mother- hood denied – is an act of sabotage against all the women (and the men) who took to heart the much different things she said three decades ago.'[3]

Now Germaine Greer 'mourns for her unborn babies'; she confesses wretchedly: 'I still have pregnancy dreams, waiting with vast joy and confidence for something that will never happen.'[4]

Completing our trio: who was it who famously described marriage as an institution of female enslavement under patriarchy, an institution under which a woman 'becomes a semi-non-person'? Who was it who some say coined the memorable phrase that 'A woman without a man is like a fish without a bicycle'? Well, the fish has found her bicycle. Gloria Steinem, another of the feminist icons, has finally married at age 66: 'Though I've worked many years to make marriage more equal', she said in her brief press statement issued via an abortion rights' political action committee, 'I never expected to take advantage of it myself. I'm happy, surprised and one day will write about it, but for now, I hope this proves what feminists have always said – that feminism is about the ability to choose what's right at each time of our lives.'[5]

But hang on – is that what young women, still introduced to early Gloria Steinem tracts in their gender and education courses, *really* believed and still believe her to be saying? One young feminist, at least, is not so sure. Hearing the news she writes: 'I was disappointed. I'm a twenty-something, single, professional woman with more interest in travel and my career than in finding a husband.' She was informed by e-mail of the marriage by one of her singleton friends, with the comment: 'There's hope for us yet!' 'Hope? Does anyone really think that Gloria Steinem sat around "hoping" she would get married? *Does my friend think that I do?*' Fighting back her Bridget Jones-esque paranoia, she notes how unsettling it is when your icons turn their back on all you thought they stood for and that have inspired you in your own goals:

> in a world that constantly throws your life into question, it would be nice to have a role model – a woman who not only lives her life on her own terms, as Steinem has, but who also has never said 'I do' to anyone other than herself. I'd always looked at Gloria Steinem as that woman. A bombshell, a single woman with brains – and a feminist to boot.

And now . . . there is no one left to guide her through her single life. What is a poor girl to do? Best get working on being the role model herself, 'living life on our own terms . . . Because soon enough, there will be a new generation of women looking to my peers and me – not Bridget Jones – for guidance.'[6]

SCHOOLS FOR INDEPENDENCE

Bridget Jones, Germaine Greer, Gloria Steinem . . . eat your hearts out: there are many feminists who would not, do not approve of all this at all. And – crucially – their message is the one that fits with the educational landscape of today. It is the themes of the early Greer, Steinem and Friedan – that independence and career are what are most important to a girl, that marriage, children and family are just so much 'domestic drudgery' – that match the curriculum and emphases of schooling for girls today. In all its aspects – denying girls subject choices, careers education that prizes female independence over all else, sex education that denies there are any differences between the ways girls and boys are, obvious bodily functions apart, pastoral care that emphasizes a girl's need to get on in the world, to be independent and career-oriented – in all these aspects Bridget Jones' dilemmas do not get a look in.

It is all so taken for granted in schools now that it can be quite easily missed. The battle has been won by feminism – that is, in terms of our distinctions in the previous chapter, by equality feminism – so much so that even to question that schooling should be about preparation of boys and girls in identical ways seems to be completely anathema. Let us ease our way in gently here: I am not saying (not yet, anyway) that girls and boys should not be prepared by schools in identical ways; just making sure that we are all aware that this is precisely what schools are compelled to do, by law. In the USA, this emphasis is dramatically illustrated in the celebrations around 25 years of Title IX – the legislation that enacted gender neutrality in all educational programmes that receive any federal funding – which, in practice, turns out to be the vast majority.[7]

What is made absolutely clear in all the pronouncements about this legislation is that what makes for successful girls and women are the same things that make for successful boys and men. The American Secretary of Education put it thus:

Women astronauts from Sally Ride to Shannon Lucid have made their mark in space even as Mia Hamm and Michelle Akers have led the women's national soccer team to Olympic glory and the

World Championship. Women have entered the medical and legal professions in record numbers and we have seen a fourfold increase in women's participation in intercollegiate athletics.

Space adventure, football and athletics – these are the things that Bridget Jones is craving to succeed in, right? These are the areas in which she and her sisters find themselves completely at sea when they reach 30 and long for guidance, correct?

The Secretary of Education, however, is oblivious to their plight: 'Somewhere in America today there are young women who are studying hard and achieving success on the athletic field who even now may be thinking hard about their careers as scientists, business owners, basketball players, or even the possibility of becoming president of the United States.' Such women 'can succeed and be part of the American Dream'. And the American Dream, let us be clear, is about achievement of women, the same as for men, in science, business, sport and politics. Family and home life are merely inconveniences, places from which women must escape in order to succeed.

And how can they escape? Just as Betty Friedan realized in *The Feminine Mystique*, it is mainly through their schooling that women and girls can 'escape the limitations of discrimination and reach their full potential'[8] – the limitations of discrimination being those that would serve to keep them in domestic roles and part-time work. This is why Title IX is so important, to liberate women from the tyranny that was their schooling in years gone by – tyranny that led to travesties such as where girls were directed 'to classes where they would learn to cook and sew', 'routinely denying' them opportunities to take 'classes in shop, manufacturing' and architectural drafting;[9] travesties such as the Connecticut judge in 1971 suggesting that 'Athletic competition builds character in our boys. We do not need that kind of character in our girls.'[10] But of course the same level of 'competitiveness' and 'controlled aggression' is needed if girls are to claim their rightful share of the American Dream.

As for the next 25 years of Title IX: there is much that has been accomplished, but still much to be done. Women need even more encouragement into the labour market where salaries are the highest, in the fields of mathematics, computer science and engineering – fields in which women are still dismally underrepresented: 'Without more equity in these fields at all levels, women will remain at the low end of positions and the pay scale in the information age.' And another dismal statistic: 'there are still about 24,000 more boys' varsity teams than girls' teams; in college, women receive only one-third of all athletic scholarships', and 'overall operating expenditure for women's college sports programs' represented less than a quarter of the total.[11] We cannot rest until girls love sport as much as boys, for only then will women be truly fulfilled, truly liberated.

President Clinton summarized the whole adventure thus: Title IX, he said, has made 'the difference . . . in the lives of millions of young girls and young women. We know about the confidence that it has built, *the expectations it has helped to set*, the achievements it has helped to inspire.' These expectations are leading girls and young women to look to their careers for fulfilment: 'We do not have a person to waste,' he declared, 'if we are to ensure the well-being of our people and the competitiveness of the nation.' 'Wasted opportunity', he proclaimed, 'diminishes all of us. As we prepare for the twenty-first century, it would be sheer folly for us not to take advantage of every ounce of energy and talent and creativity every American has to offer.' And, reiterating the themes announced by the Secretary of Education – perhaps cribbing from the same press release – he continued: 'Every girl growing up in America today should have the chance to become an astronaut or an Olympic athlete, a Cabinet Secretary or a Supreme Court Justice, a Nobel Prize winning scientist or President of the United States. For 25 years, Title IX has helped girls to realize their dreams and to achieve them.' It is only in these ways, he assures us, that 'every one of our girls and young women have the opportunities they deserve to make the most of their own lives'. Every 'young woman or girl' must be given 'a chance to make the most of her God-given abilities'; that is, God-given abilities to become astronauts or soccer players.[12] There is no mention of any other possible God-given talents here that girls might have, even talents that might be different from boys'.

As in many areas, America has led the world here. The prejudices of the early Betty Friedan, of the early Gloria Steinem, they are all there, spelled out in legislative detail to ensure gender neutrality in schooling – gender neutrality that emphasizes over and over again that the only way to success and fulfilment for women is through achievement in the worlds of business, science, sport and politics. The family does not get a look in here. As the President of the USA sternly reminded all those listening: 'Title IX is not optional. It is the law, and the law must be enforced.'[13]

In Britain it is all enshrined in law too, from the Sex Discrimination Act of 1975, just three years after Title IX, through to its final articulation in the Education Reform Act of 1988, with the feminist-oriented National Curriculum and assessment systems. Reading the speeches of politicians, we find the same sentiments expressed, and, less flamboyantly, but more insidiously, the same sentiments find their way into the small print of the legislation. For instance, the revised National Curriculum 2000 documents are quite clear that boys and girls are identical and must be treated as such, and the aims of education for each must be identical. Aim 1 of the National Curriculum is 'to provide opportunities for all pupils to learn and to achieve', and it is spelled out that the curriculum should give *all* pupils 'the opportunity to become creative, innovative, enterprising and capable of leadership to equip them for their future lives as *workers and citizens*'. The four 'main purposes' of the National Curriculum are to ensure that all pupils, *irrespective of gender*, 'develop knowledge, understanding, skills and attitudes necessary for their self-fulfilment and *development as active and responsible citizens*'.

It is subtle, perhaps easily missed: what is equally important for all students is that they are prepared for their roles *in the public domain of work and politics*. The family and the home do not get a look in here. What Bridget Jones discovers that she wants to prioritize most in her life when she hits 30 is not part of what she should be prepared for under this fundamental first aim of the curriculum.

Indeed, the only place that the home is mentioned in the curriculum documents – outlining what schools are legally required to promote – is where it is tagged on to the end of Aim 2, which spells out that the curriculum should 'promote pupils' spiritual, moral, social and cultural development', preparing them 'for the opportunities, responsibilities and experiences of life'. In passing, it is noted that this aim means the curriculum should help pupils 'to form and maintain worthwhile and satisfying relationships . . . at home, school, work and in the community'. But even this brief mention of the sphere in which many women seem to want to prioritize finding their fulfilment is made in the context that the school should 'promote equal opportunities and enable pupils to challenge discrimination and stereotyping',[14] and certainly not acquiesce in any ill-conceived notions of what home life should be all about.

Slightly less subtle is the way this approach is fleshed out in the work of the Equal Opportunities Commission. Reading its reports and aims, it is clear that its approach is fundamentally one of getting girls into masculine employment areas, the higher paid the better. It too believes that what is important for girls is the public sphere of work and politics. That women are there as so much fodder to help the economy is clear in statements such as this: 'Given the present skills shortages in the areas of science, technology and information technology . . . it is important that both girls and boys are encouraged into those areas of future employment.' But is the 'present skills shortage' something that is particularly bothering Bridget Jones? Never mind, her schooling must all be about getting competitive in the masculine world, for that above all is what is important. And when the EOC does touch on some of the issues that might strike her as more important, such as differences in personal development among boys and girls, again the solution is to break away from traditional gender stereotyping: 'Once again, these differences can be addressed by tackling inherent attitudes to gender roles. Only by changing traditional attitudes to "male" and "female" areas of the curriculum and by making these equally attractive to both sexes, will real equality be achieved.'[15] It is only through increasing gender neutrality, making boys and girls the same, eliminating difference between them, that girls can find fulfilment.

FEMINISTS CHAMPIONING GOVERNMENT

Government pronouncements are clear: they want as many women as possible to be in the workforce, and at as high a level as possible. They want as many women as possible whole-heartedly pursuing high-status pursuits in business, science and sport – so that their countries can be the greatest in the world. Hoorah! (as Bridget Jones might put it). But perhaps they can be excused for their narrow obsessions? With so few women represented at the highest levels of government, perhaps they can be excused for getting carried away with these peculiarly masculine obsessions? Perhaps, indeed, there are women writing who can help rein back some of their misplaced enthusiasms, making them realize that it is not just male pursuits that are valuable, reminding them that other things are important in life? If the reader was hoping thus, she will not find much solace in the writings of feminist educators.

What is it that makes some feminists so in tune with the things governments want from education? It is absolutely essential for the argument of this book to locate what is at stake here. What we will do is focus in detail on the arguments of *Closing the Gender Gap*, for this book, written by influential feminist academics, provides a coherent, comprehensive, and, I suggest, representative summary of the key arguments of the equality feminists about education policy. In this book can be found the key themes that support the continuing quest to eradicate gender stereotypes, to make women more like men. In this book are the major arguments in support of the reforms thus far that have made gender discrimination illegal in schools. Reviewing its arguments, I believe, unlocks the key tenets of this influential strand of feminism.

First, in *Closing the Gender Gap* we find fulsome praise for the current position of young women. The authors admit that they were wrong when they feared in the past that things were only going to get worse for girls and young women during the Thatcher years. In particular, they were wrong to doubt that life could improve for working-class girls, through the 'educational feminism' that brought so many changes to schooling and curriculum. Instead, 'Feminist teachers and educators' have been able to help girls 'to engage with the concept of woman and make it problematic'. Young women, in the 'safe haven of the school', have been freed from 'Victorian models of femininity and the patriarchal family'. This is all to be applauded, they say.

In the 1970s and 1980s, there were several major studies that interviewed working-class girls and young women about their perceptions and attitudes. However, somewhat disappointingly for the researchers, if things were bad then, the young women certainly did not recognize it themselves. Girls were 'inordinately preoccupied with romance'. They were not unhappy about their prospects, but had developed a 'romanticized future'. The girls, far from being worried about the 'domestic drudgery' that the authors of *Closing the Gender Gap* consider characterizes home life, instead immersed themselves 'in the ideology of romance and glamour as an expression of female sexuality'. Instead of being negative about 'what they took to be their *fate*' (not their aspiration or desire, note) of 'marriage and motherhood', the girls 'celebrated' it. But for the authors of *Closing the Gender Gap*, their celebration only emphasized their false consciousness, their misguidedness.

Marriage 'was used both to confer status and as an opportunity to express individuality and sexuality'. But such, say these authors, could not possibly have been a realistic appraisal of what it actually was to be like for them. These girls celebrated a 'cult of femininity', what Betty Friedan, as we saw in Chapter 1, called the 'feminine mystique'. The girls, almost universally, gave 'endorsement of the traditional female role and of femininity'. During this time, 'femininity for most girls was still more linked to boyfriends, marriage and motherhood than the wage packet'.

Closing the Gender Gap has a simple economic explanation for these girls' stubborn misapprehensions. The girls had to live in their romantic fantasies because they needed men to support them financially: 'It seemed an unavoidable and unalterable fact of life that child-rearing and childcare were to be women's responsibility. Without finance, the majority of girls would have little choice but to plan their way *out of their predicament* by ensuring marital and domestic support for their childrearing years.' In particular, say the authors, it was 'the lack of state-funded childcare' that 'had major repercussions on girls' long-term planning'.

However – and here we get the fulsome praise of these authors – young working-class girls' attitudes changed in the late 1980s and 1990s. Many are no longer prepared to put up with 'domestic drudgery' and injustice. Many became independent women, liberated from domesticity and also from their romantic illusions about marriage and family life. Of course, the authors concede that 'it would be a mistake to generalize too far'. In particular, as we have already noted, they see the '*curious contradiction*' of young women, 'no longer unaware of sex segregation and the lack of female bargaining power', who stubbornly still choose 'to work as adults within rather than outside the "realm of women's work"'. But again, they have an economic explanation for this too. It is the paucity of training places that has 'encouraged conservatism among working-class girls'. Hopefully, we infer, things will get better in this regard too, since in sum, the authors celebrate the fact that the 'liberation of women from the cult of femininity and domesticity and the traditional family . . . cannot now be reversed'.[16]

Let us repeat: these are feminists – writing in the traditions of the early Friedan, Greer and Steinem – who provide support for current government policy on education; the traditions in which they write coincide with the educational landscape of today. Some readers will find it all very positive no doubt, and will agree with the assessment of the feminist authors, and feel glad that they have such influence and power. For me, however, there are *three* important issues that arise from their arguments. These three problems will provide the structure and content for the rest of this chapter and the next, three issues that need exploration in depth.

First, there is the issue of the 'degradation of domesticity'. Is domesticity really as worthless as the feminists make out, so unfulfilling? Were the girls of yesteryear, with their romantic notions of what it could all mean, wanting to prioritize this in their lives, really as misguided as the feminists make out? This issue provides the focus for the remainder of this chapter.

Second, there is the reverse question concerning the world of men, of work and public life. Is it really as valuable as the feminists suggest? Does it really bring as much fulfilment to those within it – and can it bring that same fulfilment to the majority of women? Or is there a curious romanticization of this world, running parallel with the degradation of the domestic?

Third, there is the nagging doubt that, in their descriptions and praise of independent women, the feminists have missed out something about the mutuality, the interconnectedness, of the happiness of men and women. If in relationships girls are taught that they have to be so fiercely independent, will this not have an impact on the ways boys behave towards them? Couldn't this, indeed, have potential repercussions for the Bridget Jones Syndrome? The second and third problems provide the focus for the next chapter.

THE DEGRADATION OF DOMESTICITY

Just as Betty Friedan dismissed the way women romanticized domesticity, and strove to denigrate it, so the feminist educators, as we have seen, dismiss that girls — and working-class girls in particular — could possibly have been right to romanticize their destinies on any level. It is definitely a case of feminist knows best here. The girls were — and those who, in spite of everything, live by that *'curious contradiction'* now, still are — deceiving themselves. Bringing meaning into your lives through romance, marriage and family is all false consciousness. None of these things can possibly bring a levity into the 'domestic drudgery' of bringing up children and looking after a home. Marriage and the family cannot possibly really bring status, security and love. Family life is a *predicament* — the feminists' word — that girls have to endure. Childrearing is an 'unavoidable and unalterable' burden of life, not a joy or a vocation. For these feminists, childcare is simply another household chore, 'akin to mopping the floor'.[17]

In the bad old days, girls had to be dependent on a man to endure their lot. How much better it would have been if this dependence could be transferred to the government through 'state-funded childcare'. And how much better it is in the glorious days of the present, where girls can express their 'femininity' through 'the wage packet' rather than through love, marriage and children. How much better it is now that girls can engage in their own long-term career planning rather than planning for their families.

Indeed, such a litany is almost too familiar to repeat, so much has it pervaded our consciousness. But it is worth locating from whence it came — for within its sources lie some fascinating insights. The need to liberate women from 'domestic drudgery' to their rightful position in the workplace can usefully be traced back to Simone de Beauvoir's tirade against the housewife of 1949 in *The Second Sex*,[18] ideas translated to an American and then wider Anglo-Saxon audience by Betty Friedan in *The Feminine Mystique* of 1963.

My source initially for exploring all of this was Carolyn Graglia's polemical attack on feminism, *Domestic Tranquility*. Simone de Beauvoir, says Graglia, first sets out to establish how women have no maternal instincts, that they find their babies 'burdensome'. She then notes how the mother and housewife is 'almost always a discontented woman: sexually she is frigid or unsatisfied; socially she feels herself inferior to man'. Being a housewife is doubly unsatisfying, because she 'produces nothing'; the housewife 'is subordinate, secondary, parasitic'. Marriage 'makes women into "praying mantises", "leeches", "poisonous" creatures'. It is for the 'common welfare' of man and woman that 'the situation must be altered by prohibiting marriage as a "career" for woman': in the home, a woman cannot 'establish her existence': 'she lacks the means requisite for self-affirmation as an individual; and in consequence her individuality is not given recognition'.[19]

For Graglia, all the ideas 'advanced by contemporary feminism can be found in *The Second Sex*'. The early Betty Friedan then dressed up the same ideas in ways that were more accessible to an American — and then British — audience. For Graglia, Friedan's first book, *The Feminine Mystique* is 'an impassioned expression of overwhelming antipathy for the life of a suburban housewife'.[20] Friedan's most striking denunciation is that being a housewife leads to 'progressive dehumanization' in the 'comfortable concentration camp': 'American women are not, of course, being readied for mass extermination, but they are suffering a slow death of mind and spirit'. The work they do makes them 'dependent, passive, childlike', it 'does not require adult capabilities; it is endless, monotonous, unrewarding'. There is 'something about the housewife state itself that is dangerous'. For the women who want to be housewives 'are in as much danger as the millions who walked to their own death in the concentration camps — and the millions more who refused to believe that the concentration camps existed'. In the Nazi concentration camps, prisoners 'literally became "walking corpses"' surrendering their 'human identity': 'Strangely enough, the conditions which destroyed the human identity of so many prisoners were not the torture and the brutality, *but conditions similar to those which destroy the identity of the American housewife*.'[21]

Indeed, says Graglia, the way in which Friedan and de Beauvoir before her used the word 'parasite' to describe the housewife is probably unprecedented in American or British society, finding echoes only in the works of Hitler: 'Both *Mein Kampf* and *The Feminine Mystique* employ similar rhetoric to isolate and vilify the group each work condemns; both have succeeded, although only one author continues to receive acclaim.' With ease, she says, for the phrasing is so similar, 'Hitler's description of the Jew in German society' could be substituted for Friedan's and de Beauvoir's descriptions of the housewife.[22]

In these traditions, the feminists who have helped to create the current educational landscape proudly sit – proudly, because they have told us that they themselves were liberated from 'domestic drudgery'. It was the expansion of the education system, they say, that helped each of them 'move up and away from the narrow confines of domesticity'.[23] And they are pleased that all women, working-class as well as professional, are achieving the same too.

But is it all really as bad as all that? If it is, then clearly it is right and proper that women should be liberated from it. Why is it then that many women are still so unhappy and unfulfilled and apparently yearning to prioritize domesticity, even though they have been liberated from that need? Perhaps some answers to these questions may be found by going back to the two women who set the whole project going in the first place. I always tell my students not to rely on secondary sources for key texts, lest they be led into a game of 'Academic Chinese Whispers', where arguments become distorted and misrepresented, and the eventual outcome may bear little resemblance to what was written in the original source.[24] I try to practise what I preach, and so went back to consult de Beauvoir and Friedan themselves, rather than rely on the critic Carolyn Graglia's interpretation of them. What I found surprised me. I had to conclude that all was not quite what it seemed. Certainly each author had written what she had been quoted as saying, but there was much, much more to be said.

Betty Friedan's mea culpa

Feminist educators of today are writing firmly in the Betty Friedan tradition of the denigration of domesticity; yet, ironically, while their views fit in neatly with those in *The Feminine Mystique*, Friedan no longer abides by those extreme views. As we saw in Chapter 1, she has had a change of heart. She has been listening to the stories of women's unhappiness, of prototype Bridget Joneses in America, all wondering whether the feminist revolution was worth the candle. Was it really worth it to replace the joys of motherhood and family life with a career of dubious worth, and loneliness to boot? But Betty Friedan's change of heart does not seem to have had any impact on the feminist educators who make the policy running.

Friedan now recognizes that the comparison of the housewife to concentration camp victim was 'rather extreme'. Feminism for her never meant the 'destruction of the family, repudiation of marriage and motherhood, or implacable sexual war against men'. That was to misunderstand the whole project. Indeed, candidly, she admits that it all got rather out of hand, in part through fear of some of the more outspoken of the sisterhood: 'We were intimidated by the conformities of the women's movement', she says, intimidated by the 'powerful' 'sisterhood' more than by 'the enemy', namely, men. But she is adamant now: 'The equality we fought for isn't livable (sic), isn't workable, isn't comfortable in the terms that structured our battle.' Those women who believe it is, she says, 'who live alone, repudiating marriage and motherhood . . . are living a life defined by reaction against the family, whistling a brave tune to hide the loneliness and yearning for some form of family'. One wonders whether any of the feminist educators would be seen by Betty Friedan as fitting under this rubric.

Friedan, even as far back as 1981, could now celebrate with people like Liz, at 40 returning to the joys of domesticity by choice, who admits,

> The housewife things women can't stand doing anymore, I now love doing. Maybe it's because I do have a choice now. It has struck me the last few years how much I cling to emptying the dishwasher, folding the clean laundry. . . . It grounds me in whatever else I'm doing. I'm haunted by the women I work with who are thirty and thirty-five and are not having children, or are torn to the core about it. I had them without thinking about it,

and I'm so thankful now I did. I am absolutely the richer for it. They ground your life, keep you in touch with the fundamentals.

The woman who eschews these simple pleasures, says Friedan, loses something. Should not domesticity, she asks, 'be valued somehow?' All the things women have traditionally enjoyed – 'arranging the flowers, baking the cookies' – all the things that make 'life more pleasant', was feminism not mistaken in thinking that all these things were valueless? 'What would life be like if no one did that work?' she asks: 'What if, in reaction', a feminist 'strips her life clean of all those unmeasured, unvalued feminine tasks and frills – stops baking cookies altogether, cuts her hair like a monk, decides not to have children, installs a computer console in her bedroom?' That is far worse a fate, it would seem now, than the feminine mystique from which Friedan fought so hard to liberate women. The feminist, says Friedan, 'suffers . . . a new "crisis of confidence". She does not feel grounded in life. She shivers inside.'[25] Yet it is this 'feminist mystique' that the feminist educators seem still to be caught up in, not questioning it as Friedan has done. It is this feminist mystique that provides the foundation for our education policies, in Britain, America, Australia and elsewhere.

Simone de Beauvoir and the joys of domesticity

It is not only Friedan who has changed her mind on this issue – or rather, the other key protagonist of contemporary equality feminism seems *always* to have been in two minds about the issue. Going back to Simone de Beauvoir twenty years after first reading her was an eye-opener for me. I had an odd sense that there were *two* de Beauvoirs writing, one saying all the things that Graglia had accused her of saying, true, and that had such a resounding influence across the world; but there was another de Beauvoir struggling to get out, a woman who appeared to be delighting in all the things she was criticizing elsewhere. Reading de Beauvoir, I came across passages which seemed to be enchanted and charmed by all that women had and did, which recognized the huge importance and value of domesticity for the human condition. Finally, it is true, the critical de Beauvoir got the upper hand, but I had an uneasy sense that there was some underlying reason why this might be the case.

For, set amidst comments presenting the degradation of domestic life are passages emphasizing the delight of it all. The housewife can set up a home that has everything for her and of value beyond her. 'In the form of more or less expensive bric-a-brac she has within her four walls the fauna and flora of the world, she has exotic countries and past times; she has her husband, representing human society, and she has her child, who gives her the entire future in portable form.' For de Beauvoir sees that the home can become 'the center of the world', 'a kind of counter-universe or universe in opposition', a 'refuge, retreat, grotto, womb' that 'gives shelter from outside dangers'. With shutters closed, 'the wife feels herself queen'. Tasks within the home are valuable too: food preparation is 'agreeable'; 'gossip on doorsteps, while peeling vegetables, is a gay relief from solitude', and going to the market 'is a profound pleasure, a discovery, almost an invention'. The housewife knows that 'a solid cabbage, a ripe Camembert, are treasures that must be cleverly won from the unwilling storekeeper; the game is to get the best for the least money'. The housewife, says de Beauvoir, 'is pleased with her passing triumph as she contemplates her well-filled larder'. In the kitchen, she 'becomes a sorceress; by a simple movement, as in beating eggs, or through the magic of fire, she effects the transmutation of substances: matter becomes food'. In all of these 'alchemies' there is 'enchantment': 'there is poetry in making preserves; the housewife has caught duration in the snare of sugar'; and 'a woman can find special satisfaction in a successful cake or a flaky pastry, for not everyone can do it: one must have the gift'.

It is not just domestic 'chores' about which she waxes lyrical in places – only then to dash these pronouncements later. Motherhood is also a delight to her – again, set amongst passages that are strongly condemnatory. But when she writes that it is 'in maternity that woman fulfils her physiological destiny; it is her natural "calling", . . . the perpetuation of the species', it is hard not to discern a sincerely held passion. The woman in pregnancy 'glimpses immortality', she lends herself to 'this mystery'. 'Ordinarily life', she notes, 'is but a condition of existence'; but 'in gestation it appears as creative'. Some women, she says, 'enjoy the pleasures of pregnancy and suckling so much that they desire their indefinite repetitions'. When a women is pregnant, 'the flesh becomes root-stock, source, and blossom, it assumes transcendence, a stirring towards the future'. The woman 'is plunged anew into the mainstream of life, reunited with the wholeness of things, a link in the endless chain of generations, flesh that exists by and for another fleshly being'. In pregnancy, the woman

> is no longer a subject afflicted with the anxiety that accompanies liberty, she is one with that equivocal reality: life. Her body is at least her own, since it exists for the child who belongs to her. Society recognises her right of possession and invests it, moreover, with a sacred character.

Can this really be the same de Beauvoir who wrote of the housewife as a 'vassal', the slave and humble dependant, 'doomed' to bear children, the 'care of the home' forced 'tyrannically' upon her, her home a 'prison'? For there is not much in these alternative descriptions to support the feminist notion of 'domestic drudgery'; not much to convey the housewife as parasitical and in need of liberation. But de Beauvoir's more loving descriptions continue. As pregnancy progresses, women become even more alive:

> Many women find in their later pregnancy a marvellous peace: they feel justified. . . . They are no longer called upon for work or effort; they no longer have to think of others; the dreams of the future they cherish lend meaning to the present moment; they have only to let themselves live: they are on vacation.

De Beauvoir describes it with approving clarity: 'The pregnant woman's *raison d'être* is there, in her womb, and gives her a perfect sense of rich abundance.' One mother described it as like having 'a stove in the winter that is always lit, that is there for you alone, entirely subject to your will. It is also like a constantly gushing cold shower in the summer, refreshing you. It is there'. De Beauvoir continues, 'Thus fulfilled, the woman has also the satisfaction of feeling that she is "interesting", something that has been her deepest wish since adolescence; . . . she is the incarnation of the species, she represents the promise of life, of eternity. Her entourage respects her; her very caprices become sacred . . .' She observes that, 'Justified by the presence of an other in her womb, she at last enjoys the privilege of being wholly herself'.

De Beauvoir quotes her friend Colette *L'Étoile Vesper* at length – often returning to her descriptions, apparently lovingly – describing the 'euphoria' of her pregnancy, her 'state of pride, of vulgar grandeur', her 'cheerfulness, contentment, euphoria':

> Sixth, seventh month . . . The first strawberries, the first roses. Can I call my pregnancy anything less than a long holiday? The pangs of childbirth [now] are forgotten, but not so a long, unique holiday: I remember it all. I recall especially that slumber overcame me at odd times, and that I felt again, as in childhood, the need to sleep on the ground, on the grass, on the warm earth. It was my sole 'longing', and a wholesome one. Towards the end I was like a rat trying to make off with a stolen egg. An inconvenience to myself, I became too fatigued to go to bed. . . . For all my weight and fatigue, my holiday still continued. I was borne on a shield of privileges and attentions.

Then there is childbirth, bringing 'amazed curiosity in every young mother. It is strangely miraculous to see and to hold a living being formed within oneself and issued forth from oneself.' For many young mothers, she writes,

> The baby incarnates all nature. . . . The infant's flesh has that softness, that warm elasticity, which the woman, when she was a little girl, coveted in her mother's flesh and, later, in things everywhere. The baby is plant and animal, in its eyes are rains and rivers, the azure of sea and sky; its fingernails are coral, its hair a silky growth; it is a living doll, a bird, a kitten; 'my flower, my pearl, my chick, my lamb.' The mother murmurs almost a lover's words, and like a lover she makes avid use of the possessive case; she employs the same gestures of possession: caresses, kisses; she hugs the child to her bosom, she keeps him warm in her arms and in her bed.

Finally, 'Like the woman in love, the mother is delighted to feel herself necessary; her existence is justified by the wants she supplies; but what gives mother love *its difficulty and its grandeur* is the fact that it implies no reciprocity; the mother has to do not with man, a hero, a demigod, but with a small, prattling soul, lost in a fragile and dependent body.' Bringing up a child, says de Beauvoir, is 'the most delicate and the most serious undertaking of all: the molding of a human being'.[26]

Reading these passages, I was struck by three powerful sensations. First, I felt an overwhelming sense of awe and wonder, envy even, at what women are, and can do. I was touched by the tenderness and sensitivity, the sincerity of de Beauvoir's description. I never thought I would get this from *The Second Sex*, which I approached with some trepidation assuming that it would only be a savage attack on the female condition under patriarchy. Instead, reading her descriptions gave me a strong longing to support a woman through the process myself, that my life too was lacking if I was not involved in the process, at least by proxy, the only way a man can be involved.

But second, I was struck by incredulity that anyone could think that the world of work, politics, sport or whatever – even being an astronaut or President of the USA – could possibly compensate for the loss of any of this mystery and magic – for many women, to be sure, for no one is saying that all women will feel the same delight that de Beauvoir conveys in those selected passages. But for those who have given it up for the sake of the pay-packet and yearn for it, I felt a terrible sadness. Could it be that, under the influence of feminist-driven education policy that has enshrined the *other* voice of de Beauvoir and the early Betty Friedan in law, women now have to sacrifice this aspect of their meaning and identity? Could it be that they are not able to cherish those moments so sensitively described by this alternative de Beauvoir, but must work right up until the birth of their child, through the final stages of pregnancy when Colette slept in the grass and smelt the strawberries; and then go back to wage labour as soon as they are able afterwards, leaving their babies for some other women to murmur and coo over like a lover?

I could just about understand those in government objecting to the women enjoying their pregnancies as a 'long holiday', wanting to herd them back into the fold of productive work like so many sheep once they had done their female reproductive stuff – but why should their feminist sisters want to herd them so? Unless, as for de Beauvoir, there is something else going on – my third powerful sensation.

De Beauvoir cheated

For it seems obvious that de Beauvoir is torn by it all. In places she seems delighted by all the 'feminine mystique', revelling in the beauty of being a woman – the examples given above could be multiplied many times over – relishing in her descriptions of motherhood by proxy, as it were, delighting in the woman in love and the joys of domesticity. But then she concludes that it cannot be this way, that women cannot be dependent; they must be liberated from what they really desire.

What is going on? I am not alone, of course, in finding the text somewhat baffling and contradictory. Even sympathetic feminist commentators have called *The Second Sex* 'a fascinating, overpowering, and finally bewildering book';[27] de Beauvoir is not a writer for those of us 'who prefer their intellectuals to be coherent and uncontradictory'.[28] But wherein lies the source of these bewildering contradictions? Reading *The Second Sex* one cannot help speculating that there is something peculiar happening behind the scenes. It is almost as if there is someone reading the evolving manuscript, making sure that she curbed her real desires and thoughts to express a different, approved conclusion that she did not whole-heartedly endorse. And of course, as is well-known, Simone de Beauvoir had a lifelong affair with the existential philosopher Jean-Paul Sartre, although they never married nor shared living quarters, nor had children. It is in this relationship that we can perhaps find the root for some of the bewildering contradictions in de Beauvoir's writings on women.

For their relationship showed 'manifest inequalities', one of which speaks particularly loudly: 'it is de Beauvoir and not Sartre who is the historian of the "friendship". Sartre maintained an absolute silence on the matter, and although some of his letters to de Beauvoir have been [posthumously] published, they remain the sole testament to a relationship which lasted for over fifty years.' For one feminist commentator, 'the couple followed the age old maxim which suggests that for men love is peripheral, while for women it is their very existence'.[29] In the end, de Beauvoir is clearly not very happy with it all. At the age of 54 – hardly old age in many people's view – she wrote a 'devastating' picture of her life:

> At the age of forty I thought, 'Old age lies in wait for me at the bottom of my mirror; it's inevitable; it will take hold of me.' Now it has. I pause, aghast, before this incredible object which functions as my face. . . . I detest my own reflection; above my eyes is a kind of horrid cap and below them little pockets, my face is too full and has that sad look around the mouth which wrinkles cause. . . . I see my former face which has been damaged beyond repair by the pox of age for which there is no cure. . . . All those things I've written about and others about which I've said nothing – nothing of all that will remain. If at least my thought had given birth to – what? A hill? A rocket? But no. Nothing has taken place . . . as I look back, wondering, on the credulous adolescent that I was, I am astonished when I realize how thoroughly I have been cheated.[30]

So what would have led to this sense of being so profoundly cheated? My reading of her autobiography and feminist commentary on it suggests the following.

The young, extremely intelligent Simone de Beauvoir fell deeply in love with her 'true superior' (her words), the man whom she had been seeking from adolescence. When she first met Sartre, she tells us, 'It was the first time in my life that I felt dominated by someone else intellectually. . . . Sartre lived up exactly to the man I had dreamed of at fifteen; he was my double in whom I re-discovered all my own tastes and enthusiasms, refined to the point of incandescence; with him I could always share everything';[31] 'Day after day, and all day long I set myself up against Sartre, and in our discussions I was simply not in his class.'[32] Many women, I am told, will sympathize with her attitude. Carolyn Graglia, for instance, tells us that de Beauvoir's 'evident excitement at being bested by this superior man is familiar to women (it was not entirely with regret that I realized my future husband might beat me in an argument). This excitement can serve women well . . . losing to a superior man may enhance a woman's sexual as well as intellectual satisfaction.'[33] Moreover, 'as every reader of her autobiography knows', when Simone de Beauvoir passed her final philosophy examination 'she was placed second, . . . to Jean-Paul Sartre'.[34]

But being in love with someone as complex, as self-centred and as nihilistic as Sartre was not going to be easy, nor, as it turned out, fulfilling. De Beauvoir presumably went into the relationship with all the expectations of any young woman – she was after all a child of her generation, and in her autobiography makes it clear she has many, if not all, of the standard expectations a young woman would have of a heterosexual relationship. For instance, Part I, Chapter One of the second volume of her autobiography, *The Prime of Life* (dedicated to Sartre), opens with the young de Beauvoir immersed in the delights of domesticity,

> preparing her new, independent home in Paris and waiting for the return of Sartre to Paris after the summer holidays. There is more than an element of the young bride awaiting the arrival of her new husband in these first three pages: the new furniture is brought, the walls papered, and new clothes purchased.[35]

And then, the big event occurs: 'My new life really began when Sartre returned to Paris in mid-October.'[36]

But if she wanted to share these normal domestic delights with Sartre, her hopes were to be dashed. Sartre abhorred family life, abhorred domesticity, and abhorred the sense that anyone could be dependent on him. De Beauvoir relates how during this period she was quite content 'to *stagnate* [as she retrospectively presented it] *in happiness*'.[37] But Sartre would have none of it. He turned on her early on, chiding her: 'You used to be full of little ideas, Beaver',[38] then accused her of turning into 'a female introvert'. De Beauvoir takes this criticism very hard. He is accusing her, she writes, of becoming a 'mere housewife': 'he compared me to . . . heroines . . . who after a long battle for their independence ended up *quite content to be some man's helpmeet*. I was furious *with myself* for disappointing him in this way.'[39] If being a contented housewife led to Sartre's disapproval, then she had to change and disavow it. Thus, through disappointments like this, it is hard not to see the misogynistic views of Sartre becoming translated into the views of de Beauvoir, gestating them in readiness for exposure to the world through *The Second Sex*.

What of motherhood? The closest de Beauvoir came to having a baby was abortion[40] – and it is revealing that the first ten pages of the chapter on motherhood in *The Second Sex* are all about abortion's horrors. It seems likely from her descriptions that abortion would have been imposed on her by Sartre: 'Men tend to take abortion lightly', she wrote in *The Second Sex*,

> they regard it as one of the numerous hazards imposed on women by malignant nature, but fail to realize fully the values involved. The woman who has recourse to abortion is disowning feminine values, her values. . . . Her whole moral universe is being disrupted.[41]

For some feminists it is odd that de Beauvoir did not have children. Professor of Women's Studies, Mary Evans, for instance, puzzles that, since de Beauvoir was so enchanted by heterosexuality, 'it is remarkable that a woman who could delight so strongly in sensual pleasure (and recall the physical delights of her own childhood so vividly) was not a little more attracted to the possibility of recreating those days for herself'.[42] In the end, she takes de Beauvoir's protestations at face value that she was completely happy with Sartre, who 'was sufficient both for himself and for me . . . I never once dreamed of rediscovering myself in the child I might bear'.[43] But elsewhere we are warned to be cautious of taking at face value de Beauvoir's presentation of herself in her autobiography, and this may be one of the places where some caution is necessary.[44] At the least, one may say, logically speaking, that if abortions were imposed on de Beauvoir by Sartre, then, of course, not having his children was also imposed on her by Sartre.

However, if Sartre hated the things women desired, he certainly did not eschew the company of women. Or to be more precise, sexual relations with women. Very early on his relationship with de Beauvoir, he told her that monogamy was out, that they must both have additional sexual relationships. In practice, this meant him having as many women as he could lay his hands on, and her having the occasional fling to compensate for when he was tied up with others.

(Her celebrated affair with the American Nelson Algren, for instance, that formed the compelling love story in her novel *The Mandarins*, came about simply, de Beauvoir tells us, because Sartre told her not to return to Paris from New York because his current lover, 'M', wanted to stay longer: Sartre could not tolerate de Beauvoir in town when she was there, even though he and de Beauvoir didn't even live together![45]). But again, supporting the suggestion that de Beauvoir initially had conventional aspirations about these things that were thwarted by Sartre, 'it was essentially Sartre who explained to de Beauvoir what the nature of their relationship would be'.[46] De Beauvoir is completely frank about this. She tells us that they fought over his idea of having extra sexual relations, but, in the end, 'I acquiesced'.[47]

While we are on the subject of Sartre's relationship with 'M', there is a rather revealing passage in her autobiography where de Beauvoir comments on one of M's upsets with Sartre:

> if he loved her, how could he bear not to see her for months at a time? He listened to her complaints with remorse; he felt he was to blame. *Of course he warned her* that there could be no question of his making a life with her. *But by saying he loved her, he gave the lie to that warning, for — especially in the eyes of women — love triumphs over every obstacle. M. was not entirely in the wrong.*[48]

It is hard not to imagine the same reflections applying to de Beauvoir herself, again revealing the touchingly conventional ways that de Beauvoir would have wanted her relationship to Sartre to progress, had he been less obsessively self-centred.

So de Beauvoir learns all she needs to know about relationships between men and women from Sartre. Her strictures about independence and autonomy are nurtured during this time. Feminist commentators on her life notice this: de Beauvoir's readers 'can only conjecture that what forced de Beauvoir into true independence and autonomy . . . was the loss of the special, exclusive bond that she had previously felt between Sartre and herself',[49] says one. Says another: 'one cannot help feeling that the extreme horror of passivity, weakness, dependence, and "immanence"' of *The Second Sex* 'expresses in some way Simone de Beauvoir's reaction against a strong dependent streak in herself. Like all thinkers, she has . . . erected a theory partly from her observations and convictions, but also from her inner emotional necessities.'[50]

But, perhaps even more profoundly supporting my interpretation of events, it was Sartre's idea to write The Second Sex! By 1946, de Beauvoir had established herself as a writer, but 'felt at loose ends, eager to write but without a subject'.[51] Sartre suggested the idea of a book on women: 'I said to Sartre that for me, being a woman hadn't really counted for very much. But Sartre pointed out, "All the same, you haven't been brought up the same way as a boy; you should take a closer look at it".'[52] There was nothing unusual in this, says de Beauvoir: 'philosophically and politically the initiative has always come from him', she wrote in her autobiography, 'Sartre is ideologically creative, I am not'.

Some feminists notice the irony in all this, but 'there is no hint' that de Beauvoir did: 'Since "other women" had figured so large in the de Beauvoir/Sartre relationship . . . the suggestion now looks very much as if Sartre was handing to de Beauvoir the intellectual task of enabling him to understand women, and the pattern of his relations with them.'[53] Whatever the case,

> Once given her homework, de Beauvoir set off with great enthusiasm to find out about this extraordinary tribe called women. Her method in constructing The Second Sex was clearly to follow all entries in the library catalogue on women and then organize these entries within a theoretical framework of existentialism.

In other words, she did what Sartre told her to do, and put all she found into the theoretical structures created by Sartre. And within Sartre's existential structures, about freedom and authenticity, independence and autonomy, it was very hard to treat women at all sympathetically.

All of this leads to the important question about de Beauvoir's work during the period in which she was writing The Second Sex: 'in what sense did she express her own views, or how far did she write to please, to entertain, to seduce and – perhaps most centrally – to retain Sartre?'[54]

The odd thing is, if *The Second Sex* had actually been written *by* Jean-Paul Sartre, rather than, as seems likely, inspired in part by the difficulties of a conventional relationship *with* him, it would have been dismissed long ago as the ranting of a misogynist chauvinist, in a long tradition of abuse of women. Instead, it has been held up for acclaim by feminists. When she died in Paris in 1986, Simone de Beauvoir was 'almost universally' proclaimed as the 'mother' of contemporary feminism, 'its major twentieth century theoretician',[55] 'one of the greatest twentieth-century philosophers and writers'.[56] And *The Second Sex* is 'widely regarded as the major feminist text of the twentieth century',[57] 'one of those rare classic statements on the human condition whose power only grows as its many dimensions are discovered and interrogated'.[58] All this about a book that eventually succeeds in denigrating all that women stand for, in favour of a picture of the woman becoming as much like a man as possible. Or, to put it another way, of de Beauvoir becoming as much like Sartre as possible, to retain his affection.

One feminist wonders how different the intellectual history of twentieth-century Europe would have been 'had de Beauvoir somehow managed to scrape together that handful of extra marks and pip Sartre at the post? What might de Beauvoir not have done had it been objectively proved to her that she was cleverer than Sartre?'[59] I find another hypothetical question more interesting: what, one wonders, would have been the intellectual history of twentieth-century Europe had de Beauvoir somehow managed to fall in love with a man who wanted to give her what she wanted as a woman?

Perhaps, then, we might have avoided the particular cul-de-sac, so influential on contemporary feminism and current education policy, that de Beauvoir was led to espouse. The feminism that led to de Beauvoir's chilling prescriptions, uttered in 1975, of how to create the independent woman: 'No woman should be authorised to stay at home to raise her children. *Women should not have that choice, precisely because if there is such a choice, too many women will make that one*. It is a way of forcing women in a certain direction.'[60]

Or, as she put it 36 years earlier in *The Second Sex*: 'What is extremely demoralizing for the woman who aims at self-sufficiency is the existence of other women of like social status, having at the start the same situation and the same opportunities, who live as parasites. . . . A comfortably married or supported friend *is a temptation in the way of one who is intending to make her own success.*' With great candour, she tells us that the temptation of being a housewife is enough to stop young women pursuing their independent path: 'The hope of being one day *delivered from taking care of herself*, and the fear of having to lose that hope if she assumes this care for a time, combine to prevent her from unreservedly applying herself to her studies and her career.'[61]

And the feminist educators of today? When they attack domestic drudgery, the 'unavoidable and unalterable' burden of raising children, are they sure that they are speaking for *all* women, or just for women like themselves? And how many of those 'women-like-themselves', like de Beauvoir, are pushing back painful memories, in order to force through an agenda on women who have not been so benighted?

Is it not at least possible that when women 'exchange their femininity for the wage packet', something is lost, that making family life a priority might bring joy rather than being simply a predicament? And is it not at least possible that the working-class girls of the 1970s — and those who continue to resist the feminist onslaught — may have actually been on to something rather important that is missed by our feminist educators here?

WOMEN IN VOLUNTARY EXILE IN SERVITUDE (WIVES)

Recently, I went around to the house of a (retired) professor to talk about work unrelated to this project here. The work was interesting enough, but far more interesting was what his wife had to say as she served us tea and home-made biscuits. She described the time of her life when her children were growing up; that was when they had come to this city, and she had given up her own, rather promising academic work to look after her babies. 'It was the happiest time of my life,' she said, 'I wouldn't have swapped it for anything.' But then, perhaps realizing that such things were not said in our circles any more, she apologized: 'but of course, things are different now. My daughter, it's not what she wants. But it was wonderful for me.'

De Beauvoir knew that women had to be forced to be free,

because the feminine mystique had too strong a pull. Education, she knew, was the key to bringing this about. And through educational reforms like Title IX and the Sex Discrimination Act of the 1970s, to the National Curriculum of today, feminism has succeeded in making schooling a process of forcing women to be free. Nowhere in schools can we reflect on where a woman might gain the kind of fulfilment and joy that de Beauvoir alludes to, or that women might have different ways of finding fulfilment to men. Women, schools say today, can seek fulfilment only in the world of sport, politics, science and business, not in the home. Have we not lost something of value here? Are we sure that we would prefer to live in the world the equality feminists have created rather than the one which de Beauvoir secretly pined for, and which Friedan first condemned, only then to withdraw her condemnation? Certainly, that is what several women are arguing today. These are voices that are not heard in the gender studies' classrooms, voices that stray into 'no-go areas', as Rosalind Coward in *Sacred Cows* put it. But they deserve to be heard. I will give some of them an airing here.

Before I do so, let us be clear on one point. These voices are not saying that *all* women must value the domestic sphere and mother-hood: far from it. One of those voices, Carolyn Graglia, for instance, points to three categories of women: first, those who have no interest in marrying, or who are unable to do so, who devote themselves to careers or, in the past, to religious orders; second, those who marry and often bear children, 'but like an earlier aristocracy or elite of the entertainment industry . . . delegate to others maintenance of their household and rearing of their children and pursue careers or other interests'; and third, there are those who 'choose marriage as their primary career, devoting themselves largely to husband, children, and domesticity'.

In the past, says Graglia, there was a pact between these three groups, that they would live and let live. This was 'completely shattered' by Betty Friedan in the 1960s. And because 'women care very much what other women think', seeking their approval mainly from other women, women in the third group had their confidence shattered: 'Feminism's war against the housewife has pitted the best educated, most sophisticated, most aggressive, and most masculinized portion of the female population against women who generally possess less education and less worldly experience, who are more likely to be docile than aggressive, feminine than masculine.' Says Graglia: 'An average homemaker not only has had no forum in which to speak, but never imagined she would be called upon to defend her *raison d'être*. Until recently, society had led her to expect that repelling vicious attacks upon her worth was more the responsibility of men than women.' It is the 'insidiousness' of the women's movement that, 'while claiming – and being perceived by society – to speak for all women' it has represented only the first two groups, not the third, namely those who want to be housewives and mothers.

What these other women's voices are saying is that all the current social norms are pushing women in one direction: yes, of course feminists and society at large endorse choice, that women should be free to choose in one direction or another, to be housewives or career women. But that does not reflect the reality. As we have seen in the earlier discussion in this chapter concerning the education system in particular – and this is reflected in many other areas of our lives – the pressures are on women to 'succeed' in the 'masculine' areas, in business, science, sport and politics. And women, whether or not they would prefer to be in that third group, those 'whose natures make them less suited to striving in the workplace than concentrating on husband, children, and home', know that if they are not succeeding in those areas dictated by society, then they are not valued by the society created and endorsed by the feminist educators. Thus relegated to 'the periphery of their lives are the home and personal relationships with husband and children that they sense merit their central concern'.[62]

Women – from across different generations – such as Carolyn Graglia (*Domestic Tranquility: A Brief Against Feminism*), Danielle Crittenden (*What Our Mothers Didn't Tell Us: Why Happiness Eludes the Modern Woman*), Melanie Phillips (*The Sex-Change Society: Feminised Britain and the Neutered Male*), Jean Elshtain, (*Public Man, Private Woman*), Maureen Freely, (*What About Us? An Open Letter to the Mothers Feminism Forgot*), and Elizabeth Perle McKenna (*When Work Doesn't Work Anymore: Women, Work and Identity*),[63] are all challenging the feminist – that is, the equality feminist – domination now.

First, these women's voices are challenging the myth that women were forced to stay in the private sphere of home and family, that women would not possibly have acquiesced in it voluntarily. Melanie

Phillips argues that 'the family wage was once regarded as a *liberation* for women who, when they became mothers, tended not to want to work outside the home'.[64] Carolyn Graglia argues: 'Women's failure to take advantage of the available opportunities and exert their influence within the public arena has always been much more of a choice on women's part than feminists want to admit.' Far from being forced to stay at home, women like her – now in her seventies, having entered the world of work back in the 1950s – found that the only barrier preventing her from succeeding in the marketplace was 'her *own* willingness to constrict her maternal and domestic roles sufficiently to achieve that goal'.

As we have already noted, it is highly significant that both Simone de Beauvoir and Betty Friedan were aware of this. We have already described de Beauvoir's concern that allowing too many women to follow the domestic route would lead to 'temptation' for those who were trying to make it independently, temptation to succumb to domesticity's delights and rewards. And the key thrust of Betty Friedan's *The Feminine Mystique*, of course, is precisely the same realization. It is because of the 'mystique' of femininity that so many women are immersed in their 'false consciousness', and hence succumb to the innumerable delights of housewifery and motherhood: 'Friedan candidly acknowledges – what was clearly the fact – that college-educated women were eschewing careers and devoting ourselves to our families because this was what we wanted to do, not because we suffered discrimination.' Betty Friedan agreed that 'all professions are finally open to women in America', that there has been the 'removal of all the legal, political, economic, and educational barriers that once kept woman from being man's equal'. Even so, the problem remained for Friedan: 'so few have any purpose in life other than to be a wife and mother', because they are tricked into believing in the feminine mystique.

Carolyn Graglia's account of her own upbringing and early career certainly supports her claims:

> Within the memory of no contemporary feminist had the 'barriers of society' been strung so tightly that women could not achieve [the feminist] goal of becoming scientists and professors. When I entered college in 1947, I knew that women were

represented, albeit sparsely, in all the professions. The doctor who performed my pre-college physical examination was a woman. The lawyer who represented my mother in her divorce case in 1936 was a woman. And the president of The Trenton Trust Company, where I opened my first bank account in 1942, was a woman.

She elaborates on how she sees her early career progression:

I was a practicing lawyer in the 1950s. From the time in junior high school when I decided to become a lawyer until I ceased working in order to raise a family, I always received unstinting encouragement and support. It was scarcely possible that someone from the working class, living on the edge of poverty with a divorced mother, could have succeeded otherwise. My entire college and law school educations were funded by scholarships and my employment. Teachers and counsellors in high school and college energetically assisted in my efforts to secure these scholarships and other aid, without ever questioning the suitability of my aspirations for a woman. Not once in all the sessions where we discussed my educational options and planned how I would pay for them was this issue ever raised. . . . Contrary to the received opinion that society consistently discouraged women's market activity, I found social acquaintances were extremely supportive, while employers and many colleagues generously encouraged my pursuit of a career. . . . I was treated as well as, and I sometimes thought even better than, the men with whom I was competing.[65]

However, lest anyone should see this as an anti-feminist mischievously misrepresenting history in order to score points, we find Simone de Beauvoir making more or less precisely the same points, this time about Europe in the 1930s and 1940s. In the second volume of her autobiography, *Force of Circumstance*, she writes:

far from suffering from my femininity, I have, on the contrary, from the age of twenty-one, accumulated the advantages of both sexes; after *She Came to Stay* [her first successful novel] those

around me treated me both as a writer, their peer in the
masculine world, and as a woman; this was particularly noticeable
in America: at the parties I went to, the wives all got together
and talked to each other while I talked to the men, who
nevertheless behaved toward me with greater courtesy than they
did toward the members of their own sex.[66]

As Mary Evans puts it, like Carolyn Graglia,

looking back on de Beauvoir's life, it is possible to argue that she
actually enjoyed considerable freedom and autonomy: she did
train for an elite profession, she did live outside conventional
society with apparent ease, and to all intents and purposes she
lived that life of personal independence which she chose for
herself at an early age. Thus to speak of de Beauvoir as belonging
to some distant, essentially different, past, in which women were
absolutely un-free and subject to patriarchal domination makes a
nonsense of her life, and that of other women.[67]

No, it was certainly not the problem of workplace discrimination
that led to women ceasing to work outside the home: 'We were
impelled' says Graglia, 'to stay with our children by the strong
emotional pull they exercised on us and because we thought our
presence in the home was the single best guarantee of their well-
being. A life caring for them at home, we often discovered, was good
for us as well.' And, very importantly, 'We were confident, moreover, that society respected us and believed us to be engaged in a
valuable activity – not acting as sacrificial victims – when we
functioned as full-time homemakers.' It is this confidence of their
value that feminism has largely destroyed, 'convincing younger generations of men and women that society disdains a woman's domestic
role'.[68]

For Danielle Crittenden, some 40 years' later, it was exactly the
same: the realization that when her baby came, work palled into
insignificance, that there was little sacrifice entailed in wanting to leave
the world of work to look after her child. She writes that as modern
women, 'we are taught to anticipate many things in our lives – except
one'. And thus 'the single most profound, life-changing decision' that

the majority of women will make 'is the one we are now least prepared for – the act of having a child'. Hollywood comedies still prepare women for some of it, it is true: 'you anticipate a certain period of mayhem immediately following the baby's birth: nights without sleep, feedings, unstoppable crying, etc.' But to the modern women 'raised to believe in the importance of their work', what is totally unprepared for 'is just how much a child will dominate a mother's mind'. For 30 years or more, women have been told that they would be 'happier, more fulfilled human beings' if they left their children with child-minders and went out to work. And 'the woman with a slightly enlarged belly who announces that she plans to return to her office six weeks/six months/two years after her baby is born may genuinely believe that she will be able to do so – and in many cases, she will do so'. But, says Crittenden, if she is anything like her – and many mothers are – it will not make her happy:

> For until you are holding your actual baby in your arms – the baby you think looks *exactly* like you if you were a bald Martian – and marveling at the curve of his ear and his unearthly bright eyes that squint at you with astonishment and curiosity, you can't know how you're going to feel when you become a mother. This surprise is motherhood's greatest joy and its darkest secret: Suddenly you can't stop thinking about your child.[69]

This is something that is 'too explosive to confront' for the women's movement, but when it happens, when they finally have their child, there is something else pulling on them, far more strongly than the passing joys of work. Staying at home with their babies and young children, for women like Crittenden and Graglia, is no sacrifice at all. Graglia notes that one of the greatest injustices to such women is 'feminist's own success in convincing society to treat as a sacrifice what for some women can be the most rewarding occupation of their lives'.

Like many women of her generation, Graglia simply could not understand the criticisms of Betty Friedan's Feminine Mystique when she first came across it in 1965. She was stunned both by Friedan's 'egregious disparagement' of everything Graglia stood for, and also by her complete lack of 'imagination and initiative' to see the possibilities in a lifestyle that she found afforded 'virtually unlimited freedom – the greatest freedom I had ever known – to create a design for living for myself and family and direct its importance'. Her experience was 'diametrically opposed' to the drudgery that it was supposed to be. 'Caring for my children never seemed remotely boring, tedious, or lonely', she writes. Far from being depressing and debilitating, she experienced her years as a mother at home 'as an everyday epiphany of exquisite happiness', even down to mundane activities like wiping 'their tops and bottoms', and getting them in and out of snowsuits: 'my most common reaction was awe at how delightful they were, how fresh and exciting each of these daily activities seemed in their eyes, and how lucky I was to have the privilege of sharing in this thrilling adventure that we created out of their daily growth'. Witnessing in her children their 'depth of feeling', 'breadth of interest', and their delight and wonder in life – 'of far greater intensity than I had ever before seen in anyone' – made up 'the best learning experiences' of her life.

Nor did Graglia ever find it 'irksome' or 'humiliating' that as a housewife or mother she now became financially dependent on her husband. On the contrary, when she stopped practising law, 'an unexpected benefit was that I felt even better loved than before'. The new realization that her husband cared for her 'enough to exert himself as mightily as he did to provide so well for me and our children' gave a new glow of contentment and self-satisfaction.[70]

But it is not only women who describe themselves, like Graglia and Crittenden, as anti-feminists, who are arguing this line now. The fault line that I described in feminism at the end of Chapter 2, between 'equality' and 'liberation' feminists creates strange bedfellows – or perhaps it is a key argument of this book that there is nothing strange about this conjunction at all, that women of many political temperaments are now united in common cause against the equality feminists. For in this connection, it is hard to detect much difference between the writings of women like Graglia and Crittenden and someone who very much still calls herself a feminist: Germaine Greer. *The Whole Woman* is as considered and vigorous a plea for reclaiming the female values of domesticity and motherhood as any of the above writers. I believe she squarely belongs in this company, at least on the subject of womanhood.

Germaine Greer looks back to a better time before equality feminism: 'When the family was required to gather around the table for meals at least once a day, and snack foods were unknown, the food-provider was directly responsible for her family's quality of life. She could display both authority and skill and express her love for her family by the effort that she put into the dishes that she brought to the table.' But, she laments, that 'female role has now disappeared'. The logic of capitalism has responded, with its terrifyingly blind efficiency, to the demands of working women with the 'commercialization of food preparation'. Home cooking is now 'expressly sneered at in TV commercials'. No longer do women 'beg scraps and bones from the butcher to make stock; they don't cream sugar and butter, and eggs and flour to bake a cake. They don't go shopping every day to buy fresh vegetables and meat.' Instead, their lives imprisoned within the masculine work ethic, 'they go to the supermarket once a week and select from a vast array of prepared foods which can be kept in the freezer until it's time to defrost, heat and serve them'.

A survey for the BBC *Good Food* magazine was 'generally interpreted as bad news for feminism', notes Greer. This had found that 'more than 90 per cent of the women questioned said that they prepared supper every night for their husbands or partners'. But why should this be bad news? Greer does not think it necessarily is: 'what is to be done for the women who find giving food to the ones they love the only potentially satisfying part of their day? We do not know what proportion of the 90 per cent were defending their control of the domestic environment.' Indeed, she continues,

> Not all feminists have regarded women's traditional skills with contempt; there are feminists who see the home as a creative opportunity, who bake bread and cakes, who knit and sew, who grow fruit and vegetables and make pickles and preserves, in the forlorn hope that someone will value the work of their hands above the work of machines.

I have always taken great pleasure in reading Greer's regular columns in the *Daily Telegraph* where she lovingly describes such traditional skills and their value: 'These are the earth mother feminists, flat-footed, broad-hipped figures of fun. The reinvestment of women's traditional fields of expertise with prestige and value is one more feminist cause that is being lost.'

She values not only domesticity, but motherhood:

> The experience of falling desperately in love with one's baby is by no means universal but it is an occupational hazard for any woman giving birth. Most of the women who find themselves engulfed in the emotional tumult of motherhood are astonished by the intensity of the bliss that suddenly invades them and the keenness of the anguish they feel when their child is in pain or trouble.

Pre-equality feminist societies manage motherhood much better than ours, she says:

> Historically societies have nurtured and promoted the mother–child bond. In village India and Pakistan the new mother is still kept away from strangers, in a calm and lazy place, in close contact with her baby's body, secure in the certainty that the arrival of the new baby brought joy to everyone around her. To mark her new status and prestige she is dressed in new clothing, given new jewellery, called by a new name, feasted and feted.

And she values that in these pre-feminist societies 'girls learn mothering from their earliest years, usually by mothering their brothers and sisters'. By contrast, in the West, the quality of a woman's life 'takes a nose-dive when she has a baby', because she is inwardly compelled to juggle baby and career, with 'the foreseeable future . . . composed of equal parts of worry, guilt and exhaustion'.

Recognizing that perhaps her own earlier writing may have been influential on some of these changes, Greer writes: 'In *The Female Eunuch* I argued that motherhood should not be treated as a substitute career; now I would argue that motherhood should be regarded as a genuine career option . . .' And, to cap it all, she argues that the 'immense rewardingness of children is the best-kept secret in the western world'.[71]

These are some of the women's voices being raised against the dominant feminist description of domesticity and motherhood. They are asking for their views to be heard alongside those feminists who have won a monopoly over public policy. Reading these different descriptions, one wonders if the authors of *Closing the Gender Gap* – and of *How Schools Shortchange Girls* and the host of government documents from Britain and America – have got it completely right. These feminist authors have been liberated from their 'domestic drudgery' and want the same for other girls too, working class girls and girls of professional parents. But is what these girls are being liberated from quite as bad as the feminists make out? Perhaps, we may conclude here, the education feminists are over-egging the pudding. Perhaps there is much to be said for reclaiming the female values of domesticity and of motherhood. And perhaps our education system should be reflecting these values, rather than working for their degradation and replacement with masculine aspirations.

This is the first problem I have with the feminist agenda that gives succour and support to government policy. The second and third problems, namely looking at the overvaluing of the world of men, and the undermining of interdependence between men and women, are the focus of the next chapter.

4

'Singing and Dancing that Womanhood Is Beautiful'

On 11 September 2001 at 2 p.m. British Summer Time, 9 a.m. Eastern Standard Time, I was reading the latest book, *Misconceptions*, by Naomi Wolf, 'author of *The Beauty Myth*', as her publisher always proclaims her. The book takes the reader through Wolf's first pregnancy in painstaking detail, with each of the nine months given a chapter to itself. I was just finishing 'Fourth Month', where Wolf finds herself wishing things for her daughter, if indeed her baby is to be female:

> I wished her a medieval castle set with soldiers like the white-walled, red-roofed, turreted castle set . . . that my brother had played with when we were children, and that I had longed somehow to take part in. But his toy figures were all male knights on horseback . . . I wished my daughter the same castle, the same clever drawbridge, but, oh, I wished her . . . ladies too: ladies in Joan of Arc armour, ladies on horseback with quivers slung over their shoulders; wenches positioned on the battlements, tipping vats of boiling oil on to the siege, wenches down below hoisting a mighty pine trunk horizontally against the bolted, arched wooden doors; wenches with slingshots and wenches with crossbows. I wished her a roistering plastic figure of breast-plated Boadicea, queen of the Britons, and an army of well-equipped Roman centurions to vanquish; . . . and I wished

her figurines of a dynasty of poisoner-queens, each of whom was more deceitful than the last. I wished her villainesses as well as heroines.[1]

At the same time that I was reading this, by a horrible coincidence, 'War came to America'.[2] In Naomi Wolf's home town of New York, terrorist hijackers — perhaps aptly characterized as coming from 'a dynasty of poisoner-kings, each more deceitful than the last' — rammed two passenger jets into the twin towers of the World Trade Center, killing thousands of innocent people. And, although not quite the medieval warfare into which Naomi Wolf had wished her daughter initiated, a most terrifying conflict was unleashed on the world. As I write this, as bombs fall on the medieval fiefdom of Afghanistan, there appears no end in sight, and no one really seems to know where or how it will all end. Certainly it is possible that it may dominate Wolf's daughter's upbringing for some time to come.

What I do know, however, is that it has raised the issue of the overvaluing of the world of men in a far more powerful way than I had envisaged when I first started to write this book. In an earlier draft of this chapter, I had used as my opening gambit a rather tame story about a student who was in a 'terrible quandary', wishing she could be a full-time mother, but knowing she has to do her Ph.D. instead. Why? As a woman, she told me, the things she enjoys — 'people' things, family, friends, community — carry no status. She has to achieve in the rigours of academia in order 'to feel good about myself'. In a small way, I related, she illustrated aspects of the second problem with the feminist educators' programme, of the way the equality feminists overvalue the world of men at the expense of the female. In a much more dramatic way, the events unfolding in Afghanistan and globally graphically illustrate the same problem.

In *The Times* today, there is an article 'Should a mother report on a war?', prompted by the arrest of Yvonne Ridley by the Taliban 'government', the 43-year-old journalist from the North-East of England, mother of 9-year-old Daisy. Some tender, old-fashioned souls have raised the objection that Daisy's subsequent anguish shows that mothers have no business risking their lives in this way at the front line. But the equality feminists will have none of it:

'Two of our leading foreign correspondents' from the BBC and *The Sunday Times* 'have publicly decried the notion that Ridley had no business running around Afghanistan and getting herself captured. The male correspondents, they pointed out, have children too and no one tells them off or publishes details of their "abandoned" children.' Says Miranda Ingram, the author of the article: 'Quite so. Women have just as much business reporting from the front line.' Any other position is 'laughably outdated'. She wants to 'fiercely defend the right of any mother to head for the trouble-spots if she wants to'.

Anything he can do, a woman – even a mother of young children – can and should do too. What is sauce for the gander must be sauce for the goose too. Ingram does slightly soften her position towards the end, but her reasons for doing so are illuminating. She observes that some male journalists are now 'prepared to acknowledge their fatherhood affects their professional life', so perhaps 'it is absurd that we shouldn't admit that motherhood does too'. Equality feminists, always mindful that what men are doing is the right way of doing things, notice that some men have qualms about leaving their young children for the front line, so, all right, reluctantly, perhaps, we can permit some young mothers to feel the same pain; but only if the men feel it first.[3]

But is that really the way it should be? Is what men do in the world really so important that women should follow their lead wherever it goes – even if it means abandoning young children for the uncertain terrors of the front line? And hence, should education policy be geared to educating girls to be exactly the same as boys? Or is this whole world somehow back to front? Is this world as the equality feminists want it overvaluing what men do at the expense of the female?

The feminist war journalists certainly do not think so, and they are in esteemed company. Not only do they have Naomi Wolf wishing the wonders of war on her unborn daughter, but Simone de Beauvoir is also on their side. In *The Second Sex*, there is 'rhapsody of admiration and awe' for all that men do. Men 'transcend the mere animal condition'; women indulge and sink into it through motherhood. In an extraordinary passage de Beauvoir compares war and motherhood:

The worst curse that was laid on woman was that she should be excluded from these warlike forays. For it is not in giving life but in risking life that man is raised above the animal; that is why superiority has been accorded in humanity not to the sex that brings forth but to that which kills.[4]

But feminists are not united on this. On the other side of the argument, Germaine Greer cuts a lonely figure against her slavering sisters. She is not convinced that feminism demands the right to be so much like men, in terms of war, aggression, or, I would think, the reporting of war and aggression. When she wrote her best-seller *The Female Eunuch* in 1970, she says, 'radical women were demanding the right to aggression as a basic human right and women's groups were training in self-defence and martial arts'. This, she observes, assumed that 'Freedom had to include the right to beat your enemies up.' However, even then she saw the obvious outcome of such a 'free-for-all': 'if violence is a right the strongest and the cruellest will always tyrannize over the gentle and the loving-kind. Only those women who were strong and cruel enough could join in the butchery. The rest would be butchered.' Concerning war, she writes in her latest best-seller, *The Whole Woman*: 'repugnant as the thought may be that rich women are killing poor women for hire, *equality demands* that in a militaristic society women should be represented in the military.' But the liberation feminists question this conclusion. As one teacher at the United States Naval Academy put it: 'we no longer exclude women, but (whether we admit it or not) we still exclude the female.'

So should women 'learn to be as competitive, aggressive, lecherous and cruel as men?' asks Greer. Why should this be desirable? If women 'have historically been committed to caring; if they are now condemned to be uncaring, can this be a liberation?'[5]

With the discussion thus put into the context of the tension between equality and liberation feminism, let us now look at these issues more closely with regard to education. We return to the arguments of *Closing The Gender Gap*.

THE DUBIOUS VALUE OF THE
PURSUIT OF WORK

The feminists in *Closing the Gender Gap* — representative of a broad swathe of opinion in feminist education circles and influential on government policy — are pleased that girls, and working-class girls in particular, are leaving the domestic sphere of home and hearth and becoming increasingly independent of men through work. The education feminists think that this is the only way girls can gain status. It is only in the world of men — work, the public sphere — that women can find fulfilment and happiness, the same as it is for boys and men.

The first thing we can say is that the feminist educators have potentially rewarding jobs in higher education. But the working-class girls whom they are pleased to see liberated from domesticity probably won't have jobs linked with the privileges of academia. As academics, we have to concede, except in our most pessimistic moments, our work can be different from other jobs. We do not usually see ourselves as wage slaves, we do not need to clock on or clock off. Terms are short, times for reflection and networking are long. We do not have bosses breathing down our necks. We have a sense of responsibility and sometimes importance. We do not have many petty regulations, we can be flexible in our working hours as a matter of right, we get to travel and meet like-minded people at jolly conferences.

The working-class girls, on the other hand, are not necessarily being elevated from 'domestic drudgery' into such fine positions. Some will be, of course: there is some class mobility; but the great majority of these liberated girls will be in working-class jobs. The girls will have been liberated into being receptionists, secretaries, canteen assistants, factory workers and the like. These jobs have many differences, but the one thing that can be said about them in general is that they are not lacking in drudgery. And is it not possible that this wage-slave drudgery is perhaps as bad, or perish the thought, *even worse* than the purported drudgery of domesticity?

As the testimony of the working-class girls of the 1970s shows quite clearly, domesticity can be romanticized; perhaps these romantic myths even contained some element of truth. Perhaps these working-class girls would even find their goal of love in family in a way that these privileged academic women seem unwilling to countenance, as we discussed in the previous chapter. Perhaps love really could make their worlds go around, really could lighten the burden of domestic drudgery. Hard though anyone may try, however, it is very difficult to see how one could romanticize the joys of being a petrol pump attendant or call centre telephonist in exactly the same way.

But it is not just working-class girls about which this doubt is raised. Are professional jobs – and once the spotlight is on, perhaps even including academia – really quite as good as the feminists make out? Or are they engaged now in a equivalent 'masculinist' mystique, making out that all that men did before feminism liberated women was good, and all that women did was bad?

By 1981, Betty Friedan was having doubts along these lines too. She recounted stories of women who became disappointed when they realized that even high-flying jobs, which they had thought would be so glamorous, turned out to be so much, well, *non*-domestic drudgery. There is the woman in a high-flying bank job who says pitifully: 'I don't feel guilty. I just feel sorry that I don't see more of the children. A job is not the end. . . . It was exciting to get my job. The hard part is staying *when you discover it's just a job, that you really don't like what you're doing.*'[6]

These concerns are not, in fact, new. Margaret Mead, the feminist anthropologist, was well aware of the potential attraction of the 'masculinist' mystique that seems to have quite overcome the feminist writers. Writing in 1948, she described the way American society even then overvalued male work and activities. And she saw how women were already beginning to envy the male role, reflecting the beginnings of the devaluation of 'the sensuous creative significance of the female role of wife and mother'; she warned that when home and family are undervalued, 'women will cease to enjoy being women, and men will neither envy nor value the female role'.[7]

Mead seems to have been remarkably prescient. Modern feminists correctly saw that Western society overvalued male achievement more highly than it valued the female contribution to home and family. Instead of challenging this, 'revaluing female voices', the feminists reacted, 'unfortunately, by agreeing that this relative valuation was correct'. So today there are few feminine counterbalances to check the masculine overvaluing of what they do in the workplace and public sphere. Modern feminism has led to 'a substantial number of women' devaluing traditional roles of wife and mother and, 'out of envy of the male role', collaborating with men 'in their overvaluation of male achievements'.[8] And so we arrive at the position where, as Greer puts it, 'Our culture is far more masculinist than it was thirty years ago. . . . Football is Britain's most significant cultural activity'.[9]

But is the world of men, of work and public life, really quite as glamorous as many men would like to make out – perhaps because it is part of their own romanticization of what they do, to make it all a bit bearable for them, and, of course, to impress their womenfolk as to its importance and to the men's stature? Certainly Graglia, having worked for some years in the legal profession before giving up paid work to raise her family, does not think so. Regarding legal work she notes that this 'sometimes' provided the intellectual challenge equivalent to 'a good crossword puzzle, with the advantage that doing the puzzles well can bring handsome financial rewards'. But more commonly, legal work 'resembles alphabetizing the Manhattan phone book'. And this is said about the Law – which surely stands higher in the interest stakes than the great majority of the jobs that women have moved into from the home. In *The Feminine Mystique*, Friedan had said that it was only through paid work that women could 'feel alive': Graglia wonders if Friedan had 'any idea what it was like to read judicial decisions, draft interrogatories, write a prospectus, or draw up articles of incorporation. It's a clean way to make a good living – better than mining coal – but it's overrated as a way to make you "feel alive".' No, for feeling alive, she says, 'I would always bet on the sexual ministrations of my husband over reading judicial decisions, even of the Supreme Court'.[10]

Remarkably, given what she writes to glorify all that men do elsewhere, even Simone de Beauvoir has moments when she comes down on the same side as Carolyn Graglia. Of course, the same contradictions are there as in all of de Beauvoir's writing. Yes, she tells us that women need to be liberated into work, of whatever kind, clearly inspiring the kind of panegyrics engaged in by the authors of *Closing the Gender Gap*. As one feminist describes de Beauvoir's position:

The more interesting and challenging the occupation or profession the better of course. But even factory workers while they might find their children and their hearth more rewarding should 'liberate' themselves and stick to their lathes. Any compromise is evasion and self-deception. To become an authentic human being women must work in the same whole-hearted and total way that men do – for money. Then at last there will be a real symmetry between the sexes and man will no longer be able to regard woman as 'the other;' the humiliating dependence upon man, psychological as well as economic, will be abolished.[11]

But then, perhaps in a more reflective moment, perhaps forgetting that Jean-Paul Sartre is watching her, de Beauvoir compares the ordinary working man with the housewife, and decides that in actual fact the latter may have much more going for her. For ordinary working men are 'Destined like women to the repetition of daily tasks, identified with ready-made values, respectful of public opinions, and seeking naught on earth but a vague comfort'. Because of this, ordinary working men, de Beauvoir writes, 'are in no way superior to their accompanying females. Cooking, washing, managing her house, bringing up children, woman shows more initiative and independence than the man slaving under orders.' For the life of a working man is one in which 'he must obey his superiors, wear a white collar, and keep up his social standing'; the housewife, on the other hand, 'can dawdle around the apartment in a wrapper, sing, laugh with her neighbors'. The housewife 'gets her teeth more deeply into reality' than the ordinary working man: 'for when the office worker has drawn up his figures, or translated boxes of sardines into money, he has nothing in his hands but abstractions.' For the housewife, on the other hand, 'The baby fed and in his cradle, clean linen, the roast, constitute more tangible assets'.[12]

Another line of argument is, however, open to the feminists. Some argue that moving women into the world of men – of work and politics – will lead to an improvement in these areas, as women are able to feminize them in their own image. This does not seem to have happened at all. More importantly, it also seems that what many value about women may become lost once women move *en masse* into the public sphere. The Australian feminist Jane Kenway puts it in the context of the dangers of women losing their powers and values as they move into traditionally 'masculine' fields: 'Supposing large numbers of girls and women do gain access and success in these fields, and supposing that these fields do remain unreconstructed, despite a strong female presence, what are the likely long-term social consequences?' She thinks these are clear: 'if women are not careful, might this not also be accompanied by certain losses, for example of the "maternal thinking"?' In the workplace, having learned to 'be rational, certain, disciplined, impartial, objective, competitive, individualistic and socially mobile, we may also have *un*-learned those lateral and integrative capacities such as sensitivity and empathy, which no civilized society can afford to be without'. Such capacities, she perhaps too timidly suggests, 'might well also be regarded as a strength for society . . . females often function to provide the morality (the Moral Mother) which may be missing from the public spheres of, say, business and government.'[13]

Friedan, too, muses along similar lines in *The Second Stage*, noting how many women in the sphere of work and politics are becoming more like the men whom they previously had condemned: 'What price women's equality,' she asked, 'if its beneficiaries, by trying to beat men at their own old power games and aping their strenuous climb onto and up the corporate ladder, fall into the traps men are beginning to escape, forgoing life satisfactions basic for men and women?'[14] And Greer too:

> The notion of equality takes the male status quo as the condition to which women aspire. Men live and work in a frighteningly unfree and tyrannical society, constructed upon the oppression of junior males by senior ones, on grooming of favoured males for succession at the expense of others, on confederacies and conspiracies, on initiation and blooding rituals, on shared antisocial behaviour, on ostracisms and punishments, practical jokes, clannishness and discrimination. As soon as a woman enters a male preserve, be it the police, the military, the building site, the law, the clergy, she finds herself in an alien and repellent world which *changes her fundamentally* even as she is struggling to exert the smallest influence on it.

In any case, she says, 'The women who penetrate masculinist enclaves are usually unwelcome, kept on the periphery and treated as a sexual commodity, if they are noticed at all. Women cannot force a change in such male behaviour because, as the men don't care if they are there or not, they have no bargaining power.'[15]

But hold on: isn't this whole issue somewhat academic now? As an argument of last resort (and certainly not as one that motivated the move into work in the first place), cannot feminists argue that women have to go into the world of work now, out of economic necessity? This always strikes me as a most peculiar line to take – that in the richest societies this planet has ever known, families cannot afford the division of labour of home and working life that is simply taken for granted in even the poorest societies. Perhaps it may be true for some poorer families in our societies – and if all that has been said in this chapter is true, then this may lead to policy proposals to address these families' relative poverty to allow them the benefit of full-time mothers and housewives, if that is what the women want. But, in general, the evidence does not support this claim. In America, those families with a sole-earner husband have median incomes more or less equal to the median income for all families. And more women married to higher earning men work than those with lower earning husbands. Certainly, then, working women are not forced to go to work in order to stay on a par with the average family: they decide to work, in general, to push their family earnings far above the average. They work for luxuries, not necessities. And, in any case, the figures show, again for America, that it is not until the wife's salary rises above $60,000 that more than 20 per cent of her pay cheque remains, after paying taxes and work-related expenses.[16]

It only matters for women to be able to support themselves, of course, if men become unreliable partners. If women cannot trust their husbands to bring home the family wage, if they are wracked with insecurity about them leaving, then the feminists have a point about the need for their own economic independence. We will return to this important issue in a moment.

THE PUBLIC AND THE PRIVATE

We have arrived at the vital distinction concerning 'the public' and 'the private'. To feminists, this distinction is absolutely crucial to their arguments about women's oppression. The feminist philosopher, Carole Pateman, for instance, argues that the 'dichotomy between the private and the public is central to almost two centuries of feminist writing and political struggle'. Indeed, she affirms that the distinction 'is, ultimately, what the feminist movement is about'. The 'public' world is the sphere of politics, and work traditionally the sphere of men. The 'private' is the province of the family and home.

What makes the distinction crucial to feminism is that traditionally the 'private' sphere was considered to be the proper sphere of women because of their nature, while the 'public' was thought to be the proper sphere of men. The pretence that these two spheres were of equal value obscured 'the patriarchal reality of a social structure of inequality and the domination of women by men'. Hence, the struggle for feminists is to make women and girls as comfortable in the public sphere as men and boys, because only through this route can justice for women, and the end of domination, be achieved.[17]

Let us look more closely at this issue and see how it relates to our earlier discussion, which seems to suggest that feminists were overvaluing the public sphere at the expense of the private. For if being consigned to the private sphere constitutes oppression, as feminist philosophers argue, then perhaps we have missed something important? (We will be defining oppression more carefully in Chapter 7: for now, we will go along with an intuitive notion of what it is.) A pro-feminist male philosopher, Kenneth Clatterbaugh, tries an imaginative approach to show men just what it would feel like to be oppressed in this way:

> Imagine that our world is suddenly controlled by humanoid aliens who establish a new hegemony over the traits that are valued as human-making. They reverse or revise the traits that have been held to belong specifically to males and for which males have been socialized. An elaborate science develops that teaches that men are overly controlled by their genitals and the emotion of anger; their so-called rational abilities are, in this new world,

seen as rationalizations to support their biological and emotional demands. Male achievement in the arts, literature, philosophy, and sport are expunged from the pages of history and/or treated as trivial accomplishments. The new set of valued traits installed as human-making include many of the traits in which men have not traditionally excelled. A crisis ensues in which men lose confidence in themselves and strive to live up to the new concept, although hardly any are seen as doing so. In short, men do not fare as well as women in this new society; they are viewed as defective women and, therefore, by that norm as defective human beings. In such a world men would be oppressed.[18]

There is a clear problem with this approach, imaginative though it is. Yes, it is easy to envisage being in such a world and feeling 'oppressed' in some sense, but it is also easy to see how such an oppressive situation may be transformed to make it all much more congenial for me, say, as a man. For the problem with the society as outlined by Clatterbaugh is that there is nowhere else in which I *as a man* can gain respect and achievement. This world does not value my distinctively male attributes, values and aspirations, so I am oppressed, as a man. However, suppose that while these 'humanoid aliens' were imposing their feminized regime upon the world, a parallel world was also being created. Here men could do all their 'male achievement' stuff in arts, literature, politics, philosophy and sport, in which they could still excel and feel valued. Provided that this world were to exist as a parallel universe to the feminized world, then I, *as a man*, would surely find little to complain about. Occasionally I may look enviously over at the feminized world and wish I could be a more valued part of it. But generally I would be immersed in my own world; indeed I would probably work to help sustain the masculine mystique that it needed for its perpetuation, and all would be well.

Is not this notion – of two distinct worlds in which men and women (in general) differently flourish – precisely the public–private distinction with which feminists take umbrage, albeit seen from a crucially different angle? And is not this different angle somewhat illuminating?

While I have been writing this, I have been reading the work of the Indian novelist, Achala Moulik.[19] *The Conquerors* tells the story of the British in India from 1757 to 1867. It is written by an eminent Indian woman – as well as a novelist; she is Secretary of Education in the All India government in New Delhi – and told very much from a woman's viewpoint. Central to the plot are romance and families, the creation of dynasties and the making and breaking of marriages; oh yes, and food and internal decoration. On the periphery are battles, power struggles and the building of financial and political empires. All this peripheral activity is described either very much *en passant*, or as being precipitated because a woman has told a man to go and do it, to help build a stronger dynasty, or he is fighting over a woman's honour. Or at times there is barely concealed bafflement about why on earth the men are doing this stuff at all, and getting in the way of the central themes of family, dynasty and continuity.

The male version of Indian history, of course, tells different stories. Perhaps it tells of Indian heroes resisting the British foes, or it tells of British heroes conquering a pliant and vast subcontinent. It tells of powerful male political figures on both sides, and powerful male merchants. It tells of rulers and ruled, battles and wars. To read male versions of Indian history, it is hard to find the affairs and concerns of women mentioned at all. For the women telling the story in *The Conquerors*, however, that would miss the point. Indian history – yes, why not with some feminists, '*her*story' – is all about family and the strength of women to get men to do what they want for the sake of their families.

I am sure a similar sense could be gained from reading Jane Austen, or any of the other great women novelists of the eighteenth and nineteenth centuries. And of course, one may get exactly the same sense from reading *Bridget Jones's Diary* or its sequel. Here, there are particularly entertaining episodes about football – the girls want to watch a World Cup match to keep up with what their menfolk value, and get ready to do so, even to the extent of being entrusted with conveying the all-important final score to boyfriend Mark Darcy, who for various reasons cannot watch the match. But after enjoying momentarily the pleasurable sight of men running around in their shorts, the game somehow gets lost as the girls move on to their usual fare of relationships and self-help books; the 'inessential' gets lost to the 'essential'. And Bridget has to shamefully convey to Mark that she missed the final score, indeed any score. On another occasion, Bridget has a conversation with Mark where *she* thinks they're talking about their relationship – and she's delighted with his insights and emotional responses – but actually *he's* talking about the World Cup England vs Argentina match in which a prostate David Beckham is sent off for kicking an opponent right in front of the referee.[20]

I was reading *The Conquerors* in the same period as I read the account given by Clatterbaugh of his imagined dystopia for men. In mulling over the possibility of the alternative world where men could do the stuff they valued, I had this uncomfortable sense that these two parallel worlds were what I was reading about in the novel, and crucially, that the *important* world was *the one of the women*, the feminine, private sphere of family and dynasty. The public world, the world of men, is there to be tolerated, used as appropriate, but certainly not to be admired or envied.

I realized how much we now take it for granted, that it is the male public world that is the important one, and the women's world is secondary. This is certainly what the feminist educators want us to believe. However, as the notorious anti-feminist Stephen Goldberg pointed out, that is not always how women have seen it: 'one of the most stunning regularities' of cross-cultural data, he says,

> is the extent to which women in all societies view male preoccupation with dominance and suprafamilial pursuits in the same way as the wife in Western society views her husband's obsession with professional football – with a loving condescension and an understanding that men embrace the surrogate and forget the source.[21]

Simone de Beauvoir, again, in her more tender moments, also observes the same: she notes that 'women in markets and stores talk about domestic affairs, with a common interest, feeling themselves members of a group that . . . is opposed to the group of men *as the essential to the inessential*'. And the housewife is upset if her husband and children are not hungry, 'to the point that one wonders whether the fried potatoes are for her husband or her husband for the fried potatoes'. Indeed, everything the housewife does emphasizes this point, she says: 'she takes care of the house for her husband; but she also wants him to spend all he earns for furnishings and an electric refrigerator. She desires to make him happy; but she approves of his activities only in so far as they fall within the frame of happiness she has set up.'[22]

I had the odd thought that, if only the feminist educators would read, say, more female novelists, they might have a different picture of the world. Reading men, listening to the news, watching sports, you might get the sense that what is important is the male world. Men like to think it so. Women may take part in all those worlds, of course, but when they do, there must surely be something disconcerting to seeing their own sex either not compete in general very well against men (in politics, for instance) or having to be separated in apartheid zones, because they cannot hope to compete on equal terms. In a recent world athletics championship, for instance, the winner of the men's 100m final ran in at 9.86 seconds. The last place in the male finals was 10.29 seconds. Indeed, the slowest speed in any of the male qualifying heats was 10.48 seconds. In the women's 100m final, however, the winner ran in at 10.83 seconds. If the women and men were competing in the same race, no women would have even qualified for the second round, let alone the finals! It always seems incredibly odd to me that any women would see this as a cause for feminist celebration.

Germaine Greer cannily observes that this difference between men and women is strikingly illustrated in the BBC quiz show *University Challenge*:

> All-male teams are common and are over-represented in the high scores; most teams field a single woman who provides very few of the answers to the questions, not necessarily because she does not know them, but because she is less aggressive and shy of shouting out an answer that might be wrong. The lowest score ever achieved on *University Challenge* was scored by an all-woman team from New Hall, Cambridge.

The logic of her position is this: so much the worse for the stupidity of *University Challenge*. Why on earth would women want to bother with this masculine nonsense? The 'kind of feminism that sees getting membership of the MCC or the Garrick Club as a triumph' is a peculiar feminism indeed.

Indeed, the fact that there are now so many (usually) attractive young women on television and radio – the 'rabble of junior females, the infinitely replaceable 'hackettes'' – reporting on the predominantly male activities of sport, business and politics all adds weight to the notion that it is what the men are doing that is important. Nowhere is this more dramatically illustrated than in the reporting of war that is so ubiquitous on our television screens at the moment. Images of GMTV's Lara Logan speaking live on the videophone from the Panjshir Valley in Afghanistan, draped in an immaculate pink shawl, as bombers bomb and buildings burn, convey in the most powerful way to millions the legitimacy of the public sphere of what men do over and above the domestic lives of women.

We are so used to the feminist argument that the public–private distinction excludes women from the male world that it is instructive to view it from the opposite perspective, that the private world is first, superior, fundamental, and that men are excluded from it, banished to their own, inferior, minor, secondary world. Women look on – until recently indulgently, using it to their own advantage where and when required, and are certainly not envious of being excluded from it. Greer has a great term for the private sphere: the 'self-validating female culture'. How pitiful it is, she says, that women are so 'crazy-sad' about not being part of the male world: 'It is not so much that men won't let us into the masculine race', for clearly men will; it may even be in their interests to do so: 'it's that we want so much to join, and we take so much damage to our self-esteem before realizing that the situation is hopeless.'

Now, Germaine Greer does have a suggestion of how to revalidate the feminine – and it is here, I suppose, that her views would diverge from those of women like Carolyn Graglia and Danielle Crittenden. Noting that there is no animal society 'in which non-competitive females could wrest control from competitive males who would then submit to their sway' – indeed, such 'would be a contradiction in terms' – she observes that, instead, 'the non-competitive females choose to live as a society of females and children with or without a single male leader'. But, she decries, 'Advanced human societies regard such segregation as backward, assuming that it has been forced upon females by male tyranny'. Not so, she says. What she sees as the 'dignified alternative' to always trying to ape men in what they do 'is

103

for women to segregate themselves as men do'. Women should 'make a conscious decision not to want men's company more than men want women's. If that means segregation, so be it. If the alternative is humiliation, there is no alternative.'

But surely what our discussion here says is that this is not the only alternative; there is another, obvious alternative that she is overlooking. It is an alternative that is much more likely to appeal to many women than segregation, given that most women do not wish to simply give up men altogether. No, the 'dignified alternative' for those women who want to do so is to reinvent the public–private distinction. This would do everything that Greer wants to achieve from her segregation, namely the revaluing of the feminine, without the inconvenience of losing men altogether.

Or perhaps this is exactly what Greer means by segregation? She opens her book by telling us of how she found the 'whole woman' who inspired the title of her book: 'I gazed at women in *segregated* societies and found them in many ways stronger than women who would not go into a theatre or a restaurant without a man. . . . I learned about sexual pleasure from women who had been infibulated.' These were societies in which a woman 'would grow in authority as she aged', totally unlike our societies where youthful looks seem to count for everything. These traditional, 'segregated' societies are precisely those in which the public–private distinction is strongest. If society would again allow those women who wanted to to bring back this distinction, then Germaine Greer could again find her whole woman.

Greer notes that women should have been 'celebrating difference but, in place of singing and dancing that womanhood was beautiful, they studied'. And what have they been studying? 'They studied women and they studied gender. They set up thousands of women's studies courses in universities, and millions of students enrolled in them.'[23] They studied and they wrote books like *Closing the Gender Gap*, celebrating not women's differences but revelling in the fact that girls and women are becoming indistinguishable from boys and men.

INDEPENDENCE VERSUS CONNECTEDNESS

The public sphere is overvalued, all part of the masculine mystique that feminists have fallen for. Perhaps the same may also be said of the desire for independence in relationships, the third component of our critique of the feminist educators.

For the feminists, the working-class girls are treated as if their stories can be told in isolation from those of boys and young men. In *Closing the Gender Gap* and the government documents from both sides of the Atlantic, the girls are islands. Yes, they have the burden of children, but their individuality and self-fulfilment is what is most important. There is no mention of the *interconnectedness* between them and boys. The only hint that this might be a problem is given, not when the authors are discussing girls, but when they turn to boys. There they note, in passing, without picking it up, another element of our Bridget Jones Syndrome: girls discussed marriage in the context of boys' either 'letting you down' or not being a 'good catch'. Could part of the girls' opposition to the 'domestic burden' of marriage be because of their sense that men were no longer trustworthy? And could part of this problem have arisen because of the problem of this growing lack of interconnectedness between boys and girls?

This nagging doubt is magnified when we turn to how the feminists describe middle-class girls and young women. For these young women, individual career success is now of the utmost importance. Of course, the authors sneer, 'Domesticity as a goal' is 'viewed as a waste' of their 'human and financial resources', but these women also now look down on 'the lower status professions such as teaching and nursing', vocations that they may have countenanced in the past. Now they all want to be doctors and lawyers and high-flying executives. Most of all, they don't care how this impacts on their relationships with men. In the bad old pre-feminist education days of the 1970s and even into the 1980s, girls did not want to 'alienate men by appearing too intelligent or successful', and so developed a 'fear of success', they tell us. By the late 1990s, however, middle-class girls 'aim for and achieve the highest educational levels both at school and university, *whether or not this might alienate young men*'.[24]

Again the troublesome thought occurs that this gloating over young women's current independence ignores the possibility that they *are* alienating young men – and that this matters, or will matter, not necessarily to the young men, *but to the young women themselves*. The story of the young female professional in Chapter 1 is an illustration of this phenomenon, a story that finds numerous echoes in the study of courtship patterns of young adults for the National Marriage Project at Rutgers University.[25] It is this rejection of interdependence and *connectedness* that leaves me wondering whether the feminists are missing something rather important here.

'Connectedness' is not a word I am accustomed to using. I found it in Carrie Paechter's *Educating the Other*. We have already noted that Paechter wants us to revalue feminine ways of knowing and being, and this is one of the feminine virtues that she wants us to revalue. Reading her is like inhaling a breath of fresh air after the fierce individualism of *Closing the Gender Gap*, *See Jane Win*, and the British and American government reports. She does not spend much time on it, but when she does it seems imbued with significance. Yes, she agrees, we have to ensure 'that women have access to promotion in all fields and at all levels'; but this also means 'valuing co-operative work arrangements as well as the masculine, competitive model'. But most importantly, in terms of human relationships and the upbringing of children, her approach 'means recognizing connectedness, as much as independence'.[26]

What could this connectedness mean in practice? What could the other feminist authors be missing here? Let us see what they have to say about boys and men, to fill in the picture.

The argument of *Closing the Gender Gap* is that there is a 'crisis in masculinity', which is due in part to the fact that men have not kept up with the 'progressive' views of their female counterparts. In particular, boys and men are suspicious of women's new-found educational and career independence. Men still hark back, ridiculously, or as part of a misogynistic and oppressive 'backlash', to something that is frankly no longer attainable, and it is men who are at fault here, and who must change, not women. In their discussion of these issues, however, the feminists do reveal something rather interesting about their position, which reflects on the interdependence of men and women.

Boys and young men, it turns out, are guilty of 'romanticization' too; indeed it is the reverse side of the 'romanticization of domesticity' from which working-class girls have been liberated. Indeed, one of the 'key differences between young men and women today', the authors observe, is in support of 'Victorian models of the family, with men as breadwinners and women primarily responsible for child-rearing'. It is young men who support this 'Victorian' – used pejoratively – ideal, not young women.

Working-class boys do not share the girls' current 'unromantic realism' about family lives. Most of the boys in one recent survey 'spoke of their desire to marry'. Indeed, in one study, about half of the boys 'agreed with the statement that a woman's place is in the home looking after her family'. Boys 'wished to retain the role of male breadwinner, despite increasing evidence of male unemployment, rising female employment and girls' expectations of more equal partnerships'. A 'significant minority of young men between eighteen and thirty-four', they tell us, become 'social resisters and survivors', and 'still *cling onto old* identities attached to the male role of breadwinner and to the traditional division of labour which stresses male superiority'. But the language used here makes it clear that the authors are deriding this. These men are the 'social resisters', pitifully resisting the inevitable changes that are coming their way. The authors put it all only in a negative way: boys want to marry 'to find *the equivalent of their mothers to cook and care for them*', desiring to place their womenfolk in a 'subservient' position.

As part of their romanticization of it all, the authors note that the boys' 'attachment to traditional family life symbolizes masculinity – linking male sexuality, male work identities and family responsibilities'. Indeed, the 'main reason given by men and boys for studying and working has been to support a family'.

However, in case we might think that the boys' attitude could be a good thing – it certainly would seem to be exactly what Bridget Jones is looking for in a man – the authors add that the 'main reason given by men and boys for women having a conventional domestic role has been to support conventional versions of masculinity', and conventional versions of masculinity for the authors are definitely Neanderthal, unpleasant and to be overcome. What are required, say the authors, are 'new alternative masculinities', challenging the 'dominant forms of masculinity' in the ways done by 'feminists and gay liberation groups'.

However, perhaps there is an alternative interpretation possible, one which conveys the boys' views in a more positive light. Far from wanting to avoid the responsibilities of marriage and family – the problem very much in the forefront in *Bridget Jones's Diary* – these boys and young men are romanticizing it all, and the feminists are stamping on them for so doing. But the boys see the need for studying in order to be able to work to support a family. They want to be enmeshed in society, they want to find a worthwhile meaningful identity, and being fathers and breadwinners is a good thing that they wish to strive for. Above all, they want to be *connected* with their womenfolk. Indeed, the authors hint at this alternative explanation, but make nothing of it. They note that 'evidence of boys' greater reliance . . . on women to maintain family life suggests the greater *dependency* of men rather than their independence'.[27] They certainly fail to link this with their discussion of women's independence; indeed, they take it no further. But I would have thought it was a crucial insight. Perhaps these feminists, seeking to promote independence of women over and above any other norms, including family life and connectedness, suddenly have doubts about whether those whom they are emulating in this task – i.e. men – are actually as independent as they would like to make them out to be. But this, presumably disturbing thought is left to one side.

So Germaine Greer is completely wrong about this issue. She thinks that we have to 'proceed on the assumption that the rise in lone-female-headed families reflects what men want'.[28] Not at all. Teenage boys and young men want interdependence, they want to be able to support their wives and children. It is the feminist educators who seek to stamp out this retrograde attitude.

Let us explore this connectedness and interdependency further, since it would seem crucial to all the discussions here. And what about this sense of romance that, according to the feminist educators, has left young men out of 'synchrony' with young women?[29]

Betty Friedan, by the time of *The Second Stage*, certainly sees the interdependence aspect more clearly. Far from feminism seeking to break down relationships between men and women, she now realizes that there is something more profound linking them together. She describes some of the women whom she has met in consciousness-raising groups. One of these is Angela, 'a truly beautiful woman, a cross between Candice Bergen and Farrah Fawcett'. She is quoted as saying: 'It makes me mad that I'm so dependent on a man'; but then she suddenly realizes that this cliché fails to capture the reality of what is going on in her life: 'Twice, I've made the man utterly reliant on me, and when I take it away, the man collapses. You don't know which one is holding which up.' Why not just accept that both are holding each other up? And Friedan describes how men have put it to her: 'So he was supposed to be the big male oppressor, right? How could he admit the big secret – that maybe he needed her more than she needed him? That he felt like a baby when he became afraid she would leave?' Relationships, she now realizes, are all about mutual interdependence of men and women. And within them, women's power is very real.

For a woman's 'sexuality' and 'motherhood' itself 'are still awesome *powers* indeed,' says Friedan, 'and no man or woman who grew up in a family and has suffered or longed for or taken joy from another's touch can deny this.' Women, first as mothers and then as wives, have the 'powerful weapon over men: to give, or deny, that loving touch; to foster, by denying, that insatiable need for love in them', and this power over men was what led the men to 'power and glory-violent deeds'. She goes on:

> The very importance of children, the family, the home that is a constant of our consciousness today is based not only on the real needs of men and children for nurturing and loving care and the 'complementary', 'female' abilities of women – but also on the needs of women, equally real and basic to the human condition, for mastery, power, assertiveness, security and control.

Indeed, it is worth stressing that Friedan recognizes that the family can be a place which marvellously combines both sets of women's needs – she can be powerful and nurturing at the same time. Women, she says, do have a 'need for power, identity, status and security', as well as the need for 'love and identity, status, security and generation through marriage, children, home, the family. . . . *Both sets of needs are essential to women*'. But she tells us that the first set of needs *can be satisfied in the family and home* (providing the men are trustworthy, which we will come on to in a moment) and, moreover, that the experience of (most – not all) women trying to satisfy them in the public sphere of work leads to unhappiness and disappointment.

But there is another aspect to this interdependence – at least potentially – which the feminist educators definitely would not want to countenance, but of which, again, the later Betty Friedan is aware. She describes it thus:

> I think of women of my own generation and personal acquaintance who have spent thirty and more years married to businessmen, lawyers, doctors, writers, artists who are now successful. They all started out poor and struggling. She was his sounding board for every sentence he wrote, she kept the accounts, got the books from the library, made the plane reservations, in addition to the usual cooking, the children, the decorating, and the entertaining that everyone recognizes as part of his success. Or she filed the pictures, kept track of payments. Or was virtually full-time office-nurse-receptionist as doctor's wife. She had no separate life of her own – 'He'd follow me even to the bathroom to read his last page aloud.' Some of us who later became writers, artists, lawyers as women on our own . . . are not joking when we fantasize how much better we might be able to do ourselves 'with such a wife'.

But she is only being playful, she is not damning these arrangements at all. She says,

> As far as I can see, many of their marriages seem to work. There must be tradeoffs. Would X be a successful artist, or Y a doctor, without that constant contribution from his wife? What's wrong with doing it that way – if it works, and if neither gives up or risks too much? We used to laugh when she would say, 'We wrote five pages today,' because, in fact, we knew that *he* wrote those pages.[30]

It is this aspect of interdependence that would be complete anathema to feminist educators today, where the woman – perhaps recognizing all that has been said about the sources of her power and her fulfilment – gives up work, but still feels she lives through the work – if you like, obtaining all that she needs of the outside world by proxy – of her husband. One example of this interdependence that I came across recently is worth exploring as an example of this, to see exactly where it might be objectionable to feminists.

Rose Friedman describes her life in the wonderful memoirs, *Two Lucky People*, written with her husband Milton.[31] She would seem to be the epitome of everything that was wrong with the earlier generation and why feminism was so badly needed to change all that. Her life story is full of romantic illusions and an aversion to the independence that the feminists think is every woman's right to endure. Let us look through it and see where she went wrong and how her life could have been improved.

Although incredibly bright, and surely as clever as her future husband, as time went by Rose Friedman became increasingly less interested in her work, and more in him. When she married, she gave up work as was expected, and concentrated full time on motherhood when it quickly arrived. Usefully, just as for Carolyn Graglia, and in the same generation, she points out that it was definitely *not* imposed gender discrimination that stopped her getting work; her male profes- sors went out of their way to offer her work, which she politely declined. There was something more important for her to do.

She then raised children full time for several years, before returning to work, never equalling the fame or success of her husband Milton, not surprisingly, given the greater time commitment he had put in, except in terms of the highly successful *Free to Choose* television series. Even then many people may remember that series in terms of Milton rather than Rose.

Asked what Rose thought of her husband's success, however, and whether or not she was bitter, she says that her husband's success was her success, she had never been jealous of it. Indeed, reading the chapter describing Milton winning the Nobel Prize, where they both take it in terms excitedly to recount what had happened, it is clear that *both of them* feel it is a Friedman family achievement, shared and enjoyed by both of them equally. If you like, there was Milton as its titular head, but she shares in the Nobel Prize equally. She is the CEO of Friedman Inc., he the Chairman.

What a waste of a life! What terrible tyranny! That is what the feminists imply as they proudly assert their own independence, and want it shared by all schoolgirls and young women. But let us ask two questions about Rose and Milton Friedman, in order to challenge this perspective: would Rose's life have been better, happier or more fulfilled had she pursued her own career path more completely than her husband's? And: would Milton's and their family's lives have been better?

Of the first question, it is hard to imagine a better, happier, more fulfilled life than the one demonstrated by Rose. She certainly describes her own life in glowing terms. She certainly thinks of herself as being equally one of the 'two lucky people'. But suppose Rose had instead pursued her career as vigorously and as whole-heartedly as her husband did. Would this have made her life better, even more fulfilled? That is what feminists would tell us. But it is hard to see how we could say that it would with any certainty (and Rose explicitly herself does not believe that it would have been). For a start, pursuing her career more whole-heartedly may have left Milton unable to fulfil himself so completely, because he had to play his equal share in the childrearing, and was not so supported by her domestically. Perhaps he would not have been the great economist and policy analyst that he turned out to be. Perhaps he would not have won the Nobel Prize. Perhaps the family would not be famous and influential now, but just another normal, reasonably ambitious middle-class professional family, both parents good at their work, neither exceptional. And perhaps Rose would have felt less fulfilled by not having a Nobel Prize-winning husband, that this would have caused her *less* overall satisfaction, even though she would have got more satisfaction, we are assuming, from her career. Perhaps she would have found her relationship – let us spell it out as Graglia does – less sexually satisfying had he not been so strong and powerful in his field.

But perhaps, the feminists would argue, she would have won the Nobel Prize *herself*, or obtained whatever other academic and professional glories she may have wanted. Then all would have been well. It may have been. We will discuss the effect on Milton in a moment. But would Rose have been happier if this had been the route she had taken? Not in terms of the real Rose D. Friedman, rather than the feminist reconstruction of her. She was *not* ambitious for these things.

She wanted them in her husband. As her story makes clear, *she* was ambitious for a family and for a stable family life. Of course, she could have been made outwardly ambitious, like so many younger women are now. But then she would probably have been so much like the younger sisters whom we encountered in Chapter 1, all outwardly ambitious, but many admitting if pushed that they would drop it all tomorrow to prioritize a family if only they could find a man to have one with.

But are we perhaps asking the wrong questions here, blinded by our own false consciousness? Could not Rose have *had it all*, so that there would be no sacrifice of her Nobel Prize for her family? Possibly; but there are a few factors which would undermine that possibility. Here we turn to the second question: the impact on husband Milton and her family.

Some current feminists would object to this line of reasoning, I guess. But let us drop the assumption which pervades the feminist literature that what men feel is unimportant, bound to be suspect, compared with what women feel. If Rose had been an ambitious career woman, perhaps Milton would not have been attracted to her so much in the first place. Perhaps, like the women whose stories were recounted in Chapter 1, someone in his position would have grown tired of making sacrifices to further her career, and would instead have gone looking for a wife who *would* support him in his ambitions, so the whole thing would not have got started in the first place. But let us transport them to the present climate and norms, where a man cannot expect as of right such a luxury as a devoted full-time wife. How would he have got on with Rose Mark II, a modern career woman?

A man in this position may have been resentful that the long hours that he had to put in with the children or domesticity were stopping him from getting the Nobel Prize which he felt he deserved or could have won with a little more work. Or he may have worried more about the children, knowing that they were at some child-minder whom he did not trust, rather than with his wife whom he did. Or he may just have been psychologically uncomfortable with his successful wife, and increasingly resentful of her, without really knowing why, feeling that something was not right, but not being able to express it to her, or even to himself. Perhaps someone in his position would have felt as some of us assumed Prime Minister Tony Blair felt, when we saw photographs of himself and his wife and new baby, and then heard that Cherie Blair/Booth had gone straight back to work after the birth of baby Leo. Even though we are trained by the norms of our society not to think these things, some of us looked at Tony Blair and imagined him thinking: aren't I man enough for you? Can't I provide for you? Is the money I earn not enough to keep you and my family? Thinking these thoughts, fighting them back. (Perhaps it all rebounded on her later? Am I the only one who flinched when our new Prime Minister appeared on the steps of 10 Downing Street with his family on the morning of 8 June 2001, and Baby Leo was brought out for his father to hold for the cameras, his first public appearance? His father held baby extremely competently; his mother clearly wanted to be involved, but it appeared as though Tony was almost arching his back against her, relegating her to the fringes. She seemed incredibly small and diminished. Here was the Prime Minister, doing it all. A father, and father to the nation to boot, and the mother – well, she had forfeited her role, 'tossing off' the baby to return to work so quickly, left with no distinctive role more special than their nanny.)

Like many men, if Rose had been such a career woman, the husband may have felt that she was not unique any more, that she was, in Graglia's marvellous word, *fungible*, more easily replaced. Perhaps such a man may have turned to extra-marital relationships. He may have left her. She may have left him, turned on by others at work – perhaps those who were more successful and ruthless than the rather nondescript man her marriage had turned her husband into.

In short, perhaps there was nothing wrong with the way Milton and Rose D. Friedman chose to live their lives, namely in a gender-stereotyped fashion. And perhaps there would be nothing wrong with society if people still chose to live their lives in this way. It would seem that our feminist educators think not. They want women to be liberated to independence from their menfolk. They celebrate that independence, and dismiss anything else as soppy romanticism. And it is their views that hold sway in the educational landscape of today.

Of course, this is not to say that *everyone* has to live their lives in this way. I for one would have been deeply dismayed if Margaret Thatcher had not strode out unconventionally, leaving behind her children – perhaps even leaving them irrevocably scarred – and, by all accounts, slightly bemusing her long-suffering but devoted husband Denis. Britain and the world needed her robust views and uncompromising methods; the world definitely would, in my view, have been a worse place had she remained at home as a mother. When I travel around the world in ex-communist countries, I meet many people who would agree with this. Lady Thatcher for them sums up the spirit of the age. They acknowledge the liberating triumvirate of Gorbachev, Reagan and Thatcher, but the greatest of these was Thatcher. And the colour of British political life would have been deeply diminished, to name a second of many instances, if Betty Boothroyd had not presided as Speaker of the House of Commons for nearly a decade, if she had quietly married and raised children, and not brought her calm strength and admirable integrity to Parliament. But the exceptions will always be there. A society which allows the exceptional but does not insist that everyone has to be an exception would seem to be a tolerably good society.

Now it might be said that Rose and Milton are exceptional people themselves, and that I cannot use them as an example because it begs the question: what about less successful people? Not every Rose can be proud of her husband's achievement in getting a Nobel Prize, so perhaps this is where the argument falls down. Later we will see how women tend to choose partners whom they can look up to – for instance, an older man of the same or even lesser ability but, who has simply had more time to achieve, fits the bill nicely. So this will lead to the woman whose husband could not aspire to being a Nobel Prize-winner none the less glorifying in the accomplishment of the man getting the chair of the department, partnership in the practice, the next promotion, or simply a steady job.

Thus we are drawn back to the role of romance in it all. The feminist educators do not like their girls to share in this romance – they call it 'romanticization', a pejorative term, showing it oozing with false consciousness. Reading the feminist accounts of working-class girls romanticizing their relationships and 'domestic drudgery' back in the bad old days of the 1970s, I remembered my own experiences of that ilk. The only pre-feminist woman I have ever been out with, I suppose, who was still caught up in all that romanticization, was my very first girlfriend. It was back in 1974 or 1975; she was 15 or just 16, a few months older than me. I had come to see her, cycling over in inclement weather. I probably hadn't wanted to go, it was a cold and wet winter evening. I arrived to find that she had been baking a cake for me. The sink was piled high with dirty dishes. As I sat sipping hot tea in the kitchen with her, warmed by the paraffin heater, I apologized for putting her to such bother. Don't apologize, she said, it's very romantic. I saw it as domestic drudgery that she should have been slaving in the kitchen for me, and had all the dishes still to do, already a proto-feminist in the making. She imbued it with romance and meaning and significance. And the funny thing was, despite being cross about getting cold and wet, despite not necessarily having wanted to go over there, dragged away from my books and the warmth of my own room, because she saw it as romantic, I warmed to her immediately. In that little incident I began to know her as a mysterious 'other', yes, Carrie Paechter was right. But it was the otherness of finding romance in domesticity that I warmed to. Because she imbued simple domestic tasks with romance she made me happy, and I in my turn could made her happy too, for a while at least.

This is the romance that our feminist educators eschew. They think that the working-class girls and boys of yesteryear were completely misguided. They want life without this particular social construction of gender, to be replaced by something else altogether. It is not clear whether they are thinking on the right lines.

However, returning to Milton and Rose Friedman, there is something that the feminist educators have touched on which clearly *would* have made Rose Friedman unhappy. That is, the point about men no longer being unreliable, pointed out by the feminists in terms of girls bemused by the romance of marriage in the 1990s, pointed out very strongly, of course, in the problems Bridget Jones sees in the unreliability of men, married and unmarried. If Rose had been the devoted CEO of Friedman Inc., and *Milton had been unreliable in his role*, if such a man had gone off with his younger secretary and divorced his wife, for instance, this would have made the whole situation completely untenable. It is this kind of unreliability that the feminists might perhaps want to protect women from. But then the question is raised: How do you make men reliable in that way? And the worry is that you don't do that through the types of gender reforms the feminist educators applaud today in schools.

Roger Scruton suggests that this crisis of masculine reliability 'flows directly from the collapse of their old social role as protectors and providers'. He points out that 'Marriage was once permanent and safe; it offered the woman social status and protection, long after she ceased to be sexually attractive. And it provided a sphere in which she was dominant.' However, let us make it quite clear that that which made it valuable *to her* was a sacrifice to him; but this was itself made tolerable by the 'male monopoly of the public realm, in which men competed for money and social rewards'. Both sexes sacrificed for the sake of the greater social good of stable families: 'The two sexes respected each other's territory and recognized that each must renounce something for their mutual benefit.' But the sexual revolution changed all that. Men have now had legitimized their desires to have sex with as many women as they can. There is no social inhibition to men being serially monogamous, monopolizing a woman through her most fertile years before abandoning her for the next up-and-coming model; it all means that 'women have no secure territory of their own'.[32]

Part of this insecurity lies precisely in the arrangements that feminists have promoted in order to complete their denigration of domesticity: feminists, says Graglia,

> now indict no-fault divorce laws for causing women's insecurity within marriage, citing the risk of divorce as the reason women must abandon their traditional role in favour of career pursuits. Yet, enactment of these very laws was probably the single most important tool the women's movement employed to destroy the viability of woman's traditional role by eroding the institutional supports that had insulated women from the hazards of their marital economic dependency.[33]

No-fault divorce, says Melanie Phillips, 'actively demeans marriage. . . . If the commitment of marriage can be torn up with no good reason given, it becomes less meaningful even than a contract to buy a second-hand car.'[34] And therein lies the route of the current insecurity for married women.

Perhaps the underlying problem with the traditional arrangements is caused by the feminist revolution that has liberated men to commitment-free sex and serial monogamy, and brought in no-fault divorce to complete their liberation from interdependency. If all this is so, you cannot make women more secure by further promoting their independence through schooling.

It seems that the feminist educators are potentially short-changing girls here. By celebrating their independence from men, and pooh-poohing men's romanticization of gender roles as a throw-back to something women have long abandoned, perhaps the feminist educators are themselves engaged in creating injustice for women, the injustice that follows when women are deprived of reliable men to depend upon.

THE 'RESTLESS AND QUESTING' WOMAN

What many women seem to want to prioritize in their lives – babies, family, committed and faithful husbands – are in direct contrast to what the educational systems of today say should be the source of their fulfilment. In America, in Britain, in Australia, the education system is geared to the claim that women as much as men must gain their fulfilment and satisfaction in the workplace. It is only if one strives for the stars or to be a star – in science, business, politics and sports – that the American Dream and the dreams of all nations that ape it may be realized. And if women look for their fulfilment and satisfaction elsewhere, and particularly to prioritize childrearing, they cannot expect the education system to offer them any solace or support in their quest.

The influence of the 'early-modern' feminists, of de Beauvoir and Betty Friedan in particular, is clearly seen in this aspiration, and in the policies that now make up the educational landscape. The degradation of domesticity, the high value placed on the world of work, and the emphasis on independence of women from men and families are all themes that are spelled out clearly in *The Second Sex* and *The Feminine Mystique*. But when one looks closely at these works, or how the authors subsequently developed their views, one sees that the problems are not quite as clear as they have been presented through the feminist educators.

Betty Friedan moved on from her ideas in *The Second Stage*, recognizing that women needed families, indeed, could find the fulfilment of their need for power *and* security within the family. De Beauvoir was torn between denigrating domesticity – which it seemed she had to do, perhaps for ulterior motives – and delighting in it. Many more women's voices are now being raised in a similar vein, questioning the assumptions of the feminist educators that have found their way into policy. In particular, Carolyn Graglia's *Domestic Tranquility* and Danielle Crittenden's *What Our Mothers Didn't Tell Us* spell out an alternative gender agenda that praises women's domestic role, that questions the 'masculine' mystique which says only work is good, especially for women, and that points to men and women's interdependence as the source of fulfilment and happiness, especially for women, rather than the fierce individualism of the feminist educators. Germaine Greer's *The Whole Woman* seemed to fit squarely into this camp too. The alternative women's voices raised wonder why we need, through education, to create women who are 'restless and questing',[35] and whether it might not be better to create a society in which women are happy and fulfilled.

In other words, this and the previous chapter has suggested that the current educational landscape, while certainly consistent with, if not inspired by, the agenda of the equality feminists, is not conducive to women's happiness. In part, it leads to the restlessness of Bridget Jones. In part, it creates the questing of women who feel that they should not be fulfilled in their marriages and families, even if they feel they are, and that they should be looking outside to the world of work for their happiness, even as they doubt whether they can possibly find it there.

Doubtless there are some readers who, bursting with impatience by this point, are thinking (perhaps even scribbling in furious annotations in the margins): if domesticity is so good, why don't *you* do it, Tooley! If it is such a source of fulfilment and happiness, *you* do it, and let us women reclaim the workplace for ourselves! To be honest, I am not sure I would love domesticity as much as do the women whom I have quoted, let alone be any good at it. But this, of course, brings us back to the discussion of whether, in general, it is equally as fulfilling for men as it is for women. Clearly, there are gender differences in the way men and women respond to domesticity – for instance, the research quoted in Chapter 1 which pointed to women's increasing unhappiness in the USA and Britain spelled this out neatly.

When the results are disaggregated to explore these issues, it is clear that men 'appear to enjoy keeping house less than do women'; by contrast, unemployment 'hits a male harder than it does a female'.[36]

The feminists would argue that such differences are simply the result of socialization practices, and that therefore they are amenable to change in such practices. Men like me need more re-education, not less, in order to allow us to flourish around kitchen and hearth. We need re-education to overcome our tendency to backlash against feminism. But again, the issue is raised – and again worth exploring, if for no other reason than it is of academic interest – whether or not this is really the case. Perhaps there are biologically based differences between the sexes that could lead to the way the sexes seem to find different sources of satisfaction and fulfilment. And again, the discussions of this and the previous chapter have pointed to a more pressing need to understand the differences between men and women, biologically and culturally. It is the unhappiness that many women clearly feel in being moved away from a sphere that could be the source of their fulfilment, to a sphere that clearly is not, that creates the urgent need to find out what can be changed in society, and what may be harder to change if biologically grounded.

Are all the differences we see the result of socialization and culture, or is there something else going on? We can postpone discussion of this important issue no longer.

5

Let's Hope It's Not True

It is said that when Lady Ashley heard that Darwin's theory of evolution showed men had evolved from monkeys, she remarked: 'Let's hope it's not true; but if it is true, let's hope that it does not become widely known.' The debate about education, gender and biology today often seems to veer towards similar sentiments – from both sides of the debate.

Feminist educators tend to assume that biology plays no significant role in gender differences relevant to education. Sometimes this is explicit – as we have seen in earlier excerpts from Naomi Wolf's *Misconceptions*, the Equal Opportunities Commission and *How Schools Shortchange Girls*. More often it is implicit. For feminists, it is socialization and culture which are the causes of gender differences in education, not biology, nor even an interaction of biology and socialization.

Occasionally, efforts are made to explore the evidence, but these fall short of what might be expected in a dispassionate survey. For instance, the research commissioned by Chris Woodhead's Ofsted, *Recent Research on Gender and Educational Performance*, was supposed to look, amongst other things, at evidence for and against biological foundations for gender differences. But, curiously, the researchers examined only one book on which to base their conclusion, and this was from six years before their report was published, which is odd, given the rate at which science progresses. Odder still, while the one book chosen was the extremely important *Sex Differences in Cognitive Abilities* by Diane Halpern, the one-page summary of her findings

121

seems to arrive at the diametrically opposite position to that arrived at by Diane Halpern herself!

For, in the Preface, Halpern tells how ideas on gender differences frequently came up in classes she had been teaching on cognitive psychology and psychology of women:

> At the time, it seemed clear to me that any between-sex differences in thinking abilities were due to socialization practices, artefacts and mistakes in the research, and bias and prejudice. After reviewing a pile of journal articles that stood several feet high and numerous books and book chapters that dwarfed the stack of journal articles, *I changed my mind*. . . . the conclusions that I had expected to make had to be revised.

How did she change her mind?

> There are real, and in some cases sizable, sex differences with respect to some cognitive abilities. Socialisation practices are undoubtedly important, but *there is also good evidence that biological sex differences play a role in establishing and maintaining cognitive sex differences, a conclusion that I wasn't prepared to make when I began reviewing the relevant literature.*[1]

The British researchers, however, using only her book as a source, come to the opposite conclusion. Highlighted in a pink panel, the report notes: 'Even if biology sets limits to human abilities, there is no certainty about what these limits might be, nor *whether they are different for men and women*.' It 'is now generally acknowledged', they say, that biological explanations 'are unlikely to provide an adequate account of gender differences in academic performance'.[2] That is not what the only book they featured said at all.

This said, it is certainly not to vindicate the 'other side' in the debate. I have had a lot of time in the preceding chapters for writers such as Carolyn Graglia, Danielle Crittenden, Melanie Phillips and Roger Scruton, but on this issue, perhaps they too may be criticized for just as easily taking the opposite side of the debate. It sometimes seems as though they too take the position on trust that most suits their argument – this time, that there are biological foundations to gender differences. This is certainly the way, in any case, that feminists criticize these authors.

So, the worry with both sides of the argument is that there is too much being taken on trust, too much hoping that the opposing position is not true. Both sides may be accepting too easily the evidence that supports their position without subjecting it to the scrutiny it deserves. That at least is the way each side perceives the other. I do not wish to be tarred with the same brush in this book. I think it is an important question and genuinely wish to pursue the evidence where it leads, in this chapter and the next.

An important issue needs to be clarified at the outset. From my reading of authors on both sides of the argument, it seems that there is a coincidence between those who reject any place for biological foundations and those who are feminists; similarly, those who accept a role for biological foundations are also those who oppose the feminist arguments. I have found no exceptions to this rule; however, there is no logical reason why this should be the case. For it would be perfectly consistent – as we will explore further in Chapter 7 – for someone to be convinced that all relevant gender differences *are* biologically based, 'natural', and still want to do something about them. After all, we frequently challenge nature in ways that are somewhat parallel. I get toothache: that is a perfectly natural, biologically based phenomenon. But I still want to do something about it, because I don't like the pain. I believe there is a higher moral principle (good health, hygiene) and so rush to the dentist to get him to overrule biology's 'intentions' for me. There is no reason why someone couldn't argue the same way about gender differences. It might be accepted that these are biologically based, but if they cause injustice and oppression for women (or men), it could be argued that we must do something about them, to make the world a better place according to our higher moral principles, whatever biology might have to say about the matter.

Exactly the same is true on the other side of the argument. We could accept that all relevant gender differences are completely due to socialization and culture, that biology plays no part, but still wish to defend them, even enjoy them. This might be because we think that the way society has created the sexual division of labour is a good method of dividing things up, and it does not matter whether or not, biologically speaking, this was the way nature intended us to be. Our moral principles could again override nature, at least in principle.

The trouble with either of these alternatives, however – which is perhaps why we don't often see them expressed – is that they are hard to defend. To take a simple example: consider the gender stereotyping of courses that we discussed in Chapter 2. If it is socialization (*without any* biological foundation or interaction) that is causing boys to be more inclined to study higher mathematics and physics, then it seems plausible that we can use socialization to challenge what socialization has created. What society creates, society can take away. Thus the ideas of the equal opportunities' lobbies – the 'take your daughter to work' day, the call to parents to raise boys and girls in equal ways and so on – all make sense if socialization is the cause of these gender differences.

If on the other hand it is biology, or the interaction of biology and culture, that is causing gender differences to emerge, then it becomes more difficult to see how the differences might be challenged, on this side of genetic engineering at least. It is certainly not impossible: and if the reformers' ambitions are modest enough, it may be possible to quite adequately challenge them for all educationally relevant purposes. Boys and girls can be made to study mathematics up to the same level, and as long as the level is not set too high, and as long as it is taught and assessed in ways that allow both genders to perform reasonably well (especially if these arrangements are biased towards the gender that would naturally perform less well), then you are unlikely to come up against severe biological obstacles to equal outcomes at that level. But if your aims are more ambitious than this – as would seem to be with governments and their feminist champions, who appear to be affronted by *any* gender differences in outcomes – then it becomes much more difficult, if biology is in part the cause, to see how socialization can change things dramatically. Again, it is not saying it is impossible, but it does seem to be a much more uphill struggle. In particular, the infringements on people's liberty necessarily would seem to become much more draconian, if biology is implicated in gender differences and equal outcomes are the goal.

The converse argument is again true. If one values the traditional gender distinctions in society, values the fact that girls are feminine and boys masculine and have different roles, it may be possible to create a society where these roles emerge, even if they have nothing to do with biology – certainly feminists believe this is precisely what has happened in our current societies! But it requires constant vigilance from those who value these gender differences. All the time, our biological impulses would be leading boys and girls to be the same; we would continually have to use socialization to ensure that they are not. Again, this may need quite draconian infringements on liberty. In addition, if there is any breakdown in the consensus that these social arrangements are good, and if biology has nothing to do with gender differences, it becomes increasingly difficult to maintain the position. Once you get increasing numbers of women being astronauts and presidents of America, CEOs of business and competitive (unisex) athletes, such socialization would become increasingly untenable.

So: it is important to sort out what role, if any, biology does play in gender differences, although it will not finally decide the argument – an issue to which we will return later. But we need to know what biology says, to help us decide which is the most appropriate way forward. We must move away from simply hoping that the opposing arguments are not true.

SEX AND GENDER

To begin to explore this, we have to clarify the distinction already used in this chapter and throughout the book between *gender* and *sex*. Many writers critical of feminism (e.g. Dennis O'Keeffe in *Political Correctness and Public Finance*[3] and Christina Hoff Sommers in *The War Against Boys*[4]) are troubled by this distinction – indeed, in some circles I attend, it becomes almost a badge of honour that one does not use the politically charged word 'gender', just as in the same circles women enjoy calling themselves 'chairman' to offend the politically correct. However, I find the distinction between sex and gender to be not only wholly unexceptional, but actually to be crucial to our discussion.

It is easy enough, with rare exceptions, to distinguish the biological *sex* of a baby at birth, and this sex, again with only rare exceptions, remains with the child throughout his or her life. But then society, if you like, puts a 'spin' on these sex differences: this is *gender*. Sex is about biology, gender is based on social construction. If you ask children how men and women are different, they will say things like women wear skirts and dresses, men trousers. Women wear make-up, men don't. Women have babies, men don't. Men dig holes in the road, women don't. Some of these differences will be purely *sex* differences – women having babies, for instance – and here gender and sex do precisely coincide. But often what we see around us will be because of *gender* differences created by societal norms. It is then an open question – and indeed one of the crucial questions of this book – the extent to which these gender differences are arbitrary or the extent to which they depend on, or are influenced in important ways by, biological sex differences.

The fact that it is men who dig holes in roads (almost without exception in this country, feminist attempts to get 'Men at Work' changed to 'People at Work' in the 1970s notwithstanding) is likely to be a function of men's greater relevant muscular strength, so has a strong biological root. But, clearly, there are some women who are stronger than some men in the relevant ways, so there is no reason why there could not in fact be many women digging up roads. But the fact is they are not: the gender norm is strong enough to prevent this from happening – and one may observe that this does not seem to have been a priority of feminists to challenge, it being presumably more important to move to gender equity in plum positions like lawyers and doctors, rather than getting equal numbers of women into dirty, noisy work like digging up roads.[5]

Similarly, women wearing skirts rather than men may be a completely arbitrary gender difference – the fact that Scotsmen seem quite happy in their kilts suggests so. On the other hand, the fact that women wear make-up rather than men may not be arbitrary at all – it may be rooted in sexual differences between men and women, to do with the features that make up different physical attractiveness for men and women, as we shall explore later in this chapter.

In fact, deciding that gender and sex *are* the same thing, that there are not two distinct concepts here, seems to be a way of smuggling in the assumption that biological differences are fundamental to all the differences we see in society. This assumption is illegitimate in this book. We note that there are two concepts, sex and gender, and it is for us to decide what their connections are in the matter of educational differences. The two categories we use in gender – male and female – are the same two categories we use for sex. But it is a genuinely open question whether or not they overlap meaningfully in other ways, and how they are related.

I am reassured that I am not alone among critics of feminism in recognizing this. The philosopher Roger Scruton also spends time making this distinction. It is, regarding *sex*, 'for science to determine what it is to be male or female, and to describe the biological and functional characteristics of sexual union'. *Gender*, however, incorporates 'not only the distinct observable forms of man and woman, but also the differences in life and behaviour which cause us selectively to respond to them'.[6]

WHAT ARE THE GENDER DIFFERENCES THAT NEED EXPLAINING?

So what are the gender differences that may be relevant to our concerns here? Some might think that the only educationally relevant differences will concern cognitive ability – differences concerning ability in mathematics and languages, for instance. However, I want to cast the net more widely. For the discussion of this book has focused on the way women and men are guided towards careers and relationships at least in part by what goes on in schools, with many suggestions that this 'guidance' offends many women's preferences for what they may want to prioritize in their lives. So let us begin by looking at a selection of gender differences across a wide range of possibilities, including relationship preferences and parenting styles, as well as cognitive differences. In this way, we aim to build up a picture of the ways men and women are different that might be educationally relevant.

Before proceeding, it is crucial to be clear at the outset about *two* things. *First*, that throughout this chapter we are talking about *statistical* differences, so there will always be exceptions to these generalizations. Think of the statistical generalization that men are, on average, taller than women. This is a fact: in the USA, the average height of men and women differs by about six inches. However, no one thinks that this fact can be disputed by finding, as is the case, that *some* women are taller than *many* men. So if you as a woman read certain figures and think, 'well, I'm not like that', this does not mean to say that the figure is not true *as a generalization*. You may not be like it, but the statistic means that women in general are. The same goes for men. I labour this point because I remember seeing a highly acclaimed woman on television challenging a point about Irish women with: 'Look at me, I'm not like that, so how can it be true?' Which either shows that even she needed this point spelled out, or that she was being disingenuous (in which case hoping to hoodwink the audience, again showing the need to spell this out carefully).

Second, it is very important to realize that even *small* between-sex differences can have a *huge* effect on ratios at the extremes. Again, consider the sex difference in heights. An average height difference of six inches between men and women may not sound much, but this has a very big impact when you start to look at the tallest individuals. The male average height is about five foot ten inches. Even at this average height, there are about 30 men to every woman. Just two inches taller, at six foot, and there are *2000* men to every woman. By the time you reach six foot, eight inches, there are virtually no women at all.[7] Likewise, only a small between-gender difference in mathematical ability, say, could lead to huge differences in performance in tests, and in the proportion of men and women going into particular jobs. A small difference in mathematical ability could lead to *all* the positions that require the very highest ability in the discipline being occupied by men, without any sugges-tion of injustice or discrimination.

A recent computer simulation illustrates this graphically.[8] Suppose you have a business that uses job performance evaluation tests to promote people through the company hierarchy. Suppose that – for whatever reason – men perform, in general, slightly better on these tests than women. This difference in performance is only very slight, however, accounting for *only 1 per cent* of the variability between male and female scores. This is a very small difference, and likely to be dismissed by many as being totally insignificant. However, assuming a normal pyramidal structure within the company, with fewer top positions than lower ones, this tiny 1 per cent difference in perform-ance evaluations will produce a hierarchy in which only 35 per cent of the highest level positions are filled by women.[9] In other words, if the performance evaluation tests were fair, measuring genuine and relevant differences between the sexes, a *tiny* gender difference in ability would lead to a *huge* difference in outcome.

LOVE, SEX AND JEALOUSY

Let us now move on to the gender differences that may be educationally relevant. Remember; throughout this section, our aim is simply to catalogue these differences, to gain a sense of whether or not they are important. We are not making a judgement either way as to whether or not these differences are rooted in biology or socialization, or a combination of both – that is something we turn to in the next chapter.

Status

During the fuel shortage crisis in Britain in late 2000 – brought on by mass protests against the high rate of tax on fuel – a cartoon in a national newspaper showed a young woman positively responding to a man's advances in a pub, having initially rejected him, with the line 'Oh, I didn't realize you were a petrol pump attendant'. Petrol pump attendants were all of a sudden of a high status in society. Recent studies, however, show that men in such roles would not normally be so favourably received. One study asked men and women how they would react if someone of the opposite sex approached them for sex. This revealed two factors. First, that women and men would respond in diametrically opposed ways: 63 per cent of women said they would be insulted and 17 per cent flattered. For men, it was almost precisely reversed, 67 per cent would be flattered and 15 per cent insulted. But interestingly, how much chagrin women would feel from such sexual advances, another study showed, would depend on the social and occupational status of the man doing the harassing. On a seven-point scale, 'women would be most upset by persistent advances from construction workers (4.04), garbage collectors (4.32), cleaning men (4.19)' and our poor petrol station attendant (4.13). Conversely, they would be least upset by approaches from 'pre-medical students (2.65), graduate students (2.80) or successful rock stars (2.71)'.[10]

129

There are numerous studies that put these results into a larger context of the different characteristics men and women value in a partner, and these studies have been replicated using numerous different sources and samples over time. One finding in particular emerges dramatically. Studies show that men and women rate very differently the importance of financial prospects and social status in a partner.

A study from 1939 in America found that women 'valued good financial prospects in a mate about twice as highly as men'. On a scale from 0 (irrelevant) to 3 (indispensable), women rated it at 1.80, compared to men with 0.90. This finding was replicated in 1956 and again in 1967. Importantly, the sexual revolution of the 1960s and 1970s failed to change this sex difference preference, for, in the mid-1980s, the psychologist David Buss replicated the studies, using the same questionnaire, surveying 1491 Americans. With this study, the same twofold difference in sexual preference remains, with women now rating the financial prospects in a male slightly higher at 1.90, while men rated it at 1.02.[11]

These studies depend upon self-reporting of the subjects, which may be open to biases of one sort or another. Other evidence supports these findings from a different angle. One study investigated the characteristics sought by men and women in the 'Lonely Hearts' columns of newspapers and magazines. This study examined 1111 personal ads, and found that the female advertisers sought financial resources approximately *eleven times more* than did the male advertisers.[12]

Another very interesting piece of research asked men and women – matched for income and other socio-economic factors – to indicate what financial prospects they would seek in a partner, asking them to consider separately what they would look for if they were to start dating, have any sexual relations, go steady, and get married. The men and women were asked to rate the 'minimum percentiles' of each characteristic that they would find acceptable in a partner. This concept was explained to the participants with examples such as: 'A person at the 50th percentile would be above 50 per cent of the other people in terms of earning capacity.'[13]

The results showed that women maintain consistently higher minimum standards in their mates at each of these stages. To go on a date with a man, women wanted to know that he was at the 45th percentile; namely that he was above 45 per cent of other men in terms of earning capacity. Men would be satisfied if their date was at the 24th percentile; namely above 24 per cent of other women in earning capacity. For steady dating and marriage, both men and women raised their stakes, although women consistently wanted better financial prospects in their partners than did men. Women wanted a steady date who was above 60 per cent of other men, while men were content with 30 per cent. For marriage, women aspired to men who were above 70 per cent of other men, while men aspired only to women above 40 per cent. However, the most striking contrast was for having sex. For women, having sex required raising the stakes above what they required only for dating – they wanted a man at the 49th percentile. Men, however, did not care where their potential sexual partner came in the earnings' hierarchy, returning the zero percentile as their requirement. They would have sex with anyone.

Many of these results are from studies in America. However, it turns out that they reveal a universal phenomenon. David Buss and his colleagues conducted a cross-cultural comparison, involving 37 cultures on six continents and five islands, in populations ranging from 'coast-dwelling Australians to urban Brazilians to shantytown South African Zulus'. The study included a total of 10,047 individuals, some from monogamous, others from polygamous cultures.

Their finding was unequivocal: 'Women across all continents, all political systems (including socialism and communism), all racial groups, all religious groups, and all systems of mating (from intense polygyny to presumptive monogamy) placed more value than men on good financial prospects. Overall, women valued financial resources about 100 per cent more than men, or roughly twice as much.'[14] There were some cultural variations, but the sex difference remained the same within each group.

The study found similar results for a universal preference among women for higher social status and older men, with women highly rating ambition and industriousness, dependence and stability, athletic prowess, good health, love, and a willingness to invest in children.

Beauty

The same studies from 1939 to 1996 which looked at financial status also looked at how important women and men rated physical attractiveness in a mate. The importance of this factor has increased dramatically in America this century for both sexes, probably pointing to cultural changes. But interestingly, what has remained constant is that men rate the physical attractiveness of a female partner much more highly than women rate it in a man, although the gap is narrowing. On the scale of 0 (irrelevant) to 3 (indispensable), in the period from 1939 to 1996, men's ratings have increased from 1.50 to 2.11, while women's have increased from 0.94 to 1.67.

Parenting

Next, we turn to evidence about different parenting preferences. Perhaps the most striking evidence here is from the classic study by Lionel Tiger and Joseph Shepher, *Women in the Kibbutz*. This is particularly interesting evidence because the Israeli kibbutzim movement, founded in 1910, espoused socialist and feminist values. In the kibbutz, a new way of living was adopted. To break free from sexual inequality, women would be liberated from economic dependence upon men, released from the burdens of childcare. Children were to live in age-graded children's houses, and communal kitchens, and laundries and dining-rooms were introduced to liberate women from housewifery. Moreover, men and women were completely free to choose whatever work they wanted to do.

Tiger and Shepher studied three generations of people living in the kibbutz, a total of 34,040 people altogether. Astonishingly, they found that the division of labour was *greater* within the kibbutz than outside. Perhaps most surprisingly, this included roles over parenting. These differences resulted not from men, but from women's overwhelming preferences: gradually, over the years, women started to move away from collective childrearing. Mothers began to insist that they look after their own children, not farm them out to others. This move was initially resisted by the men, who considered it to be a retrograde move back to their rejected bourgeois values. But the mothers would not be swayed: they outvoted the men. The upshot was that the utopian experiment designed to liberate women from childrearing ended up with women reasserting their rights to motherhood.[15] In the kibbutz, says Matt Ridley, 'People have returned to stereotype'.[16]

This pattern is seen universally across cultures, and the fact that attempts to eradicate it were unsuccessful in the kibbutz at least suggests something about its origins – something we will discuss below. This impression is also reinforced by studies of the !Kung San people of the Kalahari desert in Botswana (the 'bushmen'). It is generally accepted that this society features 'equality among group members', yet despite this 'social norm of equality', again, !Kung San fathers provided less than 7 per cent of childcare, the mothers providing the majority of the remaining care.[17]

Other cross-cultural studies show this universal phenomenon of women devoting more effort towards parenting than men. This has been found in communities including the Ye'Kwana in the Venezuelan rain forests, where mothers hold infants 78 per cent of the time, and men 1.4 per cent of the time; the remainder of the time the baby is held mainly by female kin, grandmothers, sisters and aunts. Other studies from Kenya, India, Mexico, Java, Quechua, Nepal, Japan and the Philippines show that women spend up to ten times more time caring for children than do men. If passive forms of caring, such as watching over children, is taken into account, the figure rises to as much as fifteen times.[18]

Sexual interest

Research shows that males and females judge sexual intent differently. Several experiments have been conducted along these lines. For instance, in one study 98 male and 102 female college students viewed a ten-minute videotape of a conversation in which a female student visits a male professor's office to ask for more time to complete a term paper. Both roles were played by actors, who were instructed to behave in a friendly but non-flirtatious fashion. Although both men and women inferred friendliness on behalf of the female student (6.45 and 6.09 on a seven-point scale), men were significantly likely to infer sexual intentions (3.84 against 2.00) and seduction (3.38 against 1.89). Other studies have shown similar phenomena. In general, men are much more likely to interpret friendliness and smiling by women as indicating the woman's sexual interest; women are more likely to view friendliness for exactly what it is, without inferring sexual intent. A cross-cultural study compared Brazilian and American responses, and found that the sex differences in Brazil were smaller than in the USA, although still in the same direction.[19]

Competitiveness

There are considerable gender differences with regard to aggressiveness, competitiveness and status seeking. For instance, Martin Daly and Margo Wilson's work[20] on homicide found that, around the world, 'participants, both perpetrators and victims, are largely unmarried young males'.[21] Other analyses, which looked at a whole range of studies on aggression, found that males were 'moderately more' aggressive than females.[22] Again, we note that such a difference is likely to translate into quite considerable differences on the ground.

Moreover, research shows that males exhibit 'more competitive behaviour and respond more positively than females to competitive situations'.[23] While competition significantly increases the motivation of men, it does not do so for women. 'The more competitive an academic programme is perceived by women, for example, the poorer their performance, while the correlation is reversed for men.'.[24]

Males and females also differ substantially in terms of dominance behaviour. Eleanor Maccoby's[25] work has shown that males' interest in 'turf and dominance' and females' interest in maintaining social relationships are visible at an early age – as early as 3-years old. There are clear differences in the games children play too. Studies have found that about 65 per cent of the play of boys was formal games, with competitive interactions and rules, while only 35 per cent was of this type for girls.[26] In general, studies consistently show that girls prefer to cooperate rather than compete, while boys consistently prefer competition to cooperation. There is also a marked increase in girls' preference for cooperation immediately after puberty.

Researchers point out that for very young children in school when they are allowed to choose what they do, 'girls tend to predominate in indoor, family, expressive activities and boys in sand, carpentry and block-building activities'. To these researchers' dismay, they note that 'These stereotypical patterns are resistant to change'.[27]

WORDS, SPACE AND NUMBERS

Not only are there consistently found gender differences in sexual behaviour between the sexes, but there are also consistent and often large differences in cognitive abilities.

Which gender is smarter, male or female? We can throw out this question straight away. Common ways of measuring 'smartness' (i.e. general intelligence) use tests that have been *explicitly* devised so that there are no average overall differences between men and women. The early devisers of intelligence tests carefully wrote them so that, if questions were found that were answered significantly differently by males and females, they were either not used, or a question that favoured the other sex was deliberately included to balance it. Moreover, recent research by Arthur Jensen using tests that had not been deliberately so constructed found no evidence for average sex differences: 'Males, on average, excel on some factors; females on others.'[28] What we can do is break down the question of intelligence into components. Results show that there are significant differences between men and women in terms of their verbal and mathematical abilities, and also on what might be called the 'pre-cognitive' processes of perception and attention.

Perception and attention

Our sensory systems give us our information about the world – perception and attention are the 'first steps in the cognitive process'. This is an especially interesting area on which to focus initially, since, if there are gender differences to be found at this basic level of information processing, this provides a likely way of explaining gender differences at later cognitive stages. Even more importantly, no one suggests that there is likely to be socialization or cultural stereotypes operating at this basic level, for we are not really conscious of the ways in which our sensory systems function.[29] Thus any gender differences found at this stage are highly likely to be of biological, rather than socialization, in origin.

These areas have been comprehensively researched, and a wide variety of gender differences found. Girls and women are able to detect tones of one frequency ('pure tones') better than are boys and men. Girls and women can more easily detect 'sweet, sour, salty, and bitter substances' than boys and men. They are also more sensitive to being touched – one research tested touch-sensitivity on twenty body parts and found that only on the nose were males more sensitive to touch then females.[30] Other research has shown that many such gender differences in perceptual thresholds are detectable in very young babies. Newborn boys, for instance, are less sensitive to touch than are newborn girls.[31]

Diane Halpern notes that these and other differences in perception could not be attributed to socialization. Of course, the fact that boys and girls have these biologically based perceptual differences 'could create behavioural dispositions that vary as a function of sex'. That is, although such findings 'do not mean that sex differences in cognition are inevitable or unalterable', they do suggest that they 'probably have an early physiological basis'.[32]

Words

Research shows that females have superior verbal abilities to men. The size of this difference varies for the particular task in question. Given the thousands of published and unpublished research reports into gender differences, with varying results between individual experiments and surveys, how do you reach a conclusion about what is really happening in general? Meta-analysis is a sophisticated statistical way of combining the results of these numerous studies, to come up with an analysis of the many different research results. The key statistic used is in the accompanying footnote;[33] this delivers a number that gives an indication of the 'overall' size of the difference across all the numerous studies examined. For our purposes here (and we will return to this below), a number over 0.80 is considered by everyone to be large.

There have been some useful meta-analyses of gender differences in verbal abilities. For some tasks, the differences are huge. For *associational fluency* (that is, the ability to generate synonyms), there is a huge female advantage, with a huge effect size of 1.2. On tests of *consonant–vowel matching*, there is a similarly huge female advantage (1.3). As Diane Halpern puts it: 'These are enormous effect sizes – so large that tests of statistical significance are not even needed.'[34]

On *vocabulary* tests there are significant differences, although not as large as these, with some meta-analyses finding a female advantage for 19- to 25-year-old women of (0.23). For *reading comprehension*, females also have a significant advantage, with the largest difference found in children of 5 years of age and younger, with girls reading more proficiently than boys (0.31).[35]

Again, while not as large as the earlier differences, our earlier comments about size of differences should make us cautious about underestimating their impact: even tiny differences between the sexes (1 per cent in the case of the computer simulation of job hierarchy) can have enormous differences in terms of gender outcomes. Finally, boys are three to four times more likely to have problems with *stuttering* than girls, while mild *dyslexia* is five times more likely to occur in males than in females, and severe dyslexia ten times more likely.[36]

Space

Again, it is a fair summary to say that research shows that males have superior visual–spatial abilities over females. Indeed, 'findings of sex differences in visual–spatial ability are the most robust (found consistently) of the cognitive sex differences' and 'the largest sex differences are found here'.[37]

Visual–spatial abilities may be disaggregated into at least five kinds of ability: spatial perception, mental rotation, spatial visualization, spatio-temporal ability, and the generation and maintenance of a spatial image. In a recent meta-analysis of 286 studies, researchers have shown that, overall, there is an effect size of 0.37 favouring males.

But on some particular types of ability the difference is even higher, with the effect size for mental rotation being 0.56 and for spatial perception, 0.44.[38] Other studies have shown even higher effect size for mental rotation, from 0.74 to 0.90,[39] while an earlier meta-analysis showed effect sizes of 0.73, 0.44 and 0.13 for mental rotation, spatial perception and spatial visualization, respectively. Oddly, these findings were represented by their feminist researcher to suggest that they show the global generalization that 'males are superior in spatial ability' is 'simply unwarranted'[40] – because the effects are quite small in certain areas such as spatial visualization. This seems churlish. If in a triathlon an athlete wins one of the contests hands-down, one with a moderate lead, and just scrapes through on the last, would we not say that he or she is superior in the triathlon? Some feminists would not, apparently.

Numbers

In general, there is male superiority in quantitative abilities. Meta-analyses show a slight female superiority in primary school, but this soon translates into a 'moderate' male superiority in high school, college and adulthood (effect sizes of 0.29, 0.41 and 0.59 respectively).[41]

Work on mathematically gifted youth conducted at Johns Hopkins University since 1971, the Study of Mathematically Precocious Youth (SMPY), also reveals considerable gender differences[42] – again empha-sizing the way that the significance of gender differences looms larger the higher up the ability range one looks. In the USA, there are twice as many men as women scoring 500 or above on the mathematical portion of the SAT (the American college entrance exam, on which 500 is the average score for college-bound twelfth graders). By the time one reaches scores of 700 or above, however, there are thirteen times as many males as females. Importantly, these ratios 'have remained relatively stable over the past 20 years', and have been observed for 8-year-olds, and cross-culturally, although they are slightly smaller for Asians.[43]

Interesting lines of research are being opened up by work that is looking at the way quantitative ability may be related to other abilities, such as the use of visual imagery, or the ability to retrieve a formula or memorized solution. It has been found that those tasks which produce the greatest gender differences favouring males seem to require the test-takers 'to construct and mentally transform a mental representation'.[44] Perhaps this links quantitative with visual-spatial ability.

FROM GENDER TO SEX: FEMINISM'S FAULT LINE REVISITED

It is indisputable that there are significant gender differences in areas that are likely to have relevance for education. Most clearly, these are found in aspects of female verbal superiority and male mathematical superiority. However, there are also clear and undisputed gender differences in terms of what men and women seek in terms of relationships, and their different propensities for parenting and aggression, some of which may well be relevant differences for education. For now, we can feel confident in saying that any intuition we had that there are significant gender differences is well established by science, and we can be confident too that some of these differences may well be significant for educational outcomes.

But – these are *gender* differences. The key question is: How are they related to *sex* differences, to biology? For, only once we have got an answer to this question can we get a handle on how amenable these differences may be to social reform. Thus, for instance, given the well-established gender differences in visual–spatial and numerical abilities, it may come as no surprise that there are larger numbers of men than women in careers which require higher levels of mathemat- ical ability. But whether or not this should bother us would depend, in part, on whether or not it has anything to do with biology. If the outcome is because boys and girls are socialized differently, then we may feel morally obliged to do something to change the situation. If, however, the outcome is based on biological differences – even if these are 'exaggerated' in interaction with culture[45] – we might want to consider more carefully the pros and cons of trying to change things. Perhaps we cannot change much if the differences are biologi- cally rooted. Likewise for all educationally relevant gender differences.

We will try to make progress in this debate in the next chapter. Before moving on, however, something rather interesting emerges from this discussion of biology versus socialization. In an earlier chapter we distinguished between two types of feminism: 'equality' and 'liberation' (or 'rationalist' and 'celebratory' feminism). Liberation feminists, we said, welcomed gender differences and feminine values and ways of knowing, and sought to revalue these. Interestingly, one of the writers sympathetic to liberation feminism, Carrie Paechter, author of the important book *Educating the Other*, does look at evidence for biological foundations underpinning gender differences. However, she decides that observed gender differences are more likely to be the result of socialization, not of biology. This finding has a rather profound implication for feminism's fault line.

Before I say what this implication is, it is probably worth briefly addressing Paechter's argument – for if she found biological explanations for gender differences unconvincing after reviewing the evidence, surely we too might follow suit? In the end, however, I do not find her argument persuasive. Her case rests largely on discussion of children with hormonal abnormalities. All foetuses – those chromosomally female *and* male – are in some sense set to become female. It is the presence in the womb of hormones called androgens that makes chromosomally male foetuses become little boys rather than little girls. However, in rare cases of a disease called 'androgen-insensitivity', for reasons not properly understood, chromosomally male foetuses do not react to androgens in the womb, and hence potential little boys develop ambiguous sexual organs.

Paechter notes that such children – although *genetically* male – are usually *raised* as girls, and 'develop female gender identity and take on feminine gender roles'. 'Indeed', says Paechter, 'it may only be when menstruation fails to commence as expected that it is realized that there is anything unusual about them.' One of the most studied groups of these children is found in isolated villages in the Dominican Republic. Paechter notes that between 7 and 12 years of age, 'these children realized, as they became more physically masculine, that they were different from other girls, and gradually came to evolve male gender identities and roles'.[46]

The important point to note here is that these were children reared as girls by their parents, from an early age – in a society, to boot, that strictly encourages very different behaviour in boys and girls from an early age ('boys are encouraged to romp outside the home. The girls are encouraged to stay with their mothers or play in the house. At about 11 years of age, the boys seek entertainment at bars and cockfights'[47]).

According to socialization explanations for gender identity, to which Paechter is sympathetic, these children should have been perfectly happy with their gender identity as females. But they weren't. Biologically, 'as they became more physically masculine', they realized that their parents were wrong, that their nature was stronger than their nurture. In spite of their parental upbringing they adopted masculine traits. Indeed, for many researchers and commentators, this group of children provide some of the strongest evidence against a socialization theory of gender identity. Paechter does concede that some might think this way, including the researchers who have intensely studied the children, but she prefers an alternative interpretation of the evidence. Among these people, she tells us, 'initial gender assignment might well have been seen as more provisional than it is elsewhere'. Settling for one gender throughout life was 'not central to these people's conception of gender'.[48]

I find her explanation less persuasive than the one offered by the researchers themselves, and taken up by commentators such as Anthony Clare, who argues that it is the example of these children, more than anything, that shows how testosterone in puberty overrides 'the effect of rearing the boys as girls in infancy and childhood'. Indeed, 'These findings serve to illustrate the triumph of testosterone over rearing'.[49] It is biology, not upbringing, that is the determinant of their gender identity.

But, irrespective of this conclusion, the important point here – to return to the implication for feminism's fault line – is that Paechter wants to celebrate gender differences but accepts that such gender differences have arisen through socialization in oppressive patriarchal society, not through biology. I am sure she is not alone in holding both these views simultaneously. On the face of it, that seems odd to me. Why would (liberation) feminists seek to celebrate something which they say is socially constructed by patriarchy?

Perhaps there is nothing so odd about this after all. Just as grit enters an oyster and creates something of beauty and value, so I suppose it is plausible that feminine values and ways of knowing could have emerged, pearl-like, from within grubby patriarchy. I have not heard any feminist come up with this defence, however. And it does bring about the odd possibility that, just as those who value pearls must accept that, without grit bothering oysters there can be no natural pearls, so we might have to accept that, without grubby, oppressive patriarchy, we would have no feminine virtues to celebrate either.

However, these considerations do bring us to another possibility, a 'third way' for feminism. That is, within 'liberation' feminism there might be those who seek to rejoice in the feminine virtues, ways of knowing and so on but who *also* accept that these valuable differences emerge not because of socialization through patriarchy. Instead, they might celebrate female values and ways of knowing as firmly rooted in biological differences.

The only writer I have seen come close to this position – although I am not claiming that she embraces it fully – is Germaine Greer. There are hints – at least I take them as hints – that she might be amenable to such an understanding. For instance, she notes that there is 'a considerable body of evidence that no matter how gender-free their upbringing, children will invent gender for themselves', which might suggest that socialization theories are not as powerful as biological explanations for gender differences. And she argues that the 'animal world will remain sexed if not gendered, and the child would be dead from the neck up who did not wonder whether she was the kind of animal who could have puppies or not',[50] again suggesting to me that she recognizes the powerful role biology may have in gender differences.

In any case, whether or not Greer accepts it, I cannot see why such a position would create a problem for liberation feminists. For what it would do is to reclaim the valued gender differences from out of patriarchy. Valuable female qualities may be shown, wholly and unequivocally, to be because of a woman's sex as well as her gender, and nothing to do with the influence of men at all. What could be wrong with such a position? This notion of celebrating gender differences even though they might be biologically determined will inform our discussion in Chapter 8. But first, we must return to our question of whether or not there is good evidence to show biological underpinnings for gender differences before we can make any firm conclusions.

6

A Theory of Education as If Darwin Mattered

A recent television advertisement for a 'seriously smooth' beer features a boy- and girlfriend at a close friend's wedding. He quickly ascertains that the happy bride is about to throw her bouquet into the crowd. He knows that his girlfriend, resplendent in bridesmaid's dress, is waiting, eager to catch it. If she does, the custom says that she will be the next to be married, which will put awful pressure on our man to do the business of proposing to her. So the seriously smooth man quietly asks his girlfriend to hold his drink because he is bothered by his undone shoe-lace. She willingly does so, eager to please her man, full of devotion on this romantic occasion. While she holds his pint, the bouquet is thrown, and she is thwarted from jumping up to catch it. Instead it is caught by a young woman at the back of the crowd, whose boyfriend stares agonizingly at the man who should have been caught.

Such gender differences in desires for marriage and commitment are a much agonized-over feature of the Bridget Jones repertoire. However, as we saw in the last chapter, they form only a small part of a huge range of gender differences, many of which are likely to have educational implications. Science points to differences in cognitive abilities – girls and women, in general, have superior verbal abilities, while boys and men, in general, have superior visual–spatial skills and better overall mathematical aptitude. And in terms of what men and women seek in each other, we found widely accepted findings that women value high status and resources more highly in a partner, were more involved in parenting, and were less aggressive and competitive than men.

These are widely accepted *gender* differences. The key question for us is this: Could any of these gender differences be based, at least in part, on biological – that is, on chromosomal, hormonal or brain – differences between men and women, or are they likely to be products only of socialization and cultural learning? For the sake of sorting out what education reforms are desirable, we need to have a clearer idea of what the answer is here, since it makes a difference to the outcome of the argument in this book.

How can we proceed here? I could take any one of three approaches. One approach would be to undertake a detailed examination of all the arguments for and against social–cultural explanations, and then to do the same for biological ones. Diane Halpern has done this, but it took a whole book, and she looked only at cognitive differences. Such an approach seems out of the question here, for reasons of space alone. A second approach would be the opposite one. It could point to work done elsewhere that suggests a biological grounding for gender differences, and take this on trust for the purpose of the argument here. Halpern's study might be used for starters, and there are many popular books in this genre that might be used to shore up this assumption, including Matt Ridley's masterful *The Red Queen* already referred to.

Such an approach seems too easy. This book would be incomplete without some further discussion of its own on this important question. If nothing else, readers might accuse me of the same shortcoming that I have raised against feminist writers: that they take too much on trust the arguments that suit them best. For the sake of completeness we must at least make an attempt to examine the evidence.

I think there may be a possible short cut for us that could provide a reasonably satisfactory third option, since as we have noted, several of the writers I have sympathetically reviewed – such as Carolyn Graglia, Danielle Crittenden and Roger Scruton – seem persuaded that gender differences do have a biological foundation. One of the factors that seems to have persuaded them is the science of evolutionary psychology. Carolyn Graglia seems typical here. For instance, when remarking on Simone de Beauvoir's attraction to her 'superior man', Graglia notes that the evolutionary psychologist David Buss 'has established the biological basis for our attraction to the powerful, superior men best able to protect and care for us while we bear children'. Or, focusing on how men want their wives to be faithful, and get extraordinarily jealous if they are not, she notes that these 'facts of life, which are now documented by evolutionary psychologists, were always part of our cultural knowledge'. Or again, of women's unsuitability for casual sex, she notes how 'evolutionary psychology now grounds our convictions in biological facts'.[1]

Interestingly, although her sympathies finally end up in the socialization camp, Naomi Wolf too is led to thinking in terms of evolutionary psychology during her own pregnancy – insights that seem to be completely forgotten when she again stridently argues for equality once her child is born. For instance, she notes in her eighth month of pregnancy how she began to feel a *'primal'* dependency on her partner, 'a feeling of dependency I had never felt before'. This leads her to question her 'lifetime of conviction about women's ability to go it merrily alone', thinking of it as 'a complete *evolutionary howler* in the face of pregnancy'. Similarly, at around this time, many couples seem to be doing something that, she says, the evolutionary psychologists predict they will be doing, and doing it completely subconsciously. Even if the woman had kept her own name for feminist reasons, the baby was being given the name of the father: 'It seemed to me that this kind of *subconscious* make-the-man-stay behaviour was exactly what my friends and I were engaging in.' Furthermore, she notes: 'It was fascinating to see a group of women who believe fervently in women's equality *unconsciously revert* to some of the basic tenets of a patriarchy they had all their lives rebelled against – for love.' And, *'on a primal level'*, she felt the same pressures: 'I was still a feminist. But I understood, at this point in my life, that it could be dangerous to be one.'[2]

Can we follow these hints and pointers and find in evolutionary psychology a way of adjudicating between the theories of socialization and of biology as possible foundations for observed gender differences? That is the third way I will explore here. It is slightly risky, given the controversy surrounding this new science. At the outset I should stress that, if this chapter fails to convince any readers, this does not rule out the possibility of the other two approaches. Ultimately, if readers are not persuaded by the explanations of evolutionary psychology, this does not let them off the hook with regard to finding a satisfactory answer to this important question of how gender differences relate to sex.

So let us explore evolutionary psychology as a possible way of moving the debate forward. Now, my reading of philosophy of science tells me that we would need any theory to satisfy something like the following *four* conditions before we should find it persuasive.

First, of course, the theory must be consistent with *all* the available evidence. There must be no findings that simply do not fit with the theory. Thus in this case, the theory must be consistent with *all* the facts of gender differences noted in the previous chapter. *Second*, the theory must be able to offer some explanation as to *why* these *particular* differences arise. That is, we would prefer, other things being equal, a theory that can not only explain that there will be gender differences in mathematical ability, say, but also why it is that boys are better at mathematics than girls, rather than vice versa.

Third, a theory should preferably be 'parsimonious'; that is, it should be able to explain each gender difference in the same way. What we are looking for is a theory that needs the minimum amount of *ad hoc* additional explanations, that does not require an additional explanation for every additional case brought to its attention. *Finally*, and most significantly, we would require a theory to make novel or unexpected predictions that can be tested. What we want is a theory that sticks its neck out, a theory that stands out from the humdrum and says: if I'm true, then this will follow – and I bet you never thought of that! And: here's how you go about testing it. Even better, of course, would be if the testable predictions are then found to hold up to empirical scrutiny. The more novel predictions of this kind the better.

Can evolutionary psychology fit the bill here? And can it fit better than competing socio-cultural explanations? In the next section, I will try to summarize what I see as the major tenets of evolutionary psychology, before investigating how well the perspective fits the above four criteria.

PSYCHOLOGY AS IF DARWIN MATTERED

Evolutionary psychology is the research programme in science that seeks to understand our minds and behaviour from the perspective that we are evolved mammals. It is psychology as if Darwin mattered. Not many people have problems accepting that humans emerged from the apes through evolution. Not many have any problem accepting that features such as our habit of walking upright, or our handy opposable thumbs, also emerged through similar natural processes. Evolutionary psychology takes these insights a step further. Why should our minds and behaviour be exempt from evolutionary pressures?

Evolutionary psychology may be understood as being based on the central idea that natural selection evolved human psychological mechanisms as *adaptations*.[3] And, as distinctly human evolution occurred during the Pleistocene period that began about 1.6 million years ago and ended 10,000 years ago, it is to the environmental conditions of the Pleistocene – in which humans spent about 99 per cent of their evolutionary history as hunter-gatherers in Africa[4] – that we must primarily look to see how humans evolved. At the beginning of the Pleistocene, our ancestors were 'relatively small-brained apes who walked upright and made just a few crude stone tools. They were almost certainly without language, music, art, or much creative intelligence.' By the end of the period, however, our ancestors were more or less fully formed modern humans, 'identical to us in bodily appearance, brain structure, and psychology'.[5] Evolutionary psychologists argue that the *universal* human mental attributes – that is, those found among all societies – are those that are most likely to have evolved during (or possibly before) the hunter-gatherer phase of our existence.

Evolutionary theory in general has one basic assumption. Any adaptation needs to be understood in terms of the function for which it has evolved. Adaptations themselves occur through mutations in a single individual; that is, through spontaneous changes in the structure of the organism's DNA, probably arising through copying mistakes. Some mutations will simply hinder the individual, which will be disadvantaged by them and not prosper, while some mutations, some mistakes, will help the individual to thrive. Crucially, this may happen in one of *two* distinct ways.

The first way is probably the best known, leading to the process called by Darwin *natural selection*. This is simply when the mutation leads to some advantage to the organism for survival. Because it helps the individual to survive, a helpful mutation is thus likely to be passed down to later generations in growing numbers. If it continues to be successful, the mutation may spread to every member of the population. This is 'survival of the fittest', a utilitarian, somewhat grim process of genes mutating, and adaptations emerging, that sometimes lead to greater survival and hence heritable features spreading through the species population as a whole. Natural selection is about the competition for survival.

But there is another type of selection that Darwin also proposed, and which some evolutionary psychologists now think is likely to have had as great, or even greater impact on our minds and behaviour. This is *sexual selection*. In sexual selection, the mutation may lead to some advantage to the individual in the quest for reproduction. Again, if it is successful it is likely to be passed on, and if it continues to be successful, it is passed on to the whole population.

The theory of sexual selection was created by Darwin to explain some of the strange anomalies he saw in the animal world – and it is now being used by evolutionary psychologists to explain some of the chief anomalies in human behaviour and the human mind. The most puzzling anomaly for Darwin was animal ornamentation – or more particularly, *male* animal ornamentation. Darwin saw how his theory of natural selection could not account for the many expensive and unnecessary luxuries that were present in the animal kingdom, seemingly serving to undermine rather than promote the survival of the individual. Above all, these difficulties were encapsulated for Darwin in the problem of the peacock's tail. Far from contributing to the peacock's survival ability, it would seem to positively undermine it. It made the male peacock very vulnerable to predators, much more so than the modestly attired peahen.[6]

Yet, Darwin believed that evolution could explain all natural phenomena, so was forced to look elsewhere than at adaptations that were selected for their straightforward survival only. Developing his theory in *The Descent of Man, and Selection in Relation to Sex*, first published in 1871, Darwin saw that some traits might evolve as adaptations that helped in the competition for sexual mates.

In animals, Darwin noted, it is usually males who court and females who choose. To this end, males compete either by intimidating other males with a display and use of weaponry, or they seek to attract females with ornaments, or a bit of both. But what males get up to (feminists will be relieved to hear) is only half of the equation. For, Darwin noted, choosy females then decide with whom to mate once the male displays and violence are over. They prefer the stronger over the weaker, and the more attractive over the dowdier. It is fairly straightforward to explain the evolution of the male weapons and aggressiveness; Darwin's theory of sexual selection helps to explain why sexual ornamentation is so common, even though on the face of it this would hinder rather than help survival.[7]

Darwin himself was not able to explain why it is that males court and females choose. In terms of his theory, it could have been the other way around; he was merely reporting what he saw. But what he saw, he believed, was analogous to the ways humans created artificial hybrid species. He wrote in *The Descent of Man*:

> All animals present individual differences, and as man can modify his domesticated birds by selecting the individuals which appear to him the most beautiful, so the habitual or even occasional preference by the female of the more attractive males would almost certainly lead to their modification; and such modifications might in the course of time be augmented to almost any extent, compatible with the existence of the species.[8]

Sexual selection, he believed, must somehow lead to some of the most delightful male ornaments such as the peacock's tail, but he was unable to say exactly how. That had to wait until the twentieth century, and in particular for the biologist Ronald Fisher. In 1915, he published hypotheses that have provided the mainstay for our understanding ever since. He asked not only why females should bother to choose, and what evolutionary advantage it would give to them — problems that had worried Darwin — but also how sexual preferences themselves may have arisen. From this, Fisher came up with the two major themes of modern sexual selection theory. First was the 'sexual-ornament-as-fitness-indicator' theory. He speculated:

> Consider, then, what happens when a clearly marked pattern of bright feathers affords . . . a fairly good index of natural superiority. A tendency to select those suitors in which the feature is best developed is then a profitable instinct for the female bird, and the taste for this 'point' becomes firmly established.[9]

The crucial thing is that the feature in question might of itself be completely valueless, acting only as an indicator of the fitness, health and energy of the potential mate. The process works like this:

> Suppose that healthier males have brighter plumage. Females may produce more and healthier offspring if they mate with healthier males. If they happen to have a sexual preference for bright plumage, their offspring will automatically inherit better health from their highly fit fathers. Over time, the sexual preference for bright plumage would become more common because it brings reproductive benefits. Then, even if bright male plumage is useless in all other respects, it will become more common among males simply because males prefer it.[10]

Indeed, the theory has been developed to suggest that it is precisely the *high costs* of maintaining and displaying the sexual ornaments that keeps them as reliable indicators of fitness, health and energy. The peacock's tail, for instance, requires considerable investment of energy to grow, and considerable investment in time to preen. Carrying it around is tiring too. All these costs show a potential mate that the peacock is at the peak of health. The ornament, because of the costs of maintaining it, shows how fit the individual is.

Couple this process with the second theme developed by Fisher and the possibilities become endless and, to some evolutionary psychologists at least, rather exciting, through the process of 'runaway sexual selection'. Suppose female birds had settled on liking slightly brighter plumage as a fitness indicator, and males had evolved accordingly, as above. The females would still not be satisfied – they would still need some way of differentiating the fitter from less fit males; chances are they would continue doing what they 'knew best', and would seek even brighter plumage. The males, bless them, would try to keep up with their high maintenance mates' demands. Again, the females would move the goal-posts. Through this process, an 'arms race' would develop between female preferences and male-evolved ornaments.

In combination, the fitness theory and the runaway sexual selection, it is argued, plausibly show how ornaments such as the peacock's tail could evolve. Darwin's mystery has been solved. The peacock's tail is a drag on its resources. Peacocks would probably survive better if they had tails like peahens, but the peahens didn't want that; they preferred, at first, a little bit of colour, a little bit of flair. As peacocks over evolutionary time kept up with these preferences, so the peacock's tail evolved through mate choice. Its biological function is clear and simple: it is there 'to attract peahens'.[11]

In a parallel way, major contemporary work in evolutionary psychology suggests that there may have been similar processes at work in humans too. It is now argued that female choice and male competition, coupled with the more mundane features of natural selection, may explain many aspects of human behaviour too. It is worth looking in detail at some of this work to show the ways in which evolutionary psychology is developing today.

Geoffrey Miller's Mating Mind

Just as sexual selection is likely to have led to the magnificent ornamentation of the peacock's tail, the young evolutionary psychologist Geoffrey Miller, in his magnificent The Mating Mind (2000), argues that sexual selection, through female choice, is likely to have led to the development of the human brain and thence to the mind.[12] For there are three major puzzles that face the usual evolutionary 'survival' explanations for the evolution of the human brain. First, if human intelligence and creativity are such good things for survival, why did the vast majority of other animals – including our nearest ape neighbours – not develop them? Our brains are so expensive, energy-wise, to run; and most other successful animal species seem to do quite well with tiny brains.

Second, most scientists have argued that the brain's expansion was needed for human survival. But, if so, how does one explain the fact that, although brain size increased by a factor of three somewhere between 2.5 million and 100,000 years ago, 'for most of this period our ancestors continued to make the same kind of stone handaxes'? The supposed features that would enhance survival values, such as technological innovation that led to global colonization and rapid population growth, only occurred *after* our brains had stopped growing.

Finally, things we most value about the mind and which the mind is uniquely good at – humour, story-telling, gossip, art, music, self-consciousness, ornate language, imaginative ideologies, religion, morality – are not obviously related to survival: language appears far too elaborate than is 'necessary for basic survival functions alone', argues Miller. Art and music 'seem like pointless wastes of energy'. Morality seems 'irrelevant to the everyday business of finding food and avoiding predators'.

Miller proposes that his theory of the sexual selection of the brain can solve all three of these problems. His thesis is this. Amongst our apelike ancestors, males varied in 'creative intelligence' – in an embryonic form at least. This variation was heritable, so that the more creatively intelligent individuals had more creatively intelligent off-spring. For whatever reason, some female hominids developed a sexual preference for this creative intelligence. It is not important how or why they developed this taste, it could have been simply their own mutations affecting their sexual preferences. However, once developed, those males who were more creatively intelligent attracted more sexual partners and so had more offspring, who in turn inherited both higher than average creative intelligence and, in the females, the sexual preference for male creative intelligence. Note the key point here: no one need posit that the creative intelligence had any survival advantage whatsoever, only that it was sexually attractive. Through the runaway process, it could evolve purely as a sexual ornament.

But there was probably more to it than that, and here is the novel twist in Miller's theory. The brain and mind may also have evolved through sexual selection as a *fitness indicator*. Geneticists currently estimate that about 50 per cent of our genes are involved in brain development, and about 33 per cent may only be active in the brain.

Therefore the brain may both be particularly susceptible to being messed up by mutations, and – the converse – particularly good at showing that the human carrying it is *not* messed up, as it were. Thus the human brain makes for a very good fitness indicator.

But note the key, non-sexist corollary of this. Think back to peacocks for a moment. The tail of the peacock would be completely useless as a sexual ornament if the peahen was not able to appreciate it. So the peahen's *eye* evolved alongside the peacock's tail to fully appreciate it in all its beauty, and, most importantly, to be able to discriminate between more and less attractive tails, and hence identify the better fitness indicators. Exactly the same process could happen with the development of the human brain. If creative intelligence is favoured by females, and this is expressed, say, through language, music, art and wit, then they would have to be able to assess and judge that behaviour, especially as it grew more and more complex. But listening and speaking 'use many of the same language circuits'. Being able to produce and appreciate art 'probably relies on similar aesthetic capacities'. One needs to have a sense of humour in order to recognize a sense of humour in others. The bottom line is, if females are to appreciate male creative intelligence, then they too must develop creative intelligence.

If female sexual preference evolved to prefer articulate conversationalists to mumbling bores, male language abilities would improve through sexual selection, with males improving their vocabulary, syntax, plot and character. But if sexual selection is to work, female choosiness would have to increase too:

> Female language abilities would have to keep one step ahead of male abilities, to remain discerning. Females would have to be able to judge whether males used words correctly, so their vocabularies would keep pace. They would have to be able to notice grammatical errors, so their syntax abilities would keep pace. Most importantly, the females would have to understand what the males were saying to judge their meaning.

So this process, and the process of males internalizing how females will react to their displays, and females realizing just how complex are the male processes, would lead at most to only small sex differences in intelligence – unlike the case of the huge differences in the size of tails in peafowl. However, even if Geoffrey Miller is right, and the brain evolved through sexual selection in this spirited combination, surely he cannot then explain human capacities that we value, such as art, morality, language and creativity?

Let us take art first. Miller argues that the explanation for the evolution of art is difficult in terms of its survival value, but it is quite amenable to explanation in terms of sexual selection: 'The production of useless ornamentation that looks mysteriously aesthetic is just what sexual selection is good at.' Miller notes some close parallels in nature with the male bower birds in Australia and New Guinea, the 'only other animals that spend significant time and energy constructing purely aesthetic displays beyond their own bodies'. Their art displays are 'obvious products of female sexual choice'. For the male bower birds construct their enormous nests – 'large enough for David Attenborough to crawl inside' – that are used only for courtship. Once she has decided who is the most attractive nest-builder, she lets him copulate, and then off she goes to build a small, homely, practical little nest, to raise her offspring all by herself without male support, 'rather like Picasso's mistresses'.

The males decorate their bowers with a range of objects, especially those of brilliant colours, will steal from their rivals, and also try to destroy their rivals' bowers. This is 'the closest thing to human art in a non-human species'. It is clear, moreover – and this, says Miller, is likely to be the key to the evolution of human art – that bowers make good fitness indicators: 'It takes time, energy, and skill to construct the enormous bower, to gather the ornaments, to replace them when they fade, to defend them against theft and vandalism by rivals, and to attract female attention to them by singing and dancing.'

In the same way, female aesthetic taste emerged that preferred art which could have been produced only by someone of high fitness. Beauty would then equate with difficulty and high cost. We usually find most attractive art that requires the artist to possess qualities indicating high fitness, such as 'health, energy, endurance, hand–eye coordination, fine motor control, intelligence, creativity, access to rare materials, the ability to learn difficult skills' and, last but not least, 'lots of free time'.

But notice something else important that emerges here. Although

Miller's theory turns out to be decidedly non-sexist in general, it does have the corollary that it is not surprising that 'sexually mature males have produced almost all of the publicly displayed art throughout human history'. For it is males who will have been motivated to play upon aesthetic preferences 'to attract sexual partners'.

What about human altruism? Again, Miller argues that this, and in particular, charitable giving, is a particularly hard form of human activity to explain in evolutionary terms. The normal explanation is in terms of the side-effect of humans evolving 'in small tribal groups, in which any kindness would probably be reciprocated'. But charitable giving is different from this. It is giving to individuals who are unable to reciprocate, and that is precisely its point.

One of the keys to unlock this mystery for Geoffrey Miller was the observation that, after Ted Turner had said he would donate $1 billion to the United Nations, his wife, Jane Fonda, joyfully cried: 'I'm so proud to be married to you. I never felt better in my life.' As Miller wryly notes, 'At least in this case, charity inspired sexual adoration'. He believes this may have been the key to how the whole process got going. In the last chapter we saw David Buss's cross-cultural study of what men and women favour, to examine the areas where men and women diverge in these preferences. But what we saved for now is that they also converge on one factor: kindness. This was the one most important feature desired in a sexual partner, in all the 37 cultures studied, by men and women alike. It ranked higher than intelligence, beauty and status. If this is a sexual preference of both sexes, then our capacity for kindness, and from there to altruistic behaviour, may have evolved 'because our ancestors favoured sexual partners who were kind, generous, helpful and fair'.

It is hard to see how generosity to 'unrelated individuals unable to reciprocate', the essence of charity, could evolve on its own. However, bring in sexual selection, and 'such generosity can evolve easily as long as the capacity for generosity reveals the giver's fitness'. Clearly it did for Ted Turner. Indeed, it must do for anyone who engages in it, almost by definition. You cannot give money away to the poor unless you have more than enough for your own needs, as well as kindness and empathy to boot. All this suggests for Miller that 'the fact that we find kindness and generosity so appealing in sexual partners suggests that our ancestors converged on a rare and wonderful equilibrium in the game of courtship'.

Finally, what about language? Language is clearly an adaptation, a human instinct, that children develop spontaneously. But an adaptation for what? Again, the key for Miller is to observe the way language is used in human courtship, and in emphasizing human hierarchies and status. If language is viewed primarily as being information trans-mission in some reciprocal altruistic fashion – as many biologists have believed – then it will clearly bring more benefit to the listener than to the speaker: 'The speaker already knows the information being conveyed, and learns nothing new by sharing it, but the listener does gain information by listening.' In this case, biologists would predict that 'we should be a species of extremely good listeners and very good talkers. We should view silent, attentive listening as a selfish indul-gence, and non-stop talking as a saintly act of altruism.' This does not remotely describe the richness of human interaction:

> People compete to say things. They strive to be heard. When they appear to be listening, they are often mentally rehearsing their next contribution to the discourse rather than absorbing what was just said by others. Those who fail to yield the floor to their colleagues are considered selfish, not altruistic. Turn-taking rules have emerged to regulate not who gets to listen, but who gets to talk.

Sexual selection theory, on the other hand, more adequately points to the way human language is actually used, for verbal courtship is at the very heart of sexual selection in humans. It is this form of communication that has to be learned and acquired for courtship: 'As every parent of a teenage boy knows, the sudden transition from early-adolescent minimalist grunting to late-adolescent verbal fluency seems to coincide with the self-confidence necessary for dating girls.' For the boy mixing with his peers, all that is required is 'quiet, cryptic, grammatically degenerate mumbling'. But, when they start mixing with the opposite sex, boys find that the ante has been upped: 'Girls seem to demand much more volume, expressiveness, complexity, fluency, and creativity.'

Language may also have evolved to promote status, which might then also have been part of the sexual selection process. One proposal along these lines is that 'complex human language evolved through male orators competing for social status by speaking eloquently, since high status would give them reproductive success'. Certainly anthropological evidence seems to support this by showing links between verbal skill, social status and reproductive success in tribal societies.

If Miller is right and language evolved through sexual selection as a fitness indicator, then a huge problem would seem to arise for the theory. For it is women, not men, who have the higher verbal ability, as we saw in the previous chapter. But if language was sexually selected, surely it should be the other way around? As we have seen, sexual selection in most other species normally leads to the males with the larger ornaments. In terms of language, however, this is not the case. Miller has an answer to this. Recall the discussion earlier of the display of the peacock being useless without the corresponding discrimination exercised by the peahen's eyes. Peacocks may be able to *grow* bigger tails, but it is peahens who are better equipped to *see* and to *judge* tails. But then, if language was used as a sexual ornament in humans, we would, by analogy, expect there to be *female* superiority in language comprehension – the equivalent of the peahen judging cock tails – while males would be superior in language production. Miller puts it neatly:

> females should recognize more words, but males should use a larger proportion of their vocabulary in courtship, biasing their speech towards rarer, more exotic words. In this simple picture, more women might understand what 'azure' really means (so they can accurately judge male use), but more men might actually speak the word 'azure' in conversation (even if they think it means vermilion).

Finally, all this leads to reflections on what happens in the public domain, which may have educational implications. Although females are superior in language comprehension tests, clearly males seem much more motivated to produce 'public verbal displays'. 'Men write more books. Men give more lectures. Men ask more questions after lectures. Men dominate mixed-sex committee discussions. Men post more email to Internet discussion groups.' Some feminists would argue that this is self-evidently due to patriarchy, but why on earth would this be the case? 'If men control society, why don't they just shut up and enjoy their supposed prerogatives?' A much more satisfactory answer comes from the nature of sexual competition: if men did shut up, this would allow other men the chance 'to show off verbally', so they have to keep talking to compete in the sexual marketplace. For Miller, the 'ocean of male language that confronts modern women in bookstores, television, newspapers, classrooms, parliaments, and businesses' must not be seen as part of a male conspiracy to deny a voice to women. Instead, it must be seen as arising from evolutionary history 'in which the male motivation to talk was vital to their reproduction'. And women should take some amusement from the fact that men often do not know what they are talking about, for this 'only shows that the reach of their displays often exceeds their grasp'.

NOVEL PREDICTIONS

These, it seems to me, are fundamental tenets of the research programme of evolutionary psychology in some of its latest manifestations. Evolutionary theory is applied to the mind and behaviour, noting that the vast majority of our evolution is likely to have taken place while we were hunter-gatherers. But this has far from prosaic implications. Perhaps the whole of culture, art, morality and language may be explained in terms of its simple assumptions. Now: can such a theory account for the gender differences we noted in the previous chapter? And, most importantly, can it account for them in ways that are more satisfying than alternative accounts such as those which point to socialization and cultural explanations? One of the four major criteria any theory must satisfy is the ability to make novel and testable predictions. How does evolutionary psychology fare on this test?

Perhaps surprisingly for some, it seems from the literature that there is a wealth of novel predictions made. I will explore five cases here to examine the extent to which these predictions are testable and whether or not any evidence is available to support them: the case of female spatial ability; the mating preferences of economically successful women and of economically unsuccessful men; the sexual preferences of men; the evolution of parenting; and different forms of sexual jealousy.

The case of female spatial ability

Let us start with perhaps the more humdrum of these, relating to mathematics and gender, being the most obvious link back to schooling, before spicing things up a little with four cases involving sex. It turns out that the mathematics case reveals quite graphically how evolutionary psychology can make novel, and refreshingly non-sexist, predictions to aid our understanding of gender differences that may be educationally relevant.

It is a well-known truism that there is male superiority in spatial abilities, as we have discussed in the previous chapter. One explanation of these gender differences is socialization, as spelled out explicitly by a whole host of government agencies, not least the Equal Opportunities Commission, as well as feminist education writers. Girls and young women are socialized to see mathematics as being unfeminine. This leads to gender stereotyping in which mathematics and mathematically based subjects are seen as generally undesirable for girls. The feminist book *Overcoming Math Anxiety* points to the way that 'girls are encouraged to drop mathematics at an early age while social forces encourage boys to pursue such courses'.[13] It is also argued that parental influence and teachers' expectations explain why girls drop mathematics.[14] Girls and young women drop maths because they believe that they will not do well in the subject and because they think that activities and careers that need mathematics and science are less important than do their male counterparts.[15]

The evolutionary psychology of spatial differences challenges these accounts on two levels. First, it provides an underlying theoretical explanation as to why these sex differences may have occurred. Second, and most interestingly, it has made some novel predictions about peculiarly female abilities, and conducted experiments that have shown these abilities to be present.[16]

During the crucial Pleistocene period there was a sexual division of labour where males were predominantly the hunters and females predominantly the gatherers. Presumably, it is argued, this would impact differently on the sexes' cognitive development. If, for vast periods of our evolution, males were hunters and females gatherers, it is exceedingly likely that different types of cognitive skills would have evolved in each sex by natural and/or sexual selection. Hunting, the process of locating fast-moving animals, then getting into positions suitable for the kill, requires the solving of entirely different kinds of spatial problems than does gathering, the process of foraging for stationary plants, and recognizing those that are edible, remembering the seasons in which they occur and locations of good crops, and so on. Hence, adaptation is clearly likely to have favoured different spatial skills among men and women during this period.

The cognitive strengths that have been found for males reflect these differences:

> the various spatial measures showing male bias (e.g., mental rotations, map reading, maze learning) correspond to attributes that would enable successful hunting. Essentially, these attributes comprise the abilities to orient oneself in relation to objects or places, in view or conceptualised across distances, and to perform the mental transformations necessary to maintain accurate orientations during movement.[17]

Some feminists might be tempted to switch off at this stage. It is all fairly familiar, and some might assume that it will be following predictable ways. However, the evolutionary psychologists have a twist in their argument. The researchers acknowledged that much research to date had been rather male-centred; the focus of other research, perhaps conducted primarily by male scientists, looked for, and found, things that males did better than females.

It turns out that evolutionary psychologists object to the sexism of this approach. They explore a different question: If there are these male evolutionary adaptations associated with hunting, then likewise, too, shouldn't there be *female* adaptations associated with gathering? In other words, the evolutionary psychologists may be seen to be doing for spatial awareness what Carol Gilligan is praised by many feminists for doing for our moral sense, as we noted in the chapter on gender stereotyping. Gilligan suggested that male and female ways of ethical reasoning were *different*, not that there was male superiority. Or, in the context of our earlier discussion, evolutionary psychologists very definitely are challenging the way science, 'by hearing only the dominant male voice . . . has closed off potentially fertile avenues of investigation'.[18] That is exactly the approach that evolutionary psychologists are challenging with regard to mathematical abilities. For they note that nuts and berries and other food plants 'are embedded within complex arrays of vegetation'. Thus to be a successful forager would require locating food 'within such arrays and finding them in ensuing growing seasons'. These abilities would 'entail the recognition and recall of spatial configurations of objects'; that is, the female forager would need to be able to 'rapidly learn and remember the contents of object arrays and the spatial relationships of the object to one another'.[19]

Now comes the really interesting part of their programme. The evolutionary psychologists consider whether it is possible to locate such female superiority in spatial skills as predicted by their perspective. Researchers set up five studies, and find that it is.

For example, in the *first* study, subjects were shown a picture with an 'object array', namely 30 or so objects arranged in no apparent order. They were then shown the same picture, but with extra objects added, and were asked to put a cross through all the items that were not in the original array; finally, they were given a third picture which contained the original objects, but some were in different locations. The first task measures what is called 'object memory'; the second 'location memory'. The 8- to 13-year-old girls scored significantly higher than their same-age boys on the object memory task, while the older girls outperformed boys on the location memory tasks.

The *second* study was similar but in a naturalistic setting. Here subjects were not told what type of experiment they were being asked to participate in, but were led into an office furnished as a typical graduate study and told to wait for two minutes, while the experimenter finished setting up the equipment. They were then taken out of the office, and only then told that the purpose was to find out how people naturally process their environments. Hence they were asked questions about the position of objects in the office, and relationships between them. Females scored 75 per cent higher than males on this task.

The researchers conclude: 'The data of all our studies correspond closely to predictions from the hunter-gatherer model of spatial sex differences and consistently demonstrated a greater capacity by females to remember spatial configurations of objects.' Their work found that females 'are generally more alert than males to objects in the environment and their locations, whether or not these are perceived as relevant to a task at hand'.[20]

Later studies have not consistently replicated the object memory finding, but the location memory advantage has been replicated in many studies since, from paper-and-pencil tests through computer assessments to natural settings. Across each of these different conditions, the average man is outperformed by about 80 per cent of women.[21]

In my family, it is often a topic of either humour or exasperation that the menfolk can never find keys around the home, and need their wives, girlfriends or sister to help locate them. Evolutionary psychology gives us one explanation as to why this significant trait is likely to have evolved for women rather than men.[22]

While we are on the subject of these cognitive abilities, another challenge may have occurred to readers. Take a skill within a well-established area of female superiority such as reading comprehension. (Parallel objections may be made for male mathematical superiority.) Surely no evolutionary psychologist can claim that reading ability could be an *evolved* cognitive skill? For books were not invented in the Pleistocene period. So how could female advantage in reading comprehension be related to any evolutionary advantage? Some psychologists suggest that the female advantage here is based on what they call 'theory of mind': 'Girls and women appear to be more skilled, on average, than boys and men in making inferences about the emotional state, intentions, and so on of other people.' It is this advantage – that *is* explicable in terms of evolutionary adaptation – that could lead to the female advantage in reading comprehension. For the greatest advantage for girls and women relates to comprehension of literary novels, poems and dramas, where about 70 per cent of females outperform the average male: 'In many cases, comprehension of these passages involves making inferences about the nuances of social relationships.' By contrast, however, the smallest sex difference is found for passages not involving people, such as those referring to physics or town planning: 'The overall pattern suggests that the potential sex difference in theory of mind might contribute to the sex difference in overall reading comprehension scores.'[23]

Returning to mathematical ability: it turns out that evolutionary psychology not only offers a plausible explanation as to why there may be biological differences that lead to different gender outcomes, but it also makes a novel prediction, which has not been predicted by the environmentalists, that women would have evolved different kinds of spatial ability. Experiments were conducted which turned out to support this prediction. This seems to be quite a powerful finding. What then of evolutionary psychology and the battle of the sexes?

The mating preferences of economically successful women

Can evolutionary psychologists explain women's greater choosiness about sexual partners, as described in the previous chapter? And can the theory lead to any novel predictions that have not been made by the alternative, namely socialization explanations for gender differences?

The science moves to its explanations and predictions via biologist Robert Trivers' theory of 'parental investment'.[24] Parental investment is defined as the investment a parent makes in its offspring that increases the offspring's chances of survival, but at the cost of impinging upon the parent's ability to invest in other offspring. Thinking through what this means to the different sexes, Trivers predicted two main hypotheses:

1 In species in which the sexes differ in parental investment, the *higher investing sex* will be more selective in choice of mating partners.
2 Members of the *sex that invests less* parentally in offspring will be more competitive with each other for mating access to the high-investing sex.[25]

Importantly, this discussion is not yet about males and females, let alone men and women. It is only about the categories in italics, namely 'higher-' and 'lower-' investing sexes. Now, as David Buss notes, there is 'no biological law of the animal world' that dictates that 'females must invest more than males'.[26] Indeed, as Trivers found, there are species in which males invest more than females – for example, the pipefish seahorse, where females implant their eggs in the male – and crucially, the above predictions have been found to hold true for this species. The male pipefish seahorse is much more selective about who he mates with, and the female is much more competitive for the male attention. Further research has shown other 'sex-reversal' species, such as the Mormon cricket, Panamanian poison arrow frogs, red-necked phalarope and the spotted sandpiper.[27] Again, supporting Trivers' hypotheses, in each of these species, the male is found to invest more in his offspring, and there is more female competition for his attention.

Some readers may think that these sex-reversal cases illustrate that sex roles are simply arbitrary. This would be an incorrect extrapolation. What the theory of evolutionarily psychology predicts is much more subtle: the sex with the smaller parental investment – male *or* female – will be the most active in courtship, while the sex with the larger parental investment – male *or* female – will be the more choosy. It may be evolutionary arbitrary which is which, but it is not arbitrary that larger parental investment goes with greater choosiness.

In mammals, and in humans, of course, it is the female who makes the greater initial parental investment, for obvious reasons: 'Gestating, bearing, lactating, nurturing, protecting, and feeding a child are exceptionally valuable reproductive resources that are not allocated indiscriminately.' And basic economics says that those who hold valuable resources do not give them away haphazardly. For 'women in our evolutionary past', sexual intercourse led to the risk of the need for enormous investment of time and energy in raising a child – time and energy that could not be used to raise a different child. She must carry the baby for nine months, then nurse it and look after it for a couple of years. As a consequence of this, 'evolution favoured women who were highly selective about their mates'. For our ancestral women 'suffered severe costs if they were indiscriminating – they experienced lower reproductive success, and fewer of their children survived to reproductive age'. For men, on the other hand, sexual intercourse has no such implications – there really is, in nature, a gross asymmetry here. He can spend some pleasurable minutes in the act, and thereafter move on to inseminate others. Given this asymmetry, men and women are likely to have evolved completely different reproductive strategies.[28]

Regarding women's mating strategies, again it turns out that evolutionary psychologists make some novel predictions. Women have evolved preferences for, and attraction to, men who are older and higher in status and resources. If men differ in their status and resources, and are able to defend these against other men, it will benefit women to be choosy about who they mate with in terms of finding a mate with higher status and resources. In evolutionary time, this may initially have been simply because the higher status and resources would enable the woman and her children to live more comfortably and successfully (as David Buss argues). Or it may have been initially because the status and resources act as 'fitness indicators' for better genes – better strength, health, intelligence or whatever – and the actual physical resources accruing to the woman and her children were at best a happy side-effect of these (as Geoffrey Miller argues). Whichever it was, this preference would then have become an evolved preference in women, through sexual selection.

As we noted in the previous chapter, research has indeed found this preference among women, as a universal phenomenon, across many societies, and throughout the twentieth century at least. Women do express the preference, much more strongly than do men, for a potential older mating partner who has status and resources. However – and feminists might fume at this stage – that much is obvious and has a much more commonsensical, environmental explanation. Of course women will prefer men with status and resources, *because these are things that have been denied to them in the past.* If the only way women can become economically stable is to find a man able to support her, then of course she will look for someone with more status and resources than she has, by definition.

Usefully, such an attack leads to a neat prediction – and one that might potentially adjudicate between the two explanations. If the environmental explanation is correct, this would mean that as women's independence progresses, as more women enter the workforce and become economically self-sufficient, and the norms in society reinforce this process, eventually they would not need to seek higher status men on whom to be economically dependent. The evolutionary psychologist, however, would predict that it is much deeper than this, that women have evolved to look for these particular fitness indicators in their mate, and one cannot change such a deep-rooted, evolutionarily fundamental trait just by making women wealthier and of higher status themselves. So the evolutionary psychologists predict that higher status women *would seek yet still higher status men*, even though economically they don't need to do this any more. Of course there is a useful corollary about men, which often gets lost in this kind of discussion. Feminists seeking an environmentalist explanation for these gender differences would predict the opposite for men: men with fewer resources should value women with more resources. Evolutionary psychologists on the other hand would not predict this: men look for things other than high status in their mating preferences, such as youth and beauty, and these evolutionarily determined preferences cannot simply be changed as a consequence of a man finding himself poor.

Neither of the environmentalist (socialization) predictions are borne out by the evidence. For male preferences, men who are low in financial resources and status do not, as it turns out, seek wealthier women, 'any more than do financially successful men'. And, most significantly for females, the preference for older and more successful males seems to be *even more pronounced* in professionally and economically successful American women. One study looked at women who were financially successful, contrasting their mate preferences with women of lower salaries and income. The successful women often earned more than $50,000 a year, and some more than $100,000. They were well educated, often holding professional degrees, and had high self-esteem. The study showed that such successful women placed 'an even greater value than less professionally successful women on mates who have professional degrees, high social status, and greater intelligence and who are tall, independent and self-confident'. Indeed, these professional and successful women 'expressed an even stronger preference for high-earning men than did women who are less financially successful'.[29]

Another study found an identical phenomenon, that

> college women who expect to earn the most after college put
> more weight on the promising financial prospects of a potential

husband than do women who expect to earn less. Professionally successful women, such as medical and law students, also place heavy importance on a mate's earning capacity.[30]

Indeed, in discussion with economically successful female friends on this issue, I have been surprised at how obvious it is to them, to almost being a point of non-discussion. 'Of course we want a man of higher status than us! What's the issue?' And one male friend who was involved with a high-status woman related how he had wanted to engage in a sexual fantasy with her, and had begun his story, perhaps thinking of what would excite him, with: 'Pretend I'm a poor slave watching you bathe naked.' The woman had stopped him immediately: 'No, pretend you're a rich merchant or a prince.' David Buss puts it in an amusingly poignant way: recall the 1960s folk song: 'If I were a carpenter and you were a lady, would you marry me anyway, would you have my baby?' Given the cumulative evidence to date, says Buss, 'the most likely answer is: No.'[31]

While on this issue of women's preferences for high-status men, we find another novel prediction from the evolutionary psychologists that turns out to be supported by the evidence too. It may come as no surprise to some women to hear that research has shown that men who were shown pictures of beautiful and sexually provocative women 'later rated themselves as less attracted to the women with whom they were living' than did men who were shown only neutral stimuli. Some feminists might predict this would be true of women too: in fact the research showed that this phenomenon was much less pronounced for women. However, what evolutionary psychologists *would* predict is that women would do the same 'downgrading' when exposed not to attractive men, but to men who displayed signs of *social dominance*. So research was conducted that exposed men and women to images of both attractive and socially dominant members of the opposite sex in various combinations. Men were still found to be less committed to their partners after watching pictures of attractive and sexy women. However, while women reported the same level of commitment to their partners after viewing the attractiveness pictures, their commitment *did* waver when they were shown images of social dominance.[32] Again, this is another novel prediction with corroborating evidence.

The sexual preferences of men

It is a well-known phenomenon that male sexual preference is for young women. Why would this be predicted by evolutionary psychology? Because beauty as we define it in a woman is likely to be a key indicator of a woman's youth and health, and hence fertility. Men who evolved with preferences for these cues for fertility would thrive, but those who failed 'to prefer qualities that signal high fertility or reproductive value – men who preferred to marry gray-haired women with somewhat less smooth skin and less firm muscle tone – would have had fewer offspring, and their line would eventually have died out.'

So men, argue the evolutionary psychologists, are likely to have evolved common standards of beauty that focus on signals of fertility. Cross-cultural research shows this to be the case. People of different races asked to judge the facial attractiveness of Asian, Hispanic, Black and White women had tremendous consensus about who was and who was not good-looking. Importantly, this was not affected by the degree of exposure the subjects had had to Western media. Two other studies, with Taiwanese subjects and between Blacks and Whites, found similar agreement. Another piece of research supports this claim – where infants aged between 2 and 3 and 6 to 8 months were shown pictures of faces which had been independently ranked by adults in terms of attractiveness. The researchers found that 'Both younger and older infants gazed longer at the more attractive faces, suggesting that standards of beauty apparently emerge quite early in life'. These findings challenge 'the commonly held view that the standards of attractiveness are learned through gradual exposure to current cultural models. No training seems necessary for these standards to emerge.'[33]

Now, what would be an alternative explanation of male preference for youthful women? One feminist explanation put forward by Naomi Wolf in *The Beauty Myth* is that men desire younger women because they are easier to control and less dominant.

Evolutionary psychology, however, has a more specific explanation – and a novel prediction arising from this. What men desire is not youth *per se*. What they look for are features of women with fertility. For most men these features will be associated with women younger than themselves – sometimes much younger. However, this perspective leads to a rather counterintuitive prediction concerning the girls whom *adolescent* males will prefer: teenage males should prefer females who are *slightly older* than them. Why? Because, for teenagers, slightly older women will be more fertile than girls of their own age or younger.

When put to the test, research has shown that this novel prediction turns out to be well supported.[34] Male and female teenagers aged between 12 and 19 were asked what type of person they find attractive: 'Imagine you were going on a date with someone. Assume that the person would be interested in you, and that you were available to go on a date, and that things like parental permission and money aren't important.' The subjects were asked about minimum and maximum age preferences, and their ideal ages. Quite strikingly, the girls always preferred older boys – ten years older for 18-year-olds – but the boys *also* most preferred girls who were four or five years older. This occurred 'despite the fact that these older women expressed no interest at all in dating younger men'.[35] It is all rather sweet and sad.

The evolution of parenting

In the previous chapter we noted the observation – that will have come as no surprise to anyone – that women invest much more time in looking after their children than do men across a whole range of cultures. It turns out that, again, evolutionary psychology is prepared to stick its neck out here and predict that not only would women have evolved strategies to help them with the task of childrearing, but they would also have developed physiological mechanisms that enable them to enjoy and revel in this task, in a way that men will not have done. And such sexual differences have been found. When we see something that attracts us, our pupils dilate (enlarge) more than is needed to correct for the surrounding degree of illumination. Physiologists are aware of this phenomenon and have devised 'pupil dilation tests' which may be used to measure interest and attraction. Performance in such tests is, of course, immune from self-reporting biases that might influence questionnaire answers. So people will not be able to perform in ways in which they think are expected of them.

When women were shown slides of babies, 'their pupils dilated more than 17 per cent'. Men's pupils on the other hand did not dilate at all. Slides of mothers holding babies led to women's pupils dilating 24 per cent, whereas men's dilated only 5 per cent – and even that increase might be accounted for by the men's attraction to the mother rather than anything to do with the infant! Women have also been shown to identify their newborn children by smell within six hours of birth, whereas fathers can't. Women can detect and interpret facial expressions of babies such as 'surprise, disgust, anger, fear and distress', when these are shown briefly on a screen; men do so much less quickly and accurately. Significantly, women's accuracy in such predictions bears no relation to the amount of experience they have had with children. Thus women appear not only to have (gender) preferences for parenting, but also some (sex) physiological mechanisms 'that render such parenting more effective'.[36]

Surely fathers too have an interest in parenting their children – for after all, from an evolutionary perspective, offspring are a vehicle for transporting the parents' genes to succeeding generations.[37] So why is this investment less from fathers – not just in humans, but in the animal kingdom more generally? There are various possible explanations put forward to explain this, one of which is the 'Parental uncertainty hypothesis'. Mothers are 100 per cent 'sure' that their offspring is theirs; fathers are not. Research has shown 'cuckoldry rates' – that is, where the husband raises the child of another man without realizing it – are estimated at between 1 per cent and 25 per cent, depending on the population under study.[38] Thus it may be that, under some circumstances, it may be less profitable in evolutionary terms for fathers to invest in their offspring, rather than go and create some more – particularly if the fathers also have reasonable confidence that the mothers will be devoted to their children, whether or not they stay around. So, in short, 'although parental uncertainty does not preclude the evolution of male paternal care, it remains one viable cause of the widespread tendency of females to invest more in offspring than males do.'[39]

The issue of paternal uncertainty, however, leads again to some interesting novel predictions from the evolutionary psychology perspective. If men were to be 100 per cent sure – or nearly sure – that they were the fathers of the child, then they *would* have more of an evolutionary drive to stay around, to help devote resources to the child's upbringing. So the prediction from evolutionary psychology is that men will have evolved psychological mechanisms which are sensitive to help them determine whether or not they are the father of the child. It would seem, in evolutionary terms, that a man has at least two sources of possible information about his paternity (before the advent of DNA testing, that is). First, he will have evidence in terms of his partner's sexual fidelity to him during the period under question. Second, he will have evidence in terms of the child's resemblance to him. It is likely too that women will also have evolved mechanisms to convince the male of both. Evidence seems to support this – some of which we will come on to in a moment in terms of sexual jealousy.

But, most fascinatingly, in terms of the second sources of evidence, there is some interesting research showing how mothers promote a putative father's resemblance to the child. Some research used video-tape evidence of American births. In many, the quality was bad and the mother tranquillized, but there were enough of reasonable quality to focus on the explicit references made to the baby's appearance. In fully 80 per cent of these, the mothers made remarks about the resemblance to the father, against 20 per cent resemblance to her: 'It looks like you', 'feels like you', 'just like daddy', and so on, were the types of comments made.

The same researchers also conducted another study where quest-ionnaires were sent out to parents, and those who responded were asked to secure contacts with relatives to participate in the study. Among questions asked were: 'Who do you think the baby is most similar to?' Here it was found that 81 per cent of mothers said that their baby was most like the father, only 19 per cent most like themselves. Mothers' relatives also showed this bias: 66 per cent said it was most like the putative father, only 34 per cent the mother. Another study in Mexico in 1993 found exactly the same results. Clearly, this evidence is not conclusive, and a socialization-inclined feminist would be able to say, perhaps, that mothers are doing this consciously to please the fathers, rather than that there is anything to do with evolutionary-evolved ploys.

However, evolutionary psychologists have taken this further, and made an even bolder, novel prediction, and found some rather more intriguing evidence to support this hypothesis. Researchers gave photographs of children – half of them boys, half girls – at ages 1, 10 and 20, together with photos of their parents, to subjects to match each child with one of three possible mothers and one of three possible fathers (one of each of which was the real mother and father). If matchings were done randomly, correct matches would arise 33 per cent of the time. Matches of 10- and 20-year-olds with mothers and fathers came out at about this expected 33 per cent, but for the 1-year-olds, subjects matched them to the *father* 49.2 per cent of the time – boys 50 per cent and girls 48 per cent. But for the mother it was again about 33 per cent, or just in line with chance. In other words, researchers found that 1-year-olds uniquely resembled their biological fathers, but not their mothers.[40] This raises the intriguing possibility that mothers have not only evolved to say that the child is more like the father than she is, but that babies have evolved so that they *do actually* look more like their fathers at birth. Why would this happen? Perhaps because historically, babies benefited from looking like their genetic fathers, so selection favoured babies that did – presumably because there was a higher survival rate if this was the case, with the males' extra resources and protection brought to bear. Or perhaps it was because selection instead favoured those fathers who had physical 'markers' that expressed themselves genetically in their children, so stopping them from infanticide. Or perhaps selection favoured mothers who could suppress their own physical appearance in their child, because this led to the male recognizing and subsequently investing in the child.

These hypotheses await further research; but the intriguing possibility presents itself that mothers and their relatives may actually be telling the truth when they say that the baby looks 'just like daddy'.

Gender differences in sexual jealousy

Finally, on a related issue, a robust finding from research for some time was that men and women are *equally* as sexually jealous. Research from the USA, and cross-cultural studies in Hungary, Ireland, Mexico, The Netherlands, Russia, Yugoslavia and the USA consistently showed this result.[41] However, evolutionary psychology would predict something different: given their different parental investment, and the phenomenon of parental uncertainty, wouldn't men be more likely to be jealous of *sexual* involvement than women, whereas wouldn't women be more likely to be jealous of *emotional* involvement than men – as this could lead to men being less inclined to devote resources and energy to them? Does this mean that evolutionary psychology runs counter to the evidence given here?

When the types of questions asked in the existing research were examined, it turns out that it was not clear that these two types of jealousy had been adequately distinguished. This led to new tests being devised by evolutionary psychologists to explore these distinct types of jealousy. Subjects were asked for their responses to two events. First, how they would respond if they discovered their partner having sexual intercourse with someone else. Second, how they would respond upon discovering that their partner was becoming emotionally involved with someone else. 83 per cent of the women were more upset by their partner's emotional infidelity compared to only 40 per cent of the men, while 60 per cent of the men found their partner's sexual infidelity distressing, compared to only 17 per cent of the women. So by posing a more precise question about the nature of the 'sexual jealousy', another important gender difference was discovered.[42]

To check these findings, moving away from self-reporting evidence and its potential biases, another experiment was conducted with 30 men and 30 women in a laboratory, with various judiciously placed electrodes to measure frowning, sweating and pulse or heart rate. Subjects were then asked to think about cases of sexual and emotional infidelity in their partners. These brought about very different responses between the sexes, strongly supporting those above. Later work has replicated these findings in Germany, The Netherlands, Korea and Japan.[43] However, an alternative interpretation has been put forward to explain these results. What both parties fear is losing the partner, but women think that men can have sex without emotional involvement, so worry less about it, whereas men think that women will only have sex with someone when emotionally involved, so worry about it more when sex is involved. By adapting the original tests to make these two possibilities mutually exclusive, further research has found that the earlier results still reappear: men do seem to be more jealous of women's sexual involvement, whereas women do seem to be more jealous of men's emotional involvement.

A PLAUSIBLE EXPLANATION FOR GENDER DIFFERENCES?

How has evolutionary psychology succeeded in terms of the four conditions – first, that the theory must be consistent with *all* the available evidence; second, that it must be able to explain *why* these *particular* differences arise; third, that it should be 'parsimonious'; and fourth, that it should be able to make novel or unexpected predictions that can be tested and, even better, confirmed by experiments?

It seems from this, albeit brief, review that it has done rather well. It has certainly been consistent with all the phenomena of gender differences we have thrown its way. Its explanation as to why these particular differences arise has also been clear, based on the different experiences during the bulk of evolutionary time to which the different sexes would have been exposed. Moreover, it not only says that men and women will have different mathematical abilities, say, but points to the reason why men are likely in general to have different visual–spatial abilities from women – based on their different experiences as, respectively, hunters and gatherers. And the theory explains all the gender differences we see in terms of the same overriding perspective: evolutionary adaptations have occurred through natural and sexual selection, or a combination of these. Finally, and most interestingly, evolutionary psychology comes up with novel predictions arising from its perspective, and it shows how such novel predictions can be explored. And – in the five cases we have described here – the researchers have found empirical corroboration for the novel predictions.

Alternative explanations – such as theories involving 'environmentalist' or 'socialization' hypotheses – can also meet some of the four conditions, of course. But where they seem to fall down most vividly in comparison with the evolutionary psychology theory is in terms of the second and fourth conditions. For socialization theses, as noted above in terms of mathematics, cannot explain why it is that men are good at some things, and women at others. They can explain, for sure, that if men move into certain areas, these will be the ones that socialization ensures boys are initiated into, and girls not. But as to why those areas, those roles and so on are chosen in the first place, socialization theses are silent: it is arbitrary that men are better at mathematics, although not then arbitrary that mathematics acts as a critical filter in society. Evolutionary psychology overcomes that first, crucial level of arbitrariness.

And, perhaps most significantly, evolutionary psychology makes novel predictions that would not have fitted in with any socialization explanation. To give the concrete examples I have highlighted in this chapter – selected from what seemed to be hundreds of possible examples – it is hard to see how a socialization thesis could explain the difference in sexual jealousy between the sexes, or the physiological differences between the sexes in terms of responses to children, or the fact that teenage boys prefer older women, bucking the usual male preferences, or that economically-unsuccessful men do not look to economically successful women as mates, or that females have superiority in a particular form of spatial awareness. In general, the evolutionary psychology perspective seems particularly satisfying in the predictions it is making, and the way explanations for these can fit beneath the same explanatory umbrella.

None of this is conclusive, of course; but that is not the way of science. Since the time of Karl Popper's writings we know that we can never be certain that we have arrived at true theories, only that we can know that we have arrived at scientific theories which have a chance of moving us nearer to the truth.[44] By being able to make bold predictions, suggest ways in which they can be explored, and by finding corroborating evidence, I would suggest that evolutionary psychology certainly satisfies the condition of being a science.

It seems increasingly plausible that such a theory can help us adjudicate between theories of socialization and biological foundations for gender differences. But a lot hinges on this discussion. It is plausible, but it is also controversial. For the purposes of this chapter, we must examine some of the critics to see if we have missed anything important. Usefully, some of the strongest critics of evolutionary psychology have been gathered together in one volume, *Alas, Poor Darwin: Arguments Against Evolutionary Psychology*. This book has achieved great publicity and impact – as I was writing the first draft, Hilary

Rose was on BBC's *Start the Week* presenting her case to Jeremy Paxman. Big names such as Stephen Jay Gould and the key feminist critic Anne Fausto-Sterling, author of *Myths of Gender*,[45] are all lined up to counter the claims of evolutionary psychology. Another important volume of criticism was also published at around the same time, *Man, Beast and Zombie*, by Kenan Malik, in a book acclaimed by the Professor of Genetics at University College, Steve Jones, as 'A ray of common sense in a fog of pseudo-science'. It is a 'brilliant book' he says, that 'cuts through the prejudice and plain ignorance that surrounds sociobiology to show what science can and cannot say about ourselves'. If we can address the criticisms found in these books – representing strong lines of attack on evolutionary psychology – then a plausible case emerges in support of its claims.

ALAS, POOR DARWIN?

To get to Professors Hilary and Steven Rose's criticisms, unfortunately, one has to wade through quite a lot of invective that seeks to damn evolutionary psychology in terms of its pernicious influence and those with whom it is associated. 'Of course,' the Roses say, 'the claims of biology-as-destiny are as old as history itself,' with deep roots going back to Aristotle, that 'deeply patriarchal figure within Western thought'. From Aristotle it is just a short step in 'biological predestinationist' time to the 'Nazi genocide of the gypsies and the Jews', 'evil racism' and 'the horror of the death camps'. This evil, we are meant to infer, is a direct forebear of evolutionary psychology. Moreover, its 'political agenda' is 'transparently part of a right-wing libertarian attack on collectivity, above all the welfare state'. And its immediate forerunner, sociobiology 'was culturally underpinning the Thatcherite attack on the welfare state'.[46]

This line of inquisition may be dismissed fairly easily. Indeed, the explicit laying of guilt at the feet of Aristotle puts the whole thing in perspective. For that 'deeply patriarchal' figure, together with Plato, has influenced the whole of our Western thoughts and science, and nothing is immune from that influence – not even the Roses' own preferred 'restructive post-modernism' practices. If evolutionary psychology is guilty by association with Aristotle, then so, to exactly the same degree, is the biology and feminist sociology of Steven and Hilary Rose respectively. And invoking the spectre of Hitler, genocide or even Thatcher does little for the credibility of the criticisms either.

Perhaps a more interesting line of 'guilt by association' to pursue is the criticism of evolutionary psychology as *sexist*. Earlier, we noted how evolutionary psychology seemed to come up with refreshingly non-sexist predictions about human behaviour. The feminist critic, Anne Fausto-Sterling, would disagree. Evolutionary psychology presents a 'cardboard version' of women, and supports 'the stultifying politics of the status quo', she says. She objects to the domination of evolutionary psychology by sexist men who, she says, 'believe that women did not even evolve their own orgasms; it seems we just got lucky because it was so important for men to seek constant sexual gratification'.[47] To disillusion her of this misconception, she could read Geoffrey Miller's description of women not only evolving their own orgasms, but, through their preferences, men's penises too:

> Female hominids may not have preferred thicker, longer, more flexible penises per se. They may simply have liked orgasms, and larger penises led to better orgasms by permitting more varied, exciting, and intimate copulatory positions. . . . If we were a species in which males dominated the sexual system, we would have one-inch penises like dominant gorillas. The large male penis is a product of female choice in evolution. If it were not, males would never have bothered to evolve such a large, floppy, blood-hungry organ. Ancestral females made males evolve such penises because they liked them.

Perhaps Anne Fausto-Sterling's criticisms should rather be turned against Stephen Jay Gould, her companion in the Rose and Rose collection, for it is he who 'viewed the female clitoral orgasm as an evolutionary side-effect of the male capacity for penile orgasm'.[48]

Perhaps some evolutionary psychologists of the past were sexist, focused on male behaviour. But these criticisms seem to be a caricature of where evolutionary psychology is today. So what of the objections relating to evolutionary psychology as a science? Five of the most significant objections concern the assumption that all significant evolution took place during the Pleistocene period; how, indeed, we know what happened there; evolutionary psychology's neglect of environmental influences; the circularity of evolutionary psychology arguments; and the issue of whether universal traits are inevitably likely to be the products of adaptation rather than culture.

Did evolutionary time stop 10,000 years ago?

The first major criticism challenges the central premise of evolutionary psychology, that it was during the Palaeolithic period that 'fundamental human traits were fixed, and that there has not been time since to alter them'.[49] This is completely unreasonable, Rose and Rose say: 'In this architecture there have been no major repairs, no extensions, no refurbishments, indeed nothing to suggest that micro or macro contextual changes since prehistory have been accompanied by evolutionary adaptation.' This claim is 'extreme', given 'the huge changes produced by artificial selection by humans among domesticated animals – cattle, dogs and even Darwin's own favourites, pigeons – in only a few generations'. If for birds and beasts, they say, 'why not humans?'[50]

Evolutionary psychology may not be quite as stubborn as the Roses are making out, but I think their criticism does touch one raw nerve – although not perhaps the one they are aiming at. At least some evolutionary psychologists do *not* rule out that changes could have taken place more recently – only that, given 99 per cent of human evolution occurred during the Pleistocene period, *most* of our evolutionary adaptations are likely to have occurred during this period. Geoffrey Miller summarizes this position clearly: 'At the end of the Pleistocene period, just 10,000 years ago, our ancestors were already modern humans.' The evolution 'that *shaped* human nature all took place in the Pleistocene'. But in the next 10,000 years, 'humans spread around the planet, invented agriculture, money, and civilization, and grew from populations of a few million to a few billion'. While this time has been incredibly important for culture, 'Ten thousand years is only four hundred human generations, *probably not* enough time to evolve *many* new psychological adaptations'. It is, however, '*plenty of time for runaway sexual selection to make populations diverge a bit* in some aspects of body shape, facial appearance, and psychological traits'. He notes how runaway sexual selection during this period may have led to the pointed noses and whiter teeth of the Wodaabe cattle-herding nomads of Nigeria and Niger.[51] Miller is not concerned with these less significant racial and ethnic differences, but with '*universal* human mental abilities', but he – and others – make it quite clear that some evolutionary adaptations could have occurred in the later period.

It is not obvious why Steven Rose thinks the assumption 'does not bear serious inspection' that, since we spent 99 per cent of our time as hunter-gatherers, this is likely to have had a greater impact on us in evolutionary terms than the past 10,000 years. But he is welcome, in the spirit of the emerging science, to make predictions about changes that may have evolved in the past 10,000 years. But he may be opening a can of worms, which is I suspect why the evolutionary psychologists do not wish to go there. Rose and Rose do note how evolutionary psychology can at least not be accused of racism, because of 'its insistence on the unity of the human species'.[52] Indeed, there is something slightly odd about the lack of mention of race. There is not even a single index entry in David Buss's comprehensive textbook, although Buss does note that there are certain *cultural* differences between nations – for instance, that Chinese women value virginity, whereas Europeans do not to the same extent. But, as the Roses suggest, an equally plausible hypothesis might be that some differences have an evolutionary source. Indeed, it is obvious that all racial differences can *only* have evolved during the past 10,000 years, when humans branched out of Africa. With this in mind, the Roses should perhaps be careful when they criticize evolutionary psychologists for concentrating only on those features concerned with the 'unity' of mankind, lest they succeed in opening a Pandora's Box. The evolution of racial differences is not something that evolutionary psychologists seem to be interested in addressing; if the Roses had their way, perhaps they would be.

How can we find evidence to explore evolutionary psychology?

A related objection comes from Stephen Jay Gould, linked with several arguments of Kenan Malik. Gould argues that a major flaw in evolutionary psychology is that 'how can we possibly know in detail what small bands of hunter-gatherers did in Africa two million years ago?'. This difficulty presents a major problem for the science, since claims about the period in which we are supposed to have evolved 'cannot be tested in principle but only subjected to speculation'.

Is this a major problem? I am not sure that it is. It would seem somewhat analogous to a criticism that, because the physical sciences study matter that was created during the Big Bang, the only method open to these sciences is to go back billions of years and to study the origins of the universe as they happened. But the physical outcomes of the Big Bang are all around us, and therefore we can conduct experiments using materials available today. Could not a somewhat analogous situation apply to evolutionary psychology and its interest in the past?

Of course, the theory needs to have *some* evidence from the Pleistocene period. And Gould concedes that our ancestors 'left some tools and bones and palaeanthropologists can make some ingenious inferences from such evidence'.[53] David Buss agrees: 'Bone fragments secured from around the world reveal a paleontological record filled with interesting artefacts.' Carbon-dating methods give us 'rough estimates of the ages of skulls and skeletons and trace the evolution of brain size through the millennia'. Bone fragments reveal 'sources of injury, disease, and death'. There are fossilized faeces and bones from large game animals that provide information about 'features of the ancestral diet' and 'how our ancestors solved the adaptive problem of securing food'.[54] But Gould thinks that we cannot possibly go further than this and obtain 'the key information that would be required to show the validity of adaptive tales' about 'relations of kinship, social structures and sizes of groups, different activities of males and females, the roles of religion, symbolising, story-telling and a hundred other central aspects of human life that cannot be traced in fossils'.[55]

It might be thought that there is one obvious route which keeps the focus on hunter-gatherer societies. We can look to data from *existing* or recently existing hunter-gatherer societies, especially those that have remained relatively isolated from the West. Malik warns against this approach. Even the !Kung of the Botswana Kalahari, or Australian Aborigines, are likely to have 'improvised and transformed their lives' over the last tens of thousands of years, he says. Indeed, one anthropologist 'has even suggested that the !Kung are not original hunter-gatherers, but have been driven to live as they do by Bantu-speaking pastoralists, who have forced them into a life on the margins'. If this is true, they would not 'represent hunter-gatherers any more than contemporary gypsies working in a fair or a market in Europe can serve as a reliable guide to ancient nomadic civilisations'. In short, 'Human groups are not static. They develop over time. It is as unlikely that hunter-gatherers today are like their Stone Age forebears as it is that farmers today are like those of 10,000 years ago.'

These are useful points that may serve to temper over-enthusiastic evolutionary psychologists who might be tempted to think that contemporary hunter-gatherer societies will be the same as our ancestral ones. But does this apply to actual evolutionary psychologists? Malik cites major figures such as Leda Cosmides and John Tooby suggesting 'that we can *glean clues*' about our evolutionary origins through investigation of current hunter-gatherer societies; similarly, Robert Wright, author of *The Moral Animal*, is quoted as saying that to study today's hunter-gatherers 'is *to dimly glimpse* the early stages of our own cultural evolution'. 'Gleaning clues' and 'dimly glimpsing' are surely modest enough ambitions that would not run into Malik's objection?[56]

Given an acceptance of the need for a modest approach – which seems to be the approach of important figures in evolutionary psychology – how can we test hypotheses that have emerged from study of prehistory and existing primitive societies? Gould says that evolutionary psychology must inevitably be 'untestable and therefore unscientific'.[57] However, using such data collected, in conjunction with theories embedded in speculation about what life was like in the Pleistocene, we can then engage with the *present*. To explore this, let us put it into the context of the attempt by evolutionary psychology to show that gender differences evolved during the Pleistocene period, and that this period is what is most important to our current behaviour, not more recent environmental influences.

Evolutionary psychologists can proceed in at least one of two ways. First, they can start from theories about the past, and derive hypotheses and predictions that can be tested *now*. Thus, for instance, from a theory that puts human mating behaviour firmly on an evolutionary footing, parental investment theory, we may derive the hypothesis that woman – being the one who makes the greater parental investment – will be more choosy in mate selection. Second,

181

experiments can be conducted to test the prediction that a woman will impose a longer delay and more stringent standards before consenting to sex than would a man. And if the evidence supports this prediction, which it does, we can find support for the theory that women's preferences are likely to have evolved during a time when this mattered, and are relatively immune to the environmental influences under which men and women find themselves under today. Of course, this would not be conclusive on its own; it is simply part of a growing picture of evidence about the influences on human behaviour. And if we find that an environmentalist might predict similar outcomes, for different reasons, we can refine the prediction until we find some ways of adjudicating between the two possibilities. Some examples of this process taking place have already been given above. That is, evolutionary psychology does not require us to go back to our evolutionary past for all our evidence: a *theory* about what happened *then* can lead us to predictions about current behaviour *today*, which if shown to be true can then help corroborate the theory about the past.

Alternatively, evolutionary psychology can use an 'observation-driven' or 'bottom-up' approach. This starts from an observation of the current situation, and develops hypotheses that might relate these to evolutionary theory and inferences about the Pleistocene period. Thus, for instance, from the observation that men seem to place higher priority on a woman's physical appearance than women do on men, we can develop the hypothesis that women's physical appearance provided ancestral men with a clue to her fertility. From this hypothesis we are then able to conduct experiments to determine whether men's standards of attractiveness are closely based on cues to a woman's fertility. Again, if we find this to be the case – as we do – then we have more corroborating evidence for a theory that looks back to the Pleistocene period, but conducts experiments and observations *in the present*.

Circularity of arguments

On a related issue, Malik thinks there is a circularity in much evolutionary psychology reasoning. He suggests that the following is a classic example of the type of reasoning at fault: 'Violence is a universal, evolved trait. Since it is an evolved trait its earlier forms must be seen in Man's close relatives. Since analogues of human violence can be seen in our evolutionary relatives, so we have proof that violence is an evolved trait.' This is circular reasoning he says: 'If you smuggle your conclusions into your method, it is inevitable that you will end up with the answers that you want.'[58]

I am not sure that it is. What Malik is saying is that the evolutionary psychology argument has the following three steps:

1 Violence is a universal, evolved trait.
2 Since it is an evolved trait its earlier forms must be seen in man's close relatives, i.e. chimpanzees.
3 Since analogues of human violence can be seen in our evolutionary relatives, so we have proof that violence is an evolved trait.

I think he is smuggling in his own conclusion here. For it would seem that the argument is alternatively in the form of the following, much more satisfactory structure:

1 From our empirical observations, we observe that violence is a universal trait among different human groups.
2 Assumption of evolutionary psychology is that it is therefore likely to have evolved. This is the assumption that we want to test.
3 If it is an evolved trait, *we predict that* its earlier forms must be seen in man's close relatives.
4 From observation we find it in our closest evolutionary relatives, chimpanzees.
5 Hence we have corroboration for our prediction that violence is an evolved trait.

Surely this (as opposed to Malik's contrived circular version) is the kind of argument evolutionary psychologists are making, and is a legitimate scientific method. The key point is that what Malik says is simply an assumption is actually a testable hypothesis. Had evolutionary psychologists not found similar violence in our closest evolutionary relatives, then this would have been enough to seriously undermine the assumption. And crucially, had we not found it in chimpanzees, then we may have been forced to conclude that violence *has nothing to do with* our ape past, but is purely to do with our culture. And would such a finding not have aided our understanding about how to deal with violence? In the same way, knowing that it is likely to have something to do with our biology adds to our understanding of human society and how to deal with problems arising in it.

Ignoring the environment and cultural influences

A third major criticism of evolutionary psychology is that it ignores the role of the environment and the possibility that humans have evolved the ability to be adaptive to different environments. Anne Fausto-Sterling takes up this theme in the context of gender. She says that 'protohumans almost certainly found themselves in a variety of different environments', so 'the idea of a species-typical set of reproductive behaviours becomes nonsensical'. This is because it is the logic of natural selection 'that individuals should vary their reproductive behaviours as a function of the environments in which they find themselves'. 'Depending on their environments', she continues, 'both sexes can exhibit a wide range of behaviours. Changing the environment can change a set of behaviours.'

She provides one example to illustrate this hypothesis, the behaviour of eastern bluebirds – nicely ironic given her own criticisms just pages earlier of evolutionary psychologists who switch in a cavalier fashion from birds to humans and back again. She notes the 'plasticity' of the behaviour of eastern bluebirds. Nesting sites are scarce, so male bluebirds will defend these, and trade sex to allow females the use of their territory. But then people started putting up nest boxes, leading to a surplus of nesting sites, allowing females to stop having to trade sex for a home. In response, males started changing their behaviour, to differentiate them among their peers, by helping females to feed their young: 'In other words, both male and female bluebirds exhibit behavioural plasticity.' Indeed, such plasticity itself can be a 'trait under genetic control' as a mass of experimental data shows us, she says.[59]

Now one bluebird does not make a summer – it could be, for instance, that human behaviour is not as plastic as this. It may not

184

have evolved for us in the same way, perhaps because there was no one to intervene to give us the hominoid equivalent of nest boxes. But most crucially, this could lead to hypotheses that may be tested.

Certainly David Buss would not disagree with these supposed criticisms. He is at pains to stress that evolutionary psychology certainly does *not* imply that 'Human behaviour is genetically determined', that there is no room for environmental influence. Evolutionary theory, he says, actually represents 'a truly interactionist framework'. Human behaviour cannot occur without: '(1) evolved adaptations and (2) environmental input that triggers the development and activation of these adaptations.'

To illustrate this, Buss gives the example of calluses. Calluses of course have a genetic component – a callus-producing adaptation that has arisen to protect our skin. But we would not say that they are genetically determined alone, occurring regardless of whatever is happening in the environment. No, they only occur when there is the 'environmental influence of repeated friction to the skin'. So calluses are 'the result of a specific form of interaction between an environmental input (repeated friction to the skin) and an adaptation that is sensitive to repeated friction and contains instructions to grow extra new skin cells when it experiences repeated friction.' Indeed, the reason why 'adaptations evolve is that they afford organisms tools to grapple with the problems posed by the environment'.

Moreover, many seem to believe that evolutionary psychologists claim something along the lines that 'If behaviour is evolutionary, we cannot change it'. Again, this is in no way implied by the science. Consider calluses again. We don't like them, so we create relatively friction-free physical environments. Hence we don't suffer from calluses. 'Knowledge of these mechanisms and the environmental input that triggers their activation gives us the power to alter our "behavior", in this case, the number and thickness of calluses we develop'.[60]

In a similar fashion, we can derive tremendous power from knowledge of our derived sexual behaviour. For instance, there is evidence, as noted above, that a woman smiling at a man is likely to be interpreted by male observers as meaning sexual interest – more likely than by female observers. Knowing this, we have various possible ways of reducing the conflict that may arise from this mechanism – even though evolutionary psychology argues that the mechanism is likely to have evolved and so be part of our genetic make-up. We could educate men that a woman smiling does not mean sexual intent. That is the possibility Buss gives, showing off his feminist credentials. Women could of course, conversely, be educated to be more coy, not to smile at men. There are other possibilities too, such as the way found in some Muslim societies of not letting any man see a woman's smile apart from her husband.

The crucial point is that there is no disagreement here between the supposed critics and protagonists of evolutionary psychology. As Steven Rose notes, 'the biological nature of being human enables us to create individual lives and collective societies whose futures lie *at least in part* in our own hands'.[61] Certainly Buss would not disagree with that. 'In part', the future is in our own hands. Now: which part? How much of behaviour is malleable? That is one of the key questions evolutionary psychology seeks to uncover, and it is, of course, one of the key questions of this book in terms of education policy.

Universal traits and evolution

One of Malik's key criticisms challenges evolutionary psychology's argument that, if there are behaviours that are universal to all societies, then these are likely to be evolved adaptations. Malik, on the contrary, argues that many behaviours found to be universal could be cultural and social rather than innate. He considers the example of the way humanity classifies nature, often given as a universal human attribute in the literature. This could easily arise because there are actually objective relations in the real world, which would simply have been noticed by our ancestors: 'They might have noticed that animals that give birth to live young tend to suckle their offspring, whereas animals who lay eggs tend not to', and so on. The crucial thing for Malik is that if sufficient regularity exists in the living world that could have led to an evolutionary adaptation,

> then there also exists sufficient regularity and pressure for humans to create such a taxonomy empirically, without the need for innate structures . . . If nature can do it without foresight, so can

humans with a little forethought. . . . You don't need natural selection to be able to tell your ash from your elm.

Suppose Malik is right here. What follows? Notice he is not saying that such universal traits are necessarily cultural or social, 'simply that it is quite possible for them to be'. And moreover, 'clearly, many universals that might be cultural in origin nevertheless draw upon evolved traits'.

This seems to be a reasonable objection to an approach that assumes all universal human behaviour must inevitably be innate rather than learned. But does the framework of evolutionary psychology then come crashing down? It would seem not, but only serves to focus the science's attention more carefully on universals that are most likely to be innate, separating them from ones that are likely to be learned. Usefully, Malik himself provides a twofold approach to aid in distinguishing these two types of universal behaviours. The first focuses on universal behaviours 'that don't appear to be the most rational response to the problems posed either by the natural or the social worlds'. The reason for focusing on these 'irrational' behaviours is that 'it is highly unlikely that a multitude of human cultures would have hit upon the same, non-optimum response to a particular problem', hence the probability that 'such a response is evolved'. He summarizes: 'It's the quirky, bizarre, inexplicable, irrational things that all humans do that are likely to be nature's legacy – like the universal fear of creepy-crawlies (useful in the Stone Age, not particularly rational in the space age).'

The second criteria that is likely to point to an evolved trait is a universal behaviour 'that could not have been learned, either because a child has not had the opportunity to do so or because there is insufficient information in its environment to allow it to learn such behaviours'. Malik suggests that examples here include 'language acquisition, knowledge about basic physical relationships in the world, and the acceptance that all humans have minds'.[62]

On both these criteria, it would seem that universal behaviours concerning gender differences emerge strongly as likely to be innate rather than learned. We have already seen in the previous chapter how some of the foundational gender differences are present in very

187

young babies, and so could not possibly have been learned. And on the first criteria, we have noted throughout this book that it is precisely the *irrationality* of the gender differences that upsets feminists – the 'equality' feminists, I argued, could equally as well be named the 'rational feminists' for precisely this reason: Why should women prefer more higher status men than themselves, when they are now economically self-sufficient? Why should men prefer to rise to the heights of hierarchies when this is bad for their hearts and longevity? Why should girls not be as good at higher mathematics as boys, given that there are well-paying jobs at the end of it? Why should young women not pursue careers as whole-heartedly as men, given the financial and status rewards that will accrue to them? Why should women not be happy to let someone else look after their children, given the financial and status rewards they could obtain if they do? The irrationality of current gender roles, found universally throughout societies, is likely, according to Malik, to lend strong support to the notion that these behaviours are innate rather than socially learned.

So Malik's critique may be useful in rescuing us from any excessive desire of evolutionary psychology to see all universals as innate rather than recognizing that some could be socially and culturally learned. But as far as gender differences are concerned, his own criteria suggest that those which are of significance in this book are likely to fit into the biologically determined category, and not be socially learned.

MOVING THE DEBATE FORWARD

Perhaps the most surprising thing of all is that, when we get behind some of the polemic, it seems that much of what these key critics say is actually in *agreement* with the basic tenets of the evolutionary psychology arguments. For instance, Anne Fausto-Sterling agrees that David Buss's work on the different problems facing males and females and how they would differently evolve as a consequence 'has a certain plausibility'. She says, 'Let us accept that males and females are likely to have evolved different approaches to courting, mating and infant care'. But what she objects to is what the approach misses out. For example, considering the evolution of male spatial ability, she notes:

If Buss's selective scenario played, perhaps it fuelled the development of foraging skills, including the ability to hold three-dimensional maps in one's mind's eye – returning even after many years, to a spot which had previously contained a good food source. Certainly Buss can hypothesise that pregnancy and lactation led females to select males who were good providers, just as I can hypothesise that it led females to evolve well-developed spatial and memory skills. We might both be wrong or right, but without more data and a far more specific hypothesis we have no way of knowing.[63]

Here Fausto-Sterling is putting forward a hypothesis about female evolution *that has already been put forward by evolutionary psychologists*, with predictions made and experiments conducted – as has already been discussed above. With these kinds of criticisms, Fausto-Sterling is not objecting to evolutionary psychology at all, merely pointing to ways in which it might be improved, and is, in fact, already being improved.

Similarly, Stephen Jay Gould[64] actually appears similarly impressed by evolutionary psychology, arguing that it 'could be quite useful if proponents would change their propensity for cultism and ultra-Darwinian fealty for a healthy dose of modesty'. Evolutionary psychology has 'some good insights', he says. I am all for modesty and scepticism too, and if some evolutionary psychologists do get carried away with cultism, particularly in their popular writings, then this tendency needs to be brought under control. Indeed, Gould notes that 'the most promising theory of evolutionary psychology' is its

recognition that differing Darwinian requirements for males and females imply distinct adaptive behaviours centred upon male advantage in spreading sperm as widely as possible (since a male need invest no energy in reproduction beyond a single ejaculation) and female strategies for extracting additional time and attention from males (in the form of parental care or supply of provisions, etc.).

Because 'males generate large numbers of "cheap" sperm, while females make relatively few "energetically expensive" eggs', females 'must invest much time and many resources in nurturing the next generation'. 'This principle' he says, 'of differential "parental invest-ment" makes Darwinian sense and probably does underlie some different, and broadly general emotional propensities of human males and females'. Clearly Gould is broadly sympathetic to the major thrust of the evolutionary psychology enterprise.

But then he objects to the way some evolutionary psychologists elaborate this premise in terms of parenting. He says, such 'parental investment will not explain the full panoply of supposed sexual differences so dear to pop psychology'. What is his problem here? He does not want to believe that men are willing to raise children 'only because clever females beguile us'. For, he says, a 'man may feel love for a baby because the infant looks so darling and dependent and because a father sees a bit of himself in his progeny'. But this feeling, he argues, does not have to arise from 'a specifically selected Darwinian adaptation. . . . Direct adaptation represents only one mode of evolutionary origin.'

Again, attentive readers will note that Gould is mentioning an area that the evolutionary psychologists are already investigating: perhaps Gould is right, and his love for his infant is because he 'sees a bit of himself in his progeny'. But perhaps this has happened because there are *adaptations* that have evolved to this end. It is a hypothesis that has been put forward and tested. Again, it would seem that within Stephen Jay Gould's criticisms – and within those of others writing within this same critical vein, supposedly to damn the whole enterprise – are ways of helping to move evolutionary psychology forward on to even safer scientific grounds.

We looked at evolutionary psychology for a straightforward rea-son. We needed to adjudicate between biological and cultural expla-nations for gender differences. Those whose writings we had sympathetically reviewed – such as Carolyn Graglia – had found in evolutionary psychology support for their case that biology under-pinned gender differences. Others, like Naomi Wolf, had hinted that evolutionary psychology might contain useful insights into the gen-dered condition, even if it did not actually persuade them. We explored it here to see if we could provide a plausible biological foundation for gender differences. The conclusion is that it does. Not only does evolutionary psychology explain the relevant gender differences from a biological (or strictly interactivist, i.e. the interaction of biology and society) perspective, but it also puts forward novel predictions and ways of testing these that show the hallmark of a true science. Many of the novel predictions have also been shown to be corroborated by the evidence. Moreover, when some of the most compelling critics of evolutionary psychology were investigated, it seemed that their criticisms usefully exposed certain weaknesses or over-enthusiasms on the part of some evolutionary psychologists, but did not upset the whole applecart. Indeed, it would seem that some critics were basically in favour of the evolutionary psychology approach, but wanted it moved on to what they saw as more sophisticated ground – in some cases ground already moved on to by the scientists.

It thus seems increasingly plausible that evolutionary psychology provides an overarching explanation as to why many of our relevant and educationally significant gender differences are likely to be biologically based. This is the conclusion we will carry forward as we look at the ramifications for education policy in the next chapter.

7

Big Sister Is Watching You

In the heart of Bloomsbury, in the imposing foyer of University College, London, you will find in a glass case the embalmed body of the utilitarian English philosopher, Jeremy Bentham, dressed in striking nineteenth-century garb. It is said that he is wheeled into university Council meetings and marked as 'present but non-voting'. His most famous scheme for social reform was the Panopticon, the model prison architecturally designed for maximum surveillance. Night and day prisoners would be watched, their behaviour assessed and appropriate correctional procedures initiated, all to ensure that the convicts were fashioned in the image of Bentham's orderly citizen, firmly guided away from wherever their natural inclinations might otherwise tempt them.

Feminism similarly wants schools to fashion boys and girls in the image of its orderly citizen, guided away from where their natural inclinations would otherwise tempt them. Feminists want girls forced to be free. However, in order to make them thus, boys and girls must be watched night and day, their behaviour assessed and appropriate legislation enacted. Much of the legislation is already firmly in place. In schools, feminists have succeeded in enshrining in law that there must be no gender stereotyping of subject choice. The curriculum, assessment and careers advice can permit no discrimination. A girl must be informed through all channels that her wishes and desires for her future life must be the same as a boy's. And there is recourse through the courts, in both Britain and America, if this gender neutrality is violated.

But some feminists are restless and questing for more. The battle of the curriculum, the battle of careers education, these are won. But still the war rages. Feminists have turned to the ways boys and girls relate in schools. They want to refashion these in the image of equality feminism. A familiar feminist theme objects to the way boys and men 'dominate both space and time in school'. Girls, it is said, are 'marginalized' because boys seek to compete in classroom talk, to dominate the public space.[1] Harriet Harman, now firmly ensconced in the Labour Government as Solicitor General, put this style of objection in its most basic terms in her 1978 pamphlet, *Sex Discrimination in Schools and How to Fight It*. The cause of her anger? The new 'modernized' Ladybird books for children. These showed the main characters, Jane and Peter, in stereotypical roles. One illustration is of a group of boys playing ball 'while Jane cheers them in the background':

Peter has a red ball.
He plays with the boys with the red ball.
Jane looks on.
'That was good, Peter', says Jane.

Harman thinks such books are bad. They 'discriminate against women' in particularly dangerous and insidious ways, by 'reinforcing stereotyped views of male and female abilities and roles'.[2] Girls should not be looking on while boys perform. Girls should not be judging, boys acting. And Harman was part of the successful movement that succeeded in outlawing such stereotypical views.

Exactly the same objections come from America, and they are around today as much as they were in the 1970s. The famous Harvard Report by Carol Gilligan and her colleagues bemoaned the 'silencing of girls as they move from the elementary grades into junior high and high school'.[3] Feminist educators regret that 'Even today, at all levels of education, males and females often are treated differently, even by the best-intentioned teachers'. This differential treatment is again because males are 'socialized to be active and aggressive', to compete in the public space with their verbal displays, which creates 'a chilly climate that dampens female students' ambitions and diminishes their self-esteem and confidence'.[4] Feminist educators on both sides of the Atlantic want all this to be equalized, with boys discouraged from dominating the public space, and girls compelled to come out from within their fragile shells.

Males dominating the public space with verbal displays while females look on. . . . Does this sound familiar? It seems to fit in rather neatly with the way Geoffrey Miller speculated in *The Mating Mind* about the evolution of art, language and culture, as discussed in the previous chapter. Those speculations may have seemed somewhat agreeable and charming at the time. Did art evolve as male sexual ornamentation? Just as the male bower birds of Australasia strut their stuff within their magnificent arched creations into which even famous naturalists can walk, to be coolly judged by appreciative females, so too could art have emerged as male human beings competed to show off their fitness to females within the aesthetic parameters set by female sexual preferences. And could language have emerged in a parallel fashion, because women found creative intelligence sexy, and males competed to be witty and wise through their verbal displays? And could morality in general, and altruism in particular, have developed along parallel lines, with males discovering that females found kindness and charity sexually attractive, so competed to deliver what they wanted?

We looked to evolutionary psychology in the previous chapter to help adjudicate in the nature–nurture debate. We found it gave strong support to the notion that there are biological foundations to gendered behaviours that will have educational implications. But, more than that, it seems that it has freed us to look at education in new ways. If Miller is right about the origins of these attributes, then profound implications would seem to follow for the ways in which the feminists wish to control the behaviour of boys and girls in schools. If only big sister knew the evolutionary origins of all she criticizes, she would watch things in a completely different light. Wouldn't she?

Not quite yet. We are running too far ahead of ourselves. Such conclusions cannot so easily be arrived at after all. Just because biology says that men and women, boys and girls, may be different is not the end of the story. Who cares if biology says so, we can still strive for equality, for social justice! Indeed, some might argue, it makes almost no difference to the feminist struggle whether or not girls are biologically geared to desire something different from boys – for feminists, as has been illustrated throughout this book, have long argued that women have to be forced to be free. Simone de Beauvoir, Betty Friedan and many others all recognized that the life of domesticity and motherhood was far too tempting to women left to their own devices. But it was wrong to let them acquiesce in what they naturally wanted to do, because it led to women's oppression. Oppression can be there even if many women seem to want to go willingly where it leads them. So if it is biology that makes women and men the way they are, then so much the worse for biology. The struggle against women's oppression must continue, whether it is caused by socialization or biology.

Would such an approach be justified? This raises the crucial issue of 'is' versus 'ought'.

ZAPPING NATURE'S 'OUGHT'

The argument of the previous chapter suggested that gender differences which arise in schools and career choices are likely to have biological roots. That is, the gender difference of boys, in general, preferring mathematics and science, girls preferring more people-centred subjects, and many girls wanting to prioritize family life, children and so on, all of these seem likely to have biological roots. Perhaps these gender differences have evolved in the agreeable ways proposed by Geoffrey Miller through sexual selection, male ornaments in the wooing of women. Perhaps they have evolved through the division of labour in primitive society, or using both of these mechanisms. In fact it would not matter for the purposes of this chapter if, for those who cannot stomach all this talk of evolution, they were differences that were just put that way, for instance by God.

But what follows from the assumption that these differences are biological? It is tempting to simply conclude that, because of biology, we should simply accept that boys and girls are likely to have different life choice preferences, different preferences in terms of subject choices and academic abilities, and different ways of behaving in class and in the public sphere. Of course, there will be considerable overlap, and some girls will want to follow those traditionally masculine roots – just as some girls are taller than some boys. But in general, we should be happy and content that the natural world is reflected in educational and career outcomes. All's well in the world, the future is bright, the future is natural.

But we cannot move that quickly. The problem is that this approach falls foul of what philosophers call the 'naturalistic fallacy'. You cannot, philosophers say, derive an 'ought' from an 'is'. Just because the world *is* a certain way does not mean to say that it *ought* to be that way. We are rational human beings, sometimes we can change the world if we want, sometimes we can even override nature if we want to do so. It happens all the time. I get a severe pain in my back, I do not acquiesce in what nature dictates to me, I go to the doctor and eventually have the kidney stones zapped right out of my body. 'Is' does not necessarily imply 'ought'. We challenge the claims of the 'is' of nature all the time.

The 'is–ought' problem is often argued to be *the* central problem in moral philosophy,[5] raising profound difficulties. Let us look at it on a relatively commonsensical level here. In the case of the kidney stone example, why do I not simply accept the prescripts of nature, and acquiesce in nature's 'is'? Because of 'higher order' values, including the value of health. My 'ought' is focused on what I think *should* be the case, not what *is*. Not everyone, incidentally, shares that view. Some religious people, from certain Buddhists to Jehovah's Witnesses, and many in between, actually think that if we become ill it is for some God or karma-inspired reason, and that we should accept nature's 'is', even if it kills us. But most of us don't feel that way.

So: why would we not want to accept nature's 'is' in the case of gender differences? Because of the moral position that this would lead to *women's oppression*. The 'higher order' values of justice and equality would be violated – *even if it is because of nature that men and women are different*. This is important to stress, for there would be nothing at all inconsistent or illogical with someone accepting the evidence of the previous chapter and saying that this does not challenge their gender-neutral agenda. Indeed, even more so, we would want to promote a particular sort of education which emphasizes girls' dominance, girls doing maths and science, and likewise an education of boys which emphasizes nurturing behaviour, etc. The 'natural inclinations' of boys and girls to do the things they want to do leads squarely to a society which is unjust. Therefore as educators we must try to overcome these natural proclivities.

This could be a valid position to take, but it depends upon the assumption that a gendered curriculum and schooling *leads to women's oppression*. Now, especially in Chapters 3 and 4, we encountered many women who felt strongly about prioritizing domesticity, childrearing and housewifery. And the striking conclusion of all of this discussion was that, for many women, there is *no way* they would describe any of it as oppressive. Many seemed to positively delight in it – and it wasn't just Bridget Jones's craving for a husband and baby either. Simone de Beauvoir, Betty Friedan and Germaine Greer, to name but three founding figures of modern feminism, all seemed to delight in at least some of the possibilities – and initially at least wanted women prevented from going that way, because it was too attractive for them to resist.

With this in mind, it is not going to be straightforward to argue the oppression line – apart from one conclusion that drops out of the wash quite easily at this stage. Nothing in any of the discussion so far – and this has been stressed several times – suggests that *all* women feel the same way. Thus for those who do not feel that domesticity is delightful, for those who *do* want to go into the public space, of business, science, politics and sport, clearly they must be allowed to do so. A *compulsory* curriculum and schooling that forbade women from pursuing their own ideals *would* lead to their oppression. This is the first easy conclusion. This then provides an easy answer to the question raised in Chapter 2 about the curriculum and gender stereotyping. Recall that there was a pressing question raised about what kind of curriculum would satisfy the liberation feminists – our examples were Carrie Paechter, author of *Educating the Other*, and the Australian authors of *Answering Back*, Jane Kenway and Sue Willis. They did not necessarily object to girls preferring different things to boys, and having different values and ways of knowing that should occupy a place in the curriculum. So why would they object to some 'traditional' curriculum proposals, which guided boys and girls separately, in closely gender-prescribed ways?

Now an answer is obvious. Such government-sponsored curriculum proposals would be unjust – but, importantly, *not* because they would not satisfy many, indeed, possibly the majority, of girls' preferences, but because they are bound to go against what *some* girls want. And if some girls are stopped from following their individual desires, this would lead to injustice. So the answer to the question raised is clear: government-imposed gender prescriptions for the curriculum cannot be justified, because this offends individual differences in boys' and girls' desires.

But this argument aside, some readers must be thinking, we cannot get away from this idea of women's oppression so easily, since it has been a key insight of feminists for the past 30 years. For bell hooks, for instance, feminism is 'A movement to end sexist oppression'.[6] Some even say that she dropped the capital letters in her name as a statement against patriarchal hierarchy. Whatever their differences, all feminists would appear to accept that it is a fundamental tenet of feminism that women are oppressed. Surely, they would all have been writing in the full knowledge of the kind of experiences of the women we have described, and who valued domesticity and motherhood? Even if the feminists did not want domesticity themselves, presumably they were aware of many women who did? So presumably, many readers might think, they have built viable theories to show why women are oppressed taking into account that many women themselves do not feel it.

We had better explore this further. In what ways do feminist philosophers say women are oppressed, and how do these theories stand up against the likelihood of there being biological basis for gender differences?

THE SUBJECTION OF WOMEN

Reading feminist literature, there seem to be *three* versions of oppression. *First*, the 'inequality' version says that oppressed groups are prevented from gaining access to their fair share of scarce and valued resources, such as wealth, power and prestige. The philosopher Anne Phillips holds this view.[7] *Second*, there is the 'limitation' version, held by the philosopher Alison Jaggar. Here oppression is 'the imposition of unjust constraints on the freedom of individuals or groups'. A version of this theory, the one preferred by Jaggar, is where women's oppression is defined in terms of their being alienated: in 'contemporary society, men are defined as active, women as passive; men are intellectual, women are intuitive; men are inexpressive, women emotional; men are strong, women weak; men are dominant, women submissive, etc.; ad nauseam'. For Jaggar, 'to the extent that men and women conform to these definitions, they are bound to be alienated from each other, holding incompatible values and views of the world'.[8]

Third, there is the 'dehumanizing' version, where oppression is defined as 'the systematic dehumanization of an identifiable target human group'. A pro-feminist philosopher Kenneth Clatterbaugh expands on this theme:

> To dehumanize a group is to deny that members of that group possess the complete range of human abilities, needs, and wants that are valued at that time as important to being a human being. It also counts as dehumanizing to treat, overtly or covertly, a human group as if its members lack the abilities, needs, or wants of a more complete human being.[9]

Certainly, each of these definitions could lead to oppression occurring, *even if* the person herself did not actually feel oppressed. However, when these definitions are examined in the light of the finding that important gender differences are biologically based, something rather interesting starts to happen.

We will take the definitions in reverse order to see where the problem lies. The dehumanization thesis mentioned 'a *complete human being*' and '*human* abilities, needs, and wants that are valued'. Now there are some things that all men and women hold in common as human beings, the absence of which will constitute oppression. Slaves are human beings who are denied freedom, respect and dignity – all things which it is reasonable to affirm constitute 'human abilities, needs and wants'. Being an untouchable in caste India would also clearly fit into this category, where certain freedoms and dignities are not given to these humans. Men *and* women slaves, men *and* women untouchables, are oppressed, that much is clear.

The problem with using this definition to claim that women are oppressed is that it ignores the possibility raised in the previous chapter that men and women (over and above the abilities, needs and wants they share as human beings) have *different* abilities, needs and wants as men and as women. If we talk of 'a complete human being', as does Clatterbaugh, we are talking about a genderless human being, and it may not be particularly useful as a way of fine-tuning exactly whether or not oppression is taking place for women. Women, *in general* (note the important caveat, to be returned to later), are likely to have different abilities, needs and wants from men in terms of relationships, childraising and careers. This much we found in the previous two chapters. If this is true, to blithely say that women are being dehumanized because they are treated 'as if its members lack the abilities, needs, or wants of a more complete human being' is to deny that the way women want to be treated is *different* from the way men want to be treated. It may be that men and women want, need or prefer to be treated *differently* in certain significant respects, and if they *are* then treated by society differently in these respects, it would be foolish to interpret this as oppression taking place.

Of course, this is not to deny the fact that within certain societies, women may be oppressed because their fundamental freedoms, needs and so on *as human beings* are being denied. In a horribly prescient comment in the Preface to the 2000 edition of her *Sex Differences in Cognitive Abilities*, Diane Halpern notes that 'the new repressive government in Afghanistan has forbidden all girls and women from attending school or working outside the home. I hope that this stunning act of discrimination will be history by the time you are reading this book.'[10] Certainly she is not alone in arguing that the Taliban regime was oppressive to women, and many, too, argue that in countries (like Afghanistan) that practised clitoridectomy, women are or were oppressed as human beings by these practices. Certainly the British felt that the practice of *sati* (where the widow throws herself on to her husband's funeral pyre) in India was oppressive to women and so outlawed it in the nineteenth century.

The important point is that it is not clear that the practices the feminists point to *now* in Western societies constitute oppression to women as human beings. For instance, gender stereotyping of the curriculum or career choice may not have oppressive implications at all; they may just be boys and girls responding to possibilities in *different* ways as men and women, leading to wholly justifiable different life patterns later on.

The difficulties are there in each of the other versions of oppression too. In the 'limitation' version of unjust constraints, again it is not clear that current feminist grievances would satisfy this at all. Yes, women are likely to have some 'constraints' on their freedom, different from the constraints on men's freedom. For instance, if there is gender stereotyping of subject choice so that women largely go into caring, people-centred careers, eschewing science and technology, this might have an impact on their freedom to opt for certain careers in later life. But why could it be called oppressive if what women, in general, choose fits in with what women, in general, want, desire and need? Why is it oppressive if women have constraints on freedoms that they do not wish to exercise?

This objection is even more clearly there in Jaggar's preferred definition, of 'oppression as alienation'. If men and women conform to the differences expected of them in patriarchal society, she says, 'they are bound to be alienated from each other, holding incompatible values and views of the world'. But if this 'alienation' is grounded in our *biological* differences as men and women, then it is not easily changed through social reform. It may just be that men are from Mars, women are from Venus, and that we must live with, perhaps even enjoy and celebrate that difference, not see it as alienation and oppression. This was the lesson from Chapter 4, at any rate, on the public–private distinction and how this could be celebrated, and not seen as oppressive.

Finally, the same comments apply to the 'inequality' version of oppression. If women do not have equal income and wealth in society, it may be that differences in the needs and desires of men and women mitigate this potential source of oppression. When my mother was bringing up her four boys and one girl, only part-time in paid work, but of course working more than full-time in every other sense as a housewife, would she have worried that she did not, on paper, have the same income as my father? Not at all, because the way the family was structured meant that she, in reality if not on paper, had access to as much income as my father – all of his income was for the family, not for him as an individual.

Interestingly, this example reveals one way that she, and women in general, may be oppressed in some societies, and perhaps increasingly now – as we have already pointed out in Chapter 4. My mother would have been oppressed in the equality version if she had not been able to rely on my father, both in the present and in the future. If she was nervous of him leaving for a younger, unencumbered woman, abandoning us easily and quickly through no-fault divorce, then this may well have oppressed her. But in Chapter 4 it was suggested that, far from being something brought about by oppressive patriarchy, such insecurity had been foisted upon women today by feminists' easy espousal of divorce. Here it is feminism that is oppressing women, not patriarchy.

The key point is that, given gender differences, it is difficult to say that oppression is occurring when women, in general, are not treated in exactly the same ways as men, in general. To do so would smuggle in the assumption that men and women *need* or indeed *desire* to be treated in the same way. If and only if men and women had identical *desires, aspirations, things they want choices from, things they value*, might we say that observed differences in a society in all these aspects constituted oppression. But the previous chapters have suggested that, in fact, men and women are different in many important respects, and hence that if society treats them differently in these respects, this will not necessarily of itself constitute oppression.

What about the 'in general' caveat that keeps cropping up? This needs to be addressed now. Nothing in earlier chapters was meant to convey that, of course, while men and women may be different, this does not rule out that there will be a continuum on which men and women find themselves, and that there will be some overlap. If a society treats men and women differently in crucial respects, then surely, even if it is not oppressive to men and women in general, it will be oppressive to those *individuals* who do not fit closely into the stereotypes? So let us turn our focus from women as a group to individual women. Women as a group are not oppressed; but it may be that some individual women are.

I think this all depends on how society does the 'treating' of men and women differently. Suppose we have a girl who aspires to be a great mathematician, and has the ability and single-mindedness to achieve this aim. If there is a compulsory curriculum in her school which says that girls *must* do different subjects from boys, and that they *cannot* do mathematics at any higher level, then this is oppressive to her — under each of the definitions of oppression. She will be

202

unjustly limited by this imposition, will suffer inequality as a result, and will in some sense be dehumanized, because she will be unable to fulfil her human potential.

Suppose instead that her school did not insist that she could not study mathematics, but structured things in such a way as to make it difficult for her to do so? Perhaps the timetable placed higher mathematics against subjects which she was more likely to want to study than a boy. Or perhaps higher mathematics was only available by travelling to the boys' school campus, with all the practical and psychological difficulties of so doing. Forcing her to make hard choices like this, or making her uncomfortable with her choices, may also constitute oppression.

Oppression might result at both of these levels. What they point to is the need for freedom of choice and flexibility. A compulsory curriculum must not force the girl away from what she wants to do. There must be an awareness within the school that options should be kept open for those who do not fit in with the stereotypes. Thus this supports the 'easy conclusion' reached above – and the answer to the question raised in Chapter 2 about the kind of curriculum a liberation feminist might want. It is compulsory curricula – and aspects of school organization – that will lead to oppression; insisting upon curricula freedom and sensitivity of organization will mitigate this.

But perhaps some might think that this is all too simplistic, and that even with this openness towards difference and lack of compulsion, oppression could operate at a much more insidious level. Some critics might ask, wouldn't it constitute oppression if the *norms* of society assume that boys and girls will pursue different courses, even if there is neither compulsion nor a lack of flexibility? This, of course, is an objection against gender stereotyping of subjects in general. In general, the norms of the society would fit in with genuine sex differences among boys and girls, so this would not matter to most. But what about those who do not fit neatly into the gender stereotypes?

Consider again the girl who does not fit into the gender stereotypes and wants to pursue higher mathematics. She may be allowed to do so in her school, and there may be no arbitrary timetabling or similar difficulties put in her way that will prevent her from taking maths. Nevertheless, pressure comes from her parents, her mother in particular, or her friends, teachers or the media. As a girl, she will feel unfeminine if she does what she feels drawn to do. If the norms of society are saying that girls do not do that sort of thing, then is this not also oppression?

Such an argument is far too alarmist, too unnecessarily black and white, and goes against the experiences of many women over the past century. There is nothing to say that certain norms for girls and boys in general cannot coexist with an expectation that there are individuals who will be different and can be nurtured in that way. Both Carolyn Graglia's and Simone de Beauvoir's accounts of their own upbringings and early careers certainly suggests this, as we saw in Chapter 3, and it is difficult to believe that either is unique in this respect.

In other words, the discussion thus far is that it is hard to see how there is oppression for women as a group if educational arrangements in society emphasize gender differences rather than similarities. There may be oppression for individual women who do not fit into the stereotypes, but this can be alleviated, if not overridden completely, if there is curricular freedom and sensitivity to individual difference in schools and colleges. This is likely to be true even if there are expectations built up in society about the likely ways in which boys and girls will operate. And if there is no oppression, then there is no moral reason for worrying about moving from 'is' to 'ought'. We have solved that particular philosophical problem with regard to gender.

IN THE FACE OF UNCERTAINTY

The story so far suggests that there is a plausible case to be made that our educationally relevant gender differences are rooted in biological sex differences. Moreover, an education system that was sympathetic to these differences would not be oppressive. But suppose we are wrong about this? Readers are likely to be laypersons like myself, and struggling with the niceties of science. How can anyone know for sure that the arguments presented are the right ones? But, more significantly, in science we *never* can be certain, so even if the hypotheses and predictions of evolutionary psychology were well supported today, they may not be seen as true tomorrow. What should we do in the face of the inevitable uncertainty that science brings?

The pro-feminist philosopher Patrick Grim has explored this

quandary, and concluded that it is better to err on the side of caution here, and accept the current status quo of feminist-inspired 'gender-neutral' education policy. He thinks we genuinely do not know the truth of the matter regarding the origins of gender differences. They may be 'fundamental' (i.e. biological), or they may be 'social in origin'. So how should we proceed: should we assume that the differences at issue are biological 'until proven otherwise,' or 'as social in origin until and unless the evidence indicates otherwise.' What should we do in the face of our ignorance?

Grim suggests that we must decide between four possibilities, as represented in Table 1. For instance, we may assume that the biological theory is true. If it is, *in fact*, true, then we are in quadrant 1, and all is well. Similarly, if we were to assume that the social origin theory is correct – that all gender differences are caused by culture and socialization, not sex differences – and if this is, *in fact*, true, then we would be in quadrant 4 and, again, all would be well. The problem occurs if we were to end up in quadrants 2 or 3. For in quadrant 2 we are assuming that the biological theory is true, but unfortunately, the social theory is true. This would be the position we were in, feminists claim, when the curriculum unashamedly reflected gender differences in the early twentieth century, when it was compulsory for boys to be boys, very different from girls who must be girls. In quadrant 3 there is a parallel problem. Here we are assuming that the social theory is true, when in fact the biological one is true. This would be the position we are in now, if all that I have written in this book is correct.

The question then is: in the face of our ignorance, as laypersons trying to decide on policy, is it worse taking the risk of ending up in quadrant 2 or quadrant 3? Which would be the more unjust?

Table 1 'In the face of uncertainty'

		Theory true	
		Biological	Social
Theory assumed	Biological	1	2
	Social	3	4

What Grim suggests, supporting the feminist cause, is that in fact the risks we run from finding ourselves in quadrant 3 are much less significant than those we run from finding ourselves in quadrant 2. It is much better to err on the side of assuming that gender differences are in fact social, rather than biological in origin.

Why does he argue this? Some things will of course balance out between the two choices: 'If we assume either explanation for observed differences, and if we're right, other things being equal, we can expect the social programs we introduce or the social structures we build on the basis of our theories to work more smoothly overall. If our assumed theory is wrong, we can expect to suffer on the same score.'[11] Thus introducing programmes that assume men and women are the same when in fact they are different, biologically speaking, will come up against the same sort of friction as assuming men and women are different when in fact they are the same.

But the crucial difference between the two positions concerns social injustice. For Grim, this arises, *only* in quadrant 2, that is, if we are treating the differences as being biological in origin, when in fact they are social. Indeed, for Grim, this is a 'paradigm' case of injustice, where 'differences between individuals or groups, real or imagined, are taken to be inherent and fundamental' when in fact they are not. Sexism and injustice will follow us if we end up in quadrant 2.

But what about in quadrant 3? Crucially, Grim does not think that any injustice arises here. He does not explore it, he simply assumes that there is none, perhaps buoyed by the fact that the feminist literature accepts that there is none. None? This is precisely the injustice discussed in this book! If we assume that all gender differences are social in origin, and in fact they turn out to be biological, this may lead to the kind of injustices that arise in the Bridget Jones Syndrome. In schooling and education in society more generally, girls and women have been treated as if all differences are social. But the differences are biologically based, and this leads to precisely all the kinds of unhappiness described throughout the book. In my judgement, all this unhappiness and lack of fulfilment is at least as bad as any putative injustices feared by feminists.

So if we are really to take our state of ignorance seriously, there is no way that we can say, as Grim does, that the status quo of a gender-neutral schooling is to be preferred to the status quo ante. Both have serious implications for social justice. There is really no alternative but to try to do the best one can with the evidence, and move on from there, which is why I have devoted a couple of chapters to the evidence, feeling the need to get to grips with it. My discussion suggests that there is a very plausible case to be made for the differences having a biological route, and that therefore society is very likely currently to be in Grim's quadrant 3. The injustice here is very real, leading to women's present unhappiness. It is crying out to be addressed.

PERILS OF THE PRIM PANOPTICON

One final thought on women's oppression and education emerges in the light of the discussion about evolutionary psychology. What feminists object to most may be described in one word: they don't like 'patriarchy' – that is, the oppressive male dominance over women in the family and in society more generally. Our excursion into evolutionary psychology started as a way of ascertaining to what extent outcomes of this 'patriarchy' – such as gendered choices in education – could be biologically based, which would have implications for the ways in which it might be changed. Yet these discussions revealed something rather interesting. It is hard to see in the descriptions and discourses of Geoffrey Miller anything oppressive about the forces at work. His work seems a million miles away from revealing the grim oppression invoked by the feminists. Instead what we see is that some of the things which the education feminists find objectionable – male dominance of the public space, for instance – may have arisen out of *women's* desires for men of a particular sort, and men responding to these desires. What he shows us in the evolution of art and language, morality and culture, for instance, is a beautiful spiralling counterpoint of *women's desires* and men's responses. Through romance and court-ship, where women have set the parameters for what men do, much of what we value about human beings has been created. Put in these ways, is it really as objectionable as the feminists say it is? If much – perhaps all – of what we value as human beings has evolved (and presumably is still maintained) through these forces of sexual attraction, of men competing for women's affections, is it not somewhat perverse to be objecting to them?

Likewise in the work of David Buss, it is hard to find an oppressive patriarchy at work either. Again what is revealed is much of the structure of society built upon *women's* desires. Buss notes that many feminists do not seem particularly interested in where patriarchy comes from, but simply take it 'as a given', although some do point to the possibility that it arose because men are physically larger than women. But Buss instead points to male control over resources as resulting from the *co-evolution* of 'women's mate preferences and men's competitive strategies'. If women 'universally place a greater premium than do men on the resource base and resource acquisition potential of a prospective mate', then this will have led 'women to favour as mates men who possess status and resources and to disfavour as mates men who lack these assets'. So what the feminists attack as 'patriarchy' is more accurately described as a society where *women's preferences* establish the 'ground rules for men in their competition with one another'. Just as women's desire to please men has led to the huge cosmetics industry, *so women's desire* for men with resources made the acquisition of resources – and taking risks in order to acquire them – of great interest to males. Similarly, one may posit that institutions such as marriage and female fidelity evolved to mesh men firmly into family life, to help them support women and children by ensuring that they were confident of their paternity – and these again would be strategies that evolved because of *women's desires* for men to be so enmeshed.[12]

This brings two implications for the argument of this book. First, all this seems to lead to the conclusion that it makes as much sense to call what goes on in society 'patriarchy' as it does to call it 'matriarchy'. Looked at superficially, you might find some features of society pointing to male control and dominance. But looked at in detail, you find the institutions we know in society emerging through a mutual interplay of *women's desires* and men's striving to respond to these desires.

But the second implication goes directly back to where we left off at the beginning of this chapter, where it was outlined how feminists wanted to reform schools to be places of equality between the sexes, to clamp down on boys' domination of the public space in classrooms and playgrounds, to ensure that, even in their behaviour as well as in the curriculum, boys and girls were equal. But can we be confident that such an emphasis will not offend against some of the things that are of inestimable value for us as humans?

The key to these speculations is this: now that we have been relieved of the notion that the 'naturalistic fallacy' might lead to oppression for women, that there might be nothing wrong with thinking in terms of the 'is' of natural sex differences, rather than thinking in terms of the 'ought' of some contrived feminist alternative, then we are liberated to think along unfamiliar but exciting lines.

A first speculation suggests that perhaps the way the feminists have assessed the situation in schools is far too negative. Instead of being half-empty, perhaps they could instead see the glass as half-full? Looked through spectacles informed by our evolution, perhaps we could instead see the boys' classroom displays for what they are, as boys competing for attention *within the parameters set by women* over evolutionary time. And perhaps, instead of seeing only girls 'retreating', we could see if there were any girls *enjoying*, entertained yet sceptical, appraising the boys? Indeed, that is what the Australian authors of *Answering Back* report that some girls related to them, namely that they liked the boys entertaining them: ' "boys being boys" can also be sources of fun and distraction', they note; if boys were not there to amuse them, it would be 'heavy work all of the time'.[13]

It is an open empirical question. Perhaps we will still find that girls are indeed made miserable by it all, but not for the reasons that some feminists might assume. Instead, it could be because the boys in their classes are *too inept* at dominating the public space – after all, girls' preferences are for older boys. Forcibly trapped with males of their own age, perhaps they really do despise the immaturity of these young boys, but would be entertained if it were older boys doing it. This then may also have implications for the way we organize classrooms and schools.

The second speculation is this. If there is little wrong or oppressive about the way nature intended us to be, then if feminist educators were to succeed in further combating the natural propensities of boys and girls in the classroom, might this make schools places in which neither boys nor girls can really flourish? Could there not also be something delightful, even uplifting, about seeing the evolutionary construction of gender play in the classroom too? If feminists succeed in making places where boys are not allowed to entertain girls, are not allowed to compete for verbal dominance, would this not make schools and educational institutions rather grim and prim panopticons of social engineering that go against boys' *and girls'* natures? Would this not only increase disaffection in boys, if school becomes a place that tries to stamp out everything manly about them, leading to their diminishment in the eyes of girls and their reduced pleasure?

But this line of thought can also lead us along paths even more fraught in terms of offending received canons of political correctness. What the speculations of Miller point to is a theme now long neglected in education, but perhaps worth raising again – that of girls regulating the behaviour of boys. What Miller suggests is that, through evolutionary time, much of what we most value in society – art, language and morality – may have arisen precisely through the mechanism of female regulation of male behaviour. Females set the parameters, in their sexual preference for creative intelligence applied with sympathy and kindness. Males responded, competing with each other along the lines set by females. These ideas found parallels in traditional schooling, where girls too would set the parameters for boys' behaviour and aspirations. In the traditional school of my parents' and grandparents' generations, it was girls who would demand good behaviour from boys, it was they who would disapprove of boys' petty vandalism and indiscipline, and incite them to do better things with their time and energy. And boys, it is said, often responded. Indeed, as Christopher Lasch the old-style socialist observes, the nineteenth-century feminists also recognized that women could be the 'forces of organized virtue' in society, connecting with their traditional role of regulator of male behaviour, to stamp out drunkenness and debauchery, to subdue the older 'patterns of male conviviality' and domesticate males to 'bourgeois hearth and home'.[14]

Now all this has been turned on its head. Girls must not be the regulators of boys' behaviour – feminists condemn this as a retrograde step. Indeed, girls must go further, they must be as competitive and as aggressive as boys. Perhaps it is these emphases on girls that has led to the rise of 'girl power' – something else that Germaine Greer links with the rise of, among other things, equality feminism and its sinister engagement with commercialization: 'The longest revolution has many phases, false starts and blind alleys, all of which must be explored before a way through can be found', she says. One such blind alley is

> the brief and catastrophic career of 'girls', 'girls behaving badly', 'girls on top'. Though the career of the individual bad girl is likely to be a brief succession of episodes of chaotic drinking, casual sex, venereal infection and unwanted pregnancy, with consequences she will have to struggle with all her life, the cultural phenomenon is depressingly durable and the average age of acting out kinderwhores grows ever younger.

Girls can behave as badly as boys now and be endorsed by icons of equality feminism: Kidscape, the children's help-line, reported 'a 55 per cent increase in calls from girls complaining of being bullied by other girls in the 18 months up to March 1998 and put the phenomenon down to the pernicious influence of the Spice Girls'. These influences above all are felt in the 'sinister muck' of teenage magazines for girls: 'From them the emerging girl learns that the only life worth living is a life totally out of control, disrupted by debt, disordered eating, drunkenness, drugs and casual sex.'[15]

As the behaviour of girls gets worse, so young men are liberated to behave even more badly. We have lost something incredibly valuable in society if girls are encouraged to be in open competition with boys. For who then is to regulate the boys' behaviour, let alone the girls'? Are feminists tampering with such forces in schools at their peril? Perhaps it is no wonder that we see a general decline in the manners and public behaviour of boys and young men, who would be only too willing to be well behaved if this is what the girls were allowed to want from them.

Finally, and most significantly, feminists want schools to be – and have succeeded in making them – places where girls compete on (at least) equal terms with boys in preparation for the economic market-place, for the top jobs and financial rewards. But again, in terms of regulating male behaviour, this could have extremely undesirable effects, this time on society more generally. Indeed, Miller seems to be pointing to these issues when he notes that we have a 'responsibility to design social institutions that reap maximum social benefits from individual instincts for sexual competitiveness'. 'One society', he says, 'may organize human sexual competition so that individuals become alienated workaholics competing to acquire consumerist indicators of their spending ability.'[16] But Miller notes that this is not the only possible society that could be built on the foundations of our sexual competitiveness. In another, the competition might be in terms of seeking altruism, community life and environmental protection. But I believe he misses an important point here. He is right, I think, that our society has become one of 'alienated workaholics' and obsessive, conspicuous consumers. But one explanation must surely be that this is not because society has geared men to compete in this way – after all, this has always been the case, and it is only more recently that the extreme consumerism seems to have emerged – but because it has geared men *and* women to these roles. And with women made as keen to compete as men for these work-based rewards, there is no one to temper and regulate men's competitive behaviour, to remind them that there are other things more valuable in life.

Again, Lasch seemed to worry along similar things. 'Men,' he said, 'valued achievement; women, happiness and well-being.' And women were able to temper the masculine tendency for competition by showing the virtues of another kind of lifestyle.[17] As Robert Wright puts it, the Victorian wife 'could tame the animal in a man and rescue his spirit from the deadening world of work'.[18] Now, because of the way we school girls and boys, men's tendency 'to overrate their market accomplishments now prevails almost wholly unchecked by feminine counterbalance. Society has largely acquiesced in feminism's championing of this male view . . .'[19]

We looked to evolutionary psychology to help us adjudicate in the nature–nurture debate, but we have also found that it frees us to look at education in new ways. These are some of my speculations, to take forward for another time; Miller has his own ideas on education too. He argues that 'the social sciences and humanities would benefit from turning to evolutionary psychology as their conceptual basis'. And he suggests that this could challenge policies that prioritize 'academic fundamentals', for instance, skills that are there simply to 'increase worker productivity on behalf of corporate shareholders and tax-collectors', at the expense of 'extracurricular activities', such as 'sports, drama, dance, music, and art skills that increase individual sexual attractiveness'.[20] These are useful ideas to explore further, but they must be explored away from our current obsession with gender-neutral schooling. Instead we should examine these issues afresh, from an awareness of gender differences and how these can enrich and enhance our educational and social experience.

Let us not make schools into prim panopticons, where big sister is watching all that girls and boys do, judging them by the criteria of feminist political correctness. No oppression will result from letting boys be boys and girls be girls. Indeed, there is far worse injustice lying ahead if they are not allowed to be as nature guides them.

8

Celebrating the Gender Gap

Much has been made of *Bridget Jones's Diary*'s resemblance to Jane Austen's *Pride and Prejudice*. I find another literary allusion more interesting. I do not know whether Helen Fielding did it deliberately, subconsciously or whether it is just a coincidence, but *Bridget Jones: The Edge of Reason* ends with a similar dilemma to that found in the feminist classic of 1977, *The Women's Room*. This book also propelled its author, Marilyn French, into the public eye, making her an international best-seller too. It was, as I related in my confessions in Chapter 1, one of the first feminist books I ever read, and it ends with a similar dilemma to that found in *Bridget Jones*. However, the way the problem is resolved is profoundly different.

Rereading *The Women's Room* over twenty years since I first discovered it was a disconcerting experience. I could not quite work out why it was so good to read then, why women – and earnest young men like me – found it so challenging and so *liberating*. I can remember passionately discussing it on a train from Brighton to London with young male feminist friends, how it had changed the way we related to women, and how it had changed our girlfriends' attitudes to us and our unconscious and conscious sexism. (I am sure I am not alone in finding it hard to shake off those attitudes later on, even as I came to see that they are unfair to women.) Certainly the book's blurb shows me that I remembered the excitement around it correctly: 'THE NOVEL FOR EVERY WOMAN WHO EVER THOUGHT SHE KNEW HERSELF. AND FOR EVERY MAN WHO EVER THOUGHT HE KNEW A WOMAN . . .' proclaims the back cover: 'THE WOMEN'S ROOM IS the hauntingly powerful story of Mira Ward – a wife of the Fifties who becomes a woman of the Seventies. From the shallow excitements of suburban cocktail parties and casual affairs . . . to the dawning awareness of the exhilaration of liberation, the experiences of Mira and her friends crystallize those of a generation of modern women.' And finally: 'This is perhaps the most important novel yet written about the realities of life experienced by today's women. . . . [It] will establish itself as a landmark not only of literature but of our developing consciousness also.'

That was what it was all about then: of consciousness-raising, of making 'modern women' self-aware, aware of their oppression, and showing them the way to their liberation. And making their men aware of this too. The reviewers were united in their acclaim: 'Speaks from the heart to women everywhere', said one. And Fay Weldon wrote: 'The kind of book that changes lives.'

What was so exciting and *optimistic* about reading it back in the late 1970s must have been something like this: Yes, Mira ends up unhappy, that's true, but we can sacrifice her happiness for the greater good of all women. We believed we were pioneers. Romantic figures like Mira would emerge in that struggle, and through her suffering we would find the key to move forward ourselves. Eventually, society would be forced to change, so that those who followed after Mira could find the happiness that eluded her, that men would change as would employers and families, to allow those who had been liberated to flourish. All would be well, we thought, as young feminists then. And some women are still saying similar things today: Shazzer, Bridget Jones's most feminist friend, for one.[1]

In *The Women's Room*, Mira ends up 'terribly alone', 'miserable'. She 'walks the beach every day, and drinks brandy every night, and wonders if she's going mad'. She's 44, looking back over her life since that eventful year, 1968, when her life had changed, the year that she finally saw through the feminine mystique, and decided to leave her husband and children to discover herself. The year she decided to use education as a vehicle for self-discovery, to go to graduate school, to Harvard. There she had met Ben, a fellow graduate student, and spent two wonderful years with him, each helping the other to discover themselves.

Ben had spent years doing research in Africa, in a country called

'Lianu'. He 'was a combination political scientist, sociologist, and anthropologist' and older than the other graduate students, in his early thirties. For Mira, echoing the sentiments of Simone de Beauvoir when she had first met Sartre as a student, he was 'the first interesting man I've met since I've been here'. Like de Beauvoir, too, she loved looking up to him, *the* expert on Lianu – although unlike de Beauvoir, she later saw through this too, and realized that this was all part of the feminine mystique that needed to be purged like the rest of her desires: 'she understood that his superiority, her abasement, had nothing to do with them, were cultural accretions, that humanly he was not superior, she not beneath'.

Ben really loved her. He wanted to be with her, and for her to have his child. But then he was offered a job in Africa, and things fell apart. He would go on and on about it, unable to contain his excitement, and Mira became increasingly angry: 'It took Mira two weeks to isolate the source of her irritation . . . Ben had never asked her if she wanted to go to Africa, he had just assumed that she would.'

As I remarked in my introduction, I did not make that mistake when I was a young feminist. I had learned the lesson of *The Women's Room* well. On the contrary, I just assumed that my Mira *wouldn't* be going with me; and it was she, still wrestling with the feminine mystique, who innocently made the assumption that she would be coming along too.

Of course, Ben apologizes, but Mira will have none of it: ' "you simply assumed I would go with you . . . you never, never once," she rose, and her voice rose, "never thought about me! About my needs, my life, my desires! You *eradicated* me, me as a person apart from you!" ' Chance would be a fine thing, it would seem, for many young women today. And so Mira runs, weeping – yet again – into the women's room, where she does all her crying and reflecting. And eventually, she tells him no: no to Africa and no to his child.

'She loved Ben, she would have loved (once, long ago) to have his child, it would have been joy (once, long ago) to go with him to a new place and grow flowers and bake bread and talk to a little one pattering around learning to say, "Hot! Mats hot!" ' But now, this is not enough. Now 'she wanted to do her own work, she wanted to pursue this stuff, this scholarship that she loved so much. It would be a sacrifice to go to Africa – it would hurt her career, would slow her work.' And 'she could not, no, she could not have another child. Enough, she said. Enough.'

So she split up with Ben. Then 'felt utterly alone'. 'All she had to do was pick up the phone, say, Ben, I'll go, Ben, I love you. He'd be there in a moment, he'd love her the way he used to love her.' But she stops herself, because if he does not love her enough to sacrifice his ambitions then he actually does not really love her. She drinks – not glass after glass of Chardonnay, but brandy this time – for 'Truths were discovered in drunkenness sometimes'. And the truths she discovers? 'She tried to tot things up in columns. Column one – last chance for happy love; column two – what? Myself. Myself. She remembered sitting alone . . . insisting on *myself*. How horribly selfish! Maybe she was what Ben seemed to think she was.'[2] But eventually, she decides to go with her selfishness.

Bridget Jones, on the other hand, decides the opposite. At Christmas, Mark Darcy tells her that he has been asked to go away to Los Angeles. She is completely crestfallen – just as it was all going so well, why does he have to go away? No, no, he consoles her, 'I was going to ask you. . . . Will you come with me?' He is kneeling in front of her, holding her hands. Bridget Jones thinks about all the things she will miss, about her friends Jude and Shazzer, and her favourite brand-name clothes stores and coffee shops in Notting Hill Gate. She has just been offered a top job too in television; he cajoules here with thoughts of how sunny and warm it will be in California, and promises that he will wash up. Oh, all right, and she can smoke in the house. 'I looked at him, so earnest and solemn and sweet and thought that wherever he was, I didn't want to be without him. "Yes," I said happily, "I'd love to come".'[3]

The argument of this book is that government education policy is caught in a time-warp, *circa* 1977. It is still wedded to the misguided romanticism of *The Women's Room*. Government education policy has not yet caught up with Betty Friedan's change of heart of 1981. It has not caught up with a new wave of women writers, like Carolyn Graglia, Melanie Phillips and Danielle Crittenden, pleading for a revaluing of women's voices. It has complete disregard for the views of liberation feminists like Germaine Greer. And it certainly has not caught up with Bridget Jones. The plea of this book is that we allow it to catch up, that is all.

SOME HOUSEKEEPING

In Chapter 1, we started with some unhappy women. Bridget Jones, the women in the surveys from Britain and America, all the women paraded by Betty Friedan in *The Second Stage*. Friedan's women thought that they had been sold a pass. The things they valued in life – family, home, children – had become unavailable to them. And their suspicion was that it was partly the women's movement's fault. The women had followed its prescriptions for their fulfilment, pursuing independence and careers as earnestly as their male colleagues. They had resisted – and supported each other in their resistance – succumbing to the temptations afforded by domesticity, just as de Beauvoir and Friedan said they should. And then, coming into their late twenties, thirties and early forties, they wondered whether it was all worth it, because suddenly they found they had priced themselves out of the market of available men, left it too late to have children, and, to boot, seen through the masculine mystique of the worth of careers. 'A woman alone . . .' as one had put it miserably, what was she worth?

By the time we get to Bridget Jones, however, she no longer puts the blame anywhere. By the time we get to her, feminist ideas have become so commonplace, so infiltrated to the core of all that is done in society that no one really notices any more. But it is time to make people realize how schooling now militates against what many women desire. It is time to address the new problem with no name, the 'Bridget Jones Syndrome'.

The legal situation in schools, and the way this was highlighted by politicians and senior civil servants, was explored in Chapters 2 and 3. From the Sex Discrimination Act of 1975 in the UK and Title IX of the 1972 Education Act in the USA, legislation has been piled upon legislation to enforce compulsory gender equity, and to make illegal discrimination in all subjects, including, most particularly, in terms of careers education. But curiously – at least a puzzle for those engaged in promoting gender equity – as soon as boys and girls are given any choice, they stubbornly revert, in general, to the very gender stereotypes that the legislation was supposed to have outlawed.

This big problem for feminists was explored in Chapter 2. For some feminist educators, we saw how this led to a simple solution:

even more energy must be devoted to getting more girls into science and technology, into high-powered careers, and away from careers in hairdressing, teaching and nursing. But other educators were not so sure how to address the problem. Some wondered whether or not there were female ways of knowing that were more appropriate to many girls and women, whether it could be a worthwhile feminist endeavour to revalue the different ways of women. But what did that mean they wanted from the curriculum? Clearly they did object to some of the older, more traditional curriculum models, but what would they want in its place?

This distinction between two kinds of feminism was crucial to help us unpick this question, crucial too for all the arguments that followed. We found Germaine Greer's distinction between 'equality' and 'liberation' feminists a most useful one, fitting in with the distinction I had felt worth exploring between 'rationalist' and 'celebratory' feminists. It was the equality feminists who wanted to push more girls into science and technology subjects at school. It was the equality feminists who wanted girls to pursue high-powered careers, and who sought to denigrate domesticity and motherhood. And it is the ideas of the equality feminists that have become enshrined in law, that are the pivotal influences on education policy, whether through feminist power or because they fitted neatly into the interests of powerful men, or a dangerous cocktail of both.

Liberation feminists, on the other hand, do not think that women should simply ape the world of men. They think that something is very awry if female values and predilections are lost, in curriculum, in family life and society. But their voices are lost to the debates about gender equity in schools. No ministers for women take up the causes of female values. No secretaries for education champion the causes of what many women find valuable and wish to prioritize. Virtues of femaleness, like domesticity and motherhood, are put to one side.

We addressed the denigration of domesticity and motherhood in Chapter 3, followed by the ways in which equality feminists overvalued the world of men, and their undermining of the interdependence between boys and girls, men and women, in Chapter 4. These three themes, indeed, seemed to be the key planks of the equality feminists' attack on traditional schooling, the key points of their reform programme.

Bridget Jones set the context for Chapter 3, fantasizing about a baby and a family. But so, surprisingly, did thinkers such as Germaine Greer; and even Gloria Steinem seemed to have got in on the act with her autumn-of-life marriage. And then we saw how one of the mothers of modern feminism may have yearned to be a mother in a more traditional sense: Simone de Beauvoir seemed completely torn by the lure of domesticity, at one moment pining for it, at the next sternly saying that women should be forbidden its temptations. If given the choice, she observed, too many women would embrace motherhood and domesticity, not the independence that she knew was theirs by right. And the early Betty Friedan, another self-appointed mother of the women's movement (who, observed unhappy thirty-something women, happily contrived to become a *real* mother before she became a feminist, so was relieved of the terrible loneliness they found), was also aware that women were finding the temptations of domesticity rather too enticing. Of course women *technically* were free to do whatever they wanted to do, she pointed out, in terms of all careers being open to them. But they were tied by their inner voices, their false consciousness, the feminine mystique, that made housewifery and motherhood seem all too attractive to them, and they must be forced to be free. But then we saw, only a decade later, that Friedan changed her mind. We were wrong to underestimate the importance of the family and domesticity to women, she says now.

To these voices we added new ones that are emerging in the debate, asking to be heard, women's voices that apparently do not find their way on to the gender education curriculum. They were voices like Danielle Crittenden, Melanie Phillips and Carolyn Graglia, all voices saying: We speak for many women who think making domesticity a priority is fine, that the public–private distinction keeps society sane, keeps society from being caught up in the masculine-led competitive consumerism; we want, they say, to preserve and protect the private sphere. Yet we are being hindered in this, because feminism has made it seem so unattractive to young women. In part, as Friedan and de Beauvoir both knew, it has been made unattractive through the educational process, by using the powers of the state in education to get girls to be just like boys. We are hindered, in part, because girls are made to feel through their schooling and other influences that their only route to success is through a career, that if they do not immerse themselves in these pursuits when young, all will be wasted. And if they should ever succumb to doing what seems desirable to them, namely raising a family, being at home, they will always feel that what they are doing is second best, not really worthy of their talents. In school too, all the emphasis seems to be on independence, on women making it on their own, when all we really want is interconnectedness, to know that we can depend upon a man to support us and our children.

Hang on, these women are saying, we want our voices to be heard. But their voices did not seem a million miles away from the voices of feminists – liberation feminists – like Germaine Greer. Indeed, on this issue, it all seemed to mount up as an attack on all that equality feminism stands for and its pernicious influence on education.

For these women's desires and wishes, it seemed, contrasted starkly with what the education establishment wanted for girls. Following the American Secretary of State and the US President – but exactly the same things could have been said from Britain and a myriad other countries – we found the official line was that girls should buck up, and get on in school so that they could become great scientists, athletes, businessmen, astronauts even, the same as boys. The contrast between what some women seemed to be pining for and what governments were saying they should be doing seemed stark. Every young woman had to move forward her 'God-given abilities', unless these told her that she wanted to make her priorities a mother and housewife.

The curious overvaluation of the world of men was addressed in Chapter 4. Why this obsession with all that men stood for over and above what women value? Why is it that Naomi Wolf wishes her daughter to be immersed in the world of warfare rather than nurturing dolls and playing home, as Naomi before her had done? What is so great about the world of men that women must clamour for entry into it? The working-class women whom the feminists want to see liberated from the drudgery of domesticity are likely to be liberated only into working-class jobs. Is it not possible that such wage-slave drudgery is even worse than domestic drudgery, particularly as it cannot be romanticized? And even for professional jobs, just because men say they are so worthwhile does not mean that women have to acquiesce in the male valuation of them. The argument is all about the 'private–public' distinction that is so crucial to feminists' ideas on women's oppression. But by turning the argument on its head, we suggested that there was nothing oppressive about men and women in general valuing different spheres, and that this alternative valuation could lead to benefits for the whole of society.

Thus the first four chapters set out the current educational landscape of 'Bridget Jones's schooldays'. While girls seem to do very well within it, its unfairness hits them later. As the women paraded in Betty Friedan's second book seem to be saying: why on earth did my schooling not prepare me for this?

Another underlying theme ran through each of these first four chapters. We met it first in Chapter 2. If gender stereotyping persisted so stubbornly, in spite of three decades of efforts to change it, what did this say about the origins of these gender preferences, both for subjects and for post-school life? Then in Chapters 3 and 4 it raised its head above the parapet again: if so many women's voices are saying that they find careers unsatisfying and yearn to prioritize family life, did this not again raise the question of where these deep yearnings might be coming from?

Feminists are clear that the origins of each of these factors lies in social factors, in culture and in socialization. Our patriarchal society has classified things as masculine and feminine, and men have claimed the best bits for themselves. And through the powerful processes of socialization, this has led all of us, men and women alike, to internalize it all to think that these differences are something deeply rooted within our nature. But they are not. They are only as deeply-rooted as society, and what society has created, society can change. Hence we need further vigilance, further gender reform, and only then – but yes, it will be then – will we arrive at gender equity.

But we wondered whether it was all so clear-cut. Had feminists really so conclusively challenged all the arguments for biological underpinnings to gender differences? We thought we had better investigate these for ourselves, in case they had left some stone unturned.

This territory was examined in Chapters 5 and 6. The feminists did not seem to have all the answers after all. In Chapter 5, the distinction between *sex* and *gender* was clarified, noting that, while we had been speaking throughout the book of *gender* differences, clearly social constructs, nothing yet had pointed to biological sex differences that may underlie these. I then outlined the gender differences that needed some explanation – whether cultural or biological, including differences in cognitive abilities: girls had superior verbal abilities, boys superior mathematical ones – as well as differences more closely linked with our emotional lives, such our choice of partners, the ease with which men and women differently give themselves to sex, the different ways in which they value status and resources in a partner, different interests in parenting, and the male propensity to aggression, competitiveness and status-seeking. All these differences seemed likely to be relevant to the educational enterprise – especially taking it in its widest context as preparation for working and family life.

Usefully, British government sources had explored the possibility of there being some biological foundations to these gender differences, and found them unconvincing. But we in turn found their arguments entirely unconvincing. Could we do any better? Chapter 6 tried to do so, by focusing on the candidate often put forward as pointing to biological foundations for gender differences, evolutionary psychology. This theory, grounded in its assumptions of a universal human psychology, moulded and shaped by the forces of natural and sexual selection primarily during the Pleistocene period, seemed to offer a rather strong case, it turned out, for there being a biological foundation to gender differences. In particular we showed that the theory not only satisfactorily explained the relevant gender differences, but made novel predictions about subtle differences of which we might not have thought – and certainly that the alternative, namely socialization theory, had not predicted, and could not satisfactorily explain.

But our excursion into evolutionary psychology was more delightful than anticipated. Far from being a rather grim tramp through the undergrowth of grubby male achievement, of dour hunters dominating their dowdy gatherer wives, the processes of evolution seemed far more pleasing. Through satisfying women's choices during humankind's long evolution, men developed all sorts of agreeable attributes, of wit, art, music and laughter. And women evolved these too, in order better to judge the creative intelligence of their suitors.

But we did not want to easily acquiesce in these findings, delightful though they may seem. We examined some of the critics of evolutionary psychology to see if they could dissuade us of its validity. What we found, once we had passed the polemical hype, were criticisms that either showed misunderstanding of the recent work of evolutionary psychology, or pointed to ways in which the science could be improved. The critics certainly did not undermine our sense that here was a research programme that could help explain much of what was going on in terms of gender differences.

Perhaps it might help too with consideration of the way forward for education policy? Not until the crucially important issue of the 'naturalistic fallacy' was cleared up. Just because nature might say that girls and boys are different, this does not mean that we have to acquiesce in that judgement. If it leads to injustice, to oppression, then it is perfectly legitimate to fight it, whatever nature says. But given the testimony of so many women who do not find traditional roles at all oppressive, we had to look closer at what oppression means. And we found that it only makes sense to speak of traditional spheres as oppressive if we also accept that men and women are the same by nature. But the argument has led us not to be able to accept that. Indeed, the greater injustice is likely to occur if we assume men and women are the same by nature, which it turns out seems increasingly unlikely. For in assuming sameness when there is difference, the injustices of the Bridget Jones Syndrome arise.

Let us be clear exactly what is and is not being concluded. What I am *not* saying, let us make this clear (again – for someone is bound to throw this accusation at me), is that all women are the same. I am not saying that all women want, or should want, what Simone de Beauvoir (in part), Betty Friedan (Mark II), the unhappy women whose stories Betty Friedan recounts, Gloria Steinem (Mark II), Germaine Greer (Mark II), Carolyn Graglia, Danielle Crittenden and Bridget Jones (Mark I and II) want. All I am saying is that there are *many* women who clearly do want to prioritize something other than that which seems to be prioritized by their schooling. To be sure, there is a temptation to play some of the feminists at their own game here, because there is a sense from some of their writing that they think they *are* talking for all women, that all women want to eschew domesticity and pursue independence at all costs, just as the feminists do. This temptation must be resisted. Women like the authors of *Closing the Gender Gap*, and *How Schools Shortchange Girls*, the women who champion government campaigns for more women in science and technology, politics and business, such women of course have a right to pursue their goals. Women have a legitimate right not to want to have children, to eschew domesticity and family life, to eschew men altogether if they want. They have a right to be making their mark in the public space, and they are welcome to it. Or those women who do succeed in having it all – family life and career life – who really would be quite miserable being at home with the family, but nevertheless want to embrace it on their own terms, these women too, of course, are quite entitled to pursue their chosen path.

So that is what the book is not saying. All the book *is* gently asking is whether these last two groups of women have had all the running in making education policy *for all* women, and whether the first group of women's voices has not been sufficiently heard. Listening to those voices in the course of the last few years while thinking about and writing this book, it seems starkly clear that many women are not being heard, and, if anyone listened, it would be obvious that they would want a different sort of education to better prepare them for the aspirations that hit them some years after leaving school. But how to cater for these different preferences? This is a classic dilemma of liberalism, and we will point to the framework for a solution below. The way you do not do it, however, is the way we do it now.

THE TRAIN WRECK WAITING TO HAPPEN

Naomi Wolf makes a profound admission in *Misconceptions*, her latest book. She catalogues the unhappiness all around her, with young mothers angry at fathers for not pulling their weight (according to the women: we don't have any independent corroboration of this); she catalogues the impossibilities of juggling babies and careers; she points to so much depression and distress. She hears all the stories of woe, and thinks: 'Despite our degrees and our assumptions and expectations about equality, I thought with exasperation, our generation of new mothers was a train wreck waiting to happen.'

Their education has led women of her generation to come up against life's realities singularly unprepared for all that lay before them, in pregnancy and motherhood. Women of her generation seem singularly unprepared for all that it entails in being a woman. Just two incidents from numerous ones in her disturbing book illustrate this. First, there is the 'sharp demotion of status' she felt on becoming a mother. Instead of feeling proud and valued, matchless and irreplaceable, she relates feelings of 'acute social demotion'. At a party, for instance, she found herself 'chatting with a noted biographer'. He asks, 'What do you do?' and she tells him 'Well, I'm at home with a newborn, and . . .'. Before she had finished her sentence, she says, 'he had tuned out. With scarcely a murmured excuse, he moved on to more promising social pastures.' Like a train wreck waiting to happen, the young mother thinks it more important what a self-obsessed male biographer thinks of her, rather than knowing her own independent value and worth in a unique sphere. One feels like shaking her and saying: stop overvaluing the world of men, there's something much more of value for you now!

And then there is the harrowing description of when she returned to work, soon after the birth of her baby:

> It was one of those rare good days when a writer can lose herself in time. Caught up in my excitement, I stayed too long at the office. It meant that I was late for a feeding. By the time I snapped out of my state of concentration and raced out of the building to run the few blocks to cross the street to reach our house, I was very late indeed. Christine, our new care-giver, was standing on the other side of the busy boulevard, holding the baby, on her way over to come get me. . . . I felt guilty almost to the point of crying at the baby's hunger, but in the midst of my guilt, intertwined with it, was a sheer vexation, almost a childlike anger, at having had to interrupt my work. It wasn't just the one interruption, but the realization that this was a condition: interruption was now my life. I was crying because I could not win. Because, as a worker, I was turning away from my work at exactly the most important moment; yet at the same time, as a mother, I had already stayed too long at the fair.

Again, one feels like shaking the miseducation out of her. Of course you can win! The world can wait for your pearls of wisdom, Naomi, honest! Your baby cannot. To her at the moment you are irreplaceable. But she will soon be old enough not to need you, then the world can enjoy what you have to say at your leisure. Instead, it is moments like this that made her slip 'deeper into depression'.[4]

Wolf's account is sharply in contrast with what Germaine Greer commends in pre-feminist societies, where 'girls learn mothering from their earliest years, usually by mothering their brothers and sisters'.[5] But what is deeply fascinating is that, elsewhere, Wolf also yearns for the position of women in more traditional societies. What she 'longed for', she says, is cultures where pregnant women 'are treated reverentially', with 'great deference', not American society where equality feminism reigned, and women are expected to work right up to birth and back again soon thereafter. She 'longed for some sense that it was an achievement at all'.

Writing about her post-partum depression, she notes that 'there are good reasons for other cultures to treat new mothers as if they are in a heightened, vulnerable state. They are.' For mothers in America (and Britain), 'It is not the depressed new mother who is aberrant; it is her situation that is the aberration'. For in 'most other cultures, and in America in the not so distant past', in 'Greece, Guatemala, Burma, China, Japan, Malaysia and Lebanon', in 'India, Pakistan, Ecuador and Brazil', the situation is very different: and the major, decisive difference is that 'women who have given birth are expected to take it easy if circumstances permit, being *nurtured by the women of their community for some weeks postpartum. . . . while they bond* with their baby and recover from the rigours of birthing.' In traditional societies, for all their shortcomings, mothers are surrounded by a community of women, all who know that their place is supremely important, and who are not all anxiously looking over their shoulders, wishing they were making it in the men's world. It is this community of women who can nurture the new mother, help her grow into this new role. But now: there is no community of women. And why not? They're all at work, compelled there because of the superior valuation of the male sphere over and above the sphere of women.

Is that not the logic of Wolf's position, to condemn what equality feminism has delivered for women in our societies? She does admit that it is only since the 1950s 'with the advent of the socially isolated suburb, the atomisation of the extended family *and the separation of women and children from the public arena*' that women's isolation has come about.[6] But where on earth does she get the last piece of evidence from? It is surely the opposite. It is not the separation of women from the public arena that has caused the problem, but the breaking down of the public–private split that has compelled women to value the public arena over and above the arena of women. This was the lesson we learned in Chapter 4. It is the paramount lesson that Naomi Wolf seems to want to avoid.

It is fascinating that women from across feminism's fault line, the equality and the liberationists, Wolf and Greer, are both pointing to the virtues of traditional societies and their treatment of women, although not everyone is drawing what seems to be the obvious conclusion. What is also interesting is that some, conservative (and Conservative) men seem to be drawing the opposite conclusion from their glance across at traditional societies. The tousle-haired editor of *The Spectator* and MP for Henley-on-Thames, Boris Johnson, recently penned a diatribe against traditional societies and their treatment of women, prompted by the war in Afghanistan. His focus, to be fair, was on views that 'are held, with varying intensity, across the Muslim world'. But these are not so different in relevant respects from other traditional societies: 'Muslim fanatics see denatured men, and abortion, and family breakdown, and jezebels who order men around. It tempts them and appals them and, finally, enrages them.' Indeed, Mohammed Omar, the leader of the Taliban in Afghanistan, said that 'only ugly and filthy Western cultures allow women to be insulted and dishonoured as a toy'. What he means, says Johnson, 'is that only the West allows women to be treated as equals'. Johnson's choice of words is apposite. Or at least, the use of 'equals' is spot-on, for it is precisely *equality* feminism that should be in his focus. But his choice of 'allow' is wrong. What we see is that in the West, people are *compelled* to treat women as the equality feminists want, in part through their education. But, critically, many liberation feminists, too, see 'abortion, and family breakdown', and the commercialized assault on traditional female values, as women being 'insulted and dishonoured'. Not for Boris Johnson, champion of the equality feminists. He boldly states, 'It is time for concerted cultural imperialism. They are wrong about women. We are right.'[7] And on the BBC Radio 4 *Today* programme the morning after his article appeared in the *Daily Telegraph*, a simpering Sue McGregor, who was supposed to be interviewing him, readily responded to his question that, no, she would not like to be looked after and protected as women are in traditional societies. Perhaps she wouldn't, also carrying the beacon for equality feminists. But that does not mean to say that all women agree with her. Of course, most would agree that the Taliban in Afghanistan took it all to a most unwelcome extreme. But if *they* were wrong about women, Boris, that does not mean to say that *we* are right. Perhaps we in Britain and America have taken it to an opposite extreme, and that may be equally as unjust.

Naomi Wolf's predicament is simply an extension of the Bridget Jones Syndrome. One might say exactly the same of Bridget Jones, too, that she and her friends also seem like a train wreck waiting to happen. 'For all our education', you can almost hear them say, 'we have been totally unprepared for what we want to prioritize in our lives.' Their education has kept them in very good stead while they excelled through school, of course. They have had no problem with their assessments, excelled at project work and conscientiously revised for exams. They have obediently sat through all that schooling told them to do and reaped enormous rewards in the qualification paper-chase. They have then pursued their careers, obediently following all that is demanded of them by their bosses, all doing promisingly well. And then they get to thirty, and wonder if that was really all they wanted to be prioritizing during their teens and twenties.

THE RESTFUL AND FOUND WOMAN

Margaret Mead, the feminist anthropologist, wrote in *Male and Female* of the different ways in which civilizations had to confront the desires of men and women for fulfilment and achievement. In many human societies, this is accomplished by giving men the right 'to practise some activity that women are not allowed to practise', activities that are 'underwritten by preventing women from entering some field or performing some feat'. Men need this 'reassurance in achievement'. Indeed, it is always a problem for societies to find ways of giving men this 'solid sense of irreversible achievement', for they have glimpsed, through 'childhood knowledge', 'the satisfactions of childbearing', and will always be striving for something they can rate as similarly deeply fulfilling.

For women, on the other hand, Mead argued, nothing could be more simple for society: 'it is only necessary that they be permitted by the given social arrangement to fulfil their biological role, to attain this sense of irreversible achievement'. But for feminism this is not good, since women too need to be striving like men. Mead continued: '*If women are to be restless and questing, even in the face of child-bearing, they must be made so through education*', repeating the themes that we have seen in Friedan and de Beauvoir of the importance of education for the feminist project. However, few societies, she says, have 'found ways in which to give women a *divine discontent* that will demand other satisfactions than those of child-bearing.'[8] It would seem that American and British societies *have* achieved that, through their formal education systems.

But why should women be 'restless and questing'? Why should they be made to suffer a 'divine discontent'? Throughout this book, I have pointed to women's voices saying that this is not what they want. Their voices have said that there is nothing oppressive about their desires to make a priority of domesticity and family life, and nothing untoward about not seeing a career or a role in the public sphere as the most important thing for which they should strive. And our delving into philosophical and scientific literature has suggested that they might be justified in so thinking.

But the education system of today is geared to make all women restless and questing, even those who do not wish to be. What we need now, to address the Bridget Jones Syndrome, to address the unhappiness of women in large swathes of society, is an education system that allows women — at least those women who want to be this way — to be restful and fulfilled, calm and found.

How do we get away from the miseducation of women? This is not the place to make detailed policy proposals. I have wanted to open up the debate, offer an opening gambit, not the final end-game. But the theme of any solution is freedom, and in this way the argument here fits into the theme of my earlier book, *Reclaiming Education*.[9] The argument here is that we need to reclaim from government our sex and our gender, since government, through its interventions in schooling, has tried to dictate in what ways these can be expressed. But government does not know best about this, its inertia has left it stuck in the equality feminism of yesteryear that wants to compel all girls to be like boys, all women to be like men. It has not learned the lesson of liberation feminism, that women and men are different, have different values and priorities. Nor has it learned from science that shows liberation feminism's intuitions about difference to be well grounded – perhaps not where they thought they would be, or indeed wanted them to be, but there none the less – in biological sex differences. We called it feminism's 'third way'. Now we see it for what it could be: a celebration of gender differences, as the liberation feminists want, not because these differences have been created by corrupting and polluting patriarchy, but because they have been created out of the sex of women. Unless we reclaim our education from the meddling of government, we will be immersed in injustice, the injustice of the Bridget Jones Syndrome (and its close cousin, Naomi Wolf's train wreck). The theme is freedom: perhaps to conclude I may venture five modest proposals that flesh out this theme?

First, we must allow open discussion of this crucial issue. The pros and cons of gender stereotyped educational opportunities need to be aired now, not pushed out of bounds by feminists who claim to speak for all women, but clearly do not. There must be no 'no-go' areas. There must be no sacred cows. Crucially, we must not think that there is only one legitimate feminist line on education. I have deliberately followed what I see as popular usage and used the 'feminist' label on its own when I mean the equality feminists. But this must not be allowed to cloud the truth that there are many different, profoundly conflicting views of what the good life is for women. The public, the press, the media, all seem to take it for granted that there is only one line on education: there isn't. The debate must be opened up so that other women's voices are heard too.

Second, let us liberate ourselves from our morbid fascination with national worrying about the lack of girls entering one field or another, or of the lack of boys in other areas. There should be no Royal Commissions, no Reports to Congress, fretting anxiously over why there aren't more girls in science or maths. No more government ministers must worry about too many girls taking up hairdressing. We have had enough of all this over the years, this inane puzzling over the wrong territory for solutions to a non-existent problem. There aren't more girls in maths and science because it does not fit in, in general, with their natural preferences. That's the end of the matter.

Third, we must free educational institutions from the fetters of the Sex Discrimination Act and Title IX, and from the fetters of a gender-neutral National Curriculum, as well as national tests that are aimed at the strengths of only one sex. The legislative framework must neither impose gender neutrality nor, of course, one particular gender bias.

Fourth, educational institutions can be encouraged to innovate along the lines of gender differences when it comes to learning styles, assessment, curriculum and pedagogy. Some are doing this already, in terms of girls' and boys' own teaching – mainly as a way of dealing with boys' underachievement. These experiments should be extended. The British government is seeking a drive towards 'diversity' and innovation in its new White Paper, *Schools: Achieving Success*.[10] That rubric should be extended to allow innovation along the lines of gender too. Perhaps boys and girls are better assessed, in general, in different ways from each other? Perhaps they would prefer to learn different things, in general, during school hours, or to have different emphases even when studying the same subject areas? Perhaps we even need to look closely at the ages at which boys and girls start school, since differences in early childhood development suggest that girls are ready for school much sooner than boys, and pushing boys into schools too early may only encourage disaffection. Above all, we should allow a thousand flowers to bloom here, to find what works best for girls and boys, and not assume that it will always be the same for each sex. Only that will enable boys and girls truly to flourish as individuals.

Finally, perhaps most crucially, let us feel relaxed about the fact – for it is a fact – that girls and boys in general may want to prioritize different things later in their lives, and, most importantly, they may prefer to start planning for such differences even while they are still at school. Indeed, many girls may decide that they want to plan a completely different path through life from the one that manifestly suits boys, but may not suit girls at all, with profound implications for the way schooling is organized. And so to the most far-reaching suggestion, that schools should allow girls to consider radically differ-ent alternatives for their life plans.

Danielle Crittenden, in *What Our Mothers Didn't Tell Us*, explores possibilities along these lines. She notes the 'self-defeating' way women currently plan their lives:

> Right now women are leading lives that are exactly backward. We squander our youth and our sexual passion upon men who are not worth it, and only when we are older and less sexually powerful do we try and find a man who *is* worth it. We start our careers in our twenties, when we are at our most physically fertile and yet are neither old enough nor experienced enough to get anywhere professionally. Then we try to have babies when our jobs are financially starting to go somewhere but our bodies are less receptive to pregnancy.

She tentatively explores the solution, extraordinarily difficult to convey in today's climate: 'I wonder if we shouldn't consider leading our lives the other way around . . . getting married and having babies when our grandmothers would have, in our early twenties, and pursuing our careers later, when our children are in school.' She sees many advantages in this idea. A young woman in her late teens and twenties would 'feel less pressure' to sleep with her boyfriends, 'if she knew she would soon be choosing one of them'. Seriously respecting marriage 'at an earlier age, she would be less likely to waste her time, or her heart, upon men with whom she couldn't imagine spending the rest of her life'. And the more her friends followed this route, the more there would be a 'shrinkage in the number of sexually available young women', which would impact on men: 'Sexual conquests would be harder, depriving them of their current easy ability to persuade women to share their beds without sharing their lives.'

Crittenden agrees that, to modern women, 'this surrender of youthful freedom might seem unimaginable'. But the gains surely outweigh any lost partying time: 'By the time her second child is toddling off to nursery school, she'd still be only twenty-nine or thirty.' Then she could easily enter the workforce 'with an easier conscience because her children would need her less than before'. She would be able to get into her stride at work without having to make 'the agonizing choice at thirty-two or thirty-three to stop everything now and drop out for a few years to have a baby – or spend six weeks with her infant and then deliver it into the hands of a nanny or day-care center',[11] with all the unhappiness that leads to, as dismally related by Naomi Wolf.

Interestingly, although it certainly does not want to embrace this option, the equality feminist manual *See Jane Win* does mention the same alternative pattern for women. Sylvia Rimm calls it the 'Late Bloomer' model, one that does not involve women juggling careers and children, but allows them to wait to start their careers when their children are older. There is no suggestion that it was a conscious choice for those women who typified this model in her case studies: 'These women were thrust into the parenting or work worlds early, and only much later and very gradually did they accomplish their education and move into successful careers.' Indeed, Dr Rimm admonishes, 'This is not a recommended career path for your daughters' – daughters, that is, who are to be high-flying career girls, 'because there is much risk that they will not be able to overcome their late start'. On the other hand, she does agree with Crittenden, that for modern women,

> thirty-five or forty is not too old for beginning a career. . . . Although women may not be able to accomplish all at once everything that the feminist movement encourages them to do, their remodelled lives may permit them to accomplish what they wish to accomplish in alternating sequences.[12]

This might indeed be the key way forward for liberation feminism. Perhaps we can be less tentative than Crittenden, certainly less apologetic than Rimm. The current model of the progression of school, college and career was unequivocally made in the image of men, after all. It suits them very well. And when a minority of women were involved in the professions, then it suited that minority well too. But putting it in those terms starkly reveals how it might not be suited to the majority of women. School, college and career – so where is family and home, things that many women want to prioritize? Why do they not feature on the life plan chart that forms the model for schooling? They don't because it was made to suit men. Liberation feminists need not acquiesce in that model at all.

With these five steps, schools could become places that *respect* girls and boys equally, without the proviso that they then have to assume girls and boys *want* the same things equally. With these five steps, we could again start to revalue female voices, and liberate women from the perils of the Bridget Jones Syndrome.

Bridget Jones had one suggestion for curriculum reform: that all boys and girls should be made to read *Men are from Mars and Women are from Venus*, 'so both sides of opposing armies understand each other'.[13] She is thinking along the right lines. What we need is to be rid of the coercion aimed at closing the gender gap. Instead we should be free to celebrate our gender differences; differences that may have created so much of what we value in human culture. Differences that could enrich our sense of ourselves, in our educational endeavour and in the lives we lead in public and private worlds.

Notes

1 THE BRIDGET JONES SYNDROME

1. Nicola Shulman, *Times Literary Supplement*, blurb of Fielding 1996.
2. Faulder and Brown, 1982, p. 15.
3. Friedan, 1963, pp. 13, 311, 318, 331.
4. *Financial Times*, Quotes of the Year, 31 January 2000.
5. Fielding, 1996, pp. 2, 41, 42, 60, 78, 148, 213; Fielding, 1999, pp. 98, 39; Fielding, 1996, pp. 119, 42, 21.
6. Hoff Sommers, 2000; Marks, 2001.
7. *Top Santé*, July 2001, 'Bad day at work?', pp. 96–7.
8. Greer, 2000, p. 221.
9. Women with children 'working longer hours than ever', *Financial Times*, 19 September 2001.
10. Blanchflower and Oswald, 2000, pp. 8, 12, 16.
11. Friedan, 1982, pp. 83, 33, 21, 22, 52, 71, 22–3, 90, 91, 26–7, 28.
12. Faludi, 1991.
13. Friedan, 1982, pp. 28, 34–5 (emphasis added), 35 (emphasis added), 65, 66, 67.
14. Clare, 2000; Faludi, 1999; Skelton, 2001.
15. Whitehead, 1999.
16. Fielding, 1996, p. 20.
17. *Daily Telegraph*, 17 May 2001.
18. Lyndon, 1982; BBC Radio 4, *On the Ropes*, 25 June 2001.

2 STUBBORN GIRLS

1. Whyte *et al.*, 1985.
2. Arnot *et al.*, 1999, pp. 74, 78, 78–9.
3. Equal Opportunities Commission, 1985, p. 12.
4. Arnot *et al.*, 1999, p. 113.
5. DfEE and QCA, 1999, pp. 32, 12, 31.
6. Equal Opportunities Commission, 1985, p. 4.
7. Title IX: 'A Sea Change in Gender Equity in Education', p. 3, www.ed.gov/pubs/TitleIX/part3.html
8. Arnot *et al.*, 1999, p. 22.
9. All quotations are from the EOC website: www.eoc.org.uk (emphasis added)
10. Arnot *et al.*, 1998; Ofsted and EOC, 1996.
11. Ofsted and EOC 1996, p. 13 (emphasis added).
12. Arnot *et al.*, 1998, p. 31.
13. American Association of University Women (AAUW), 1995, pp. 43, 44, 45, 49, 147.
14. Rimm *et al.*, 1999, pp. 10–11.
15. *Daily Telegraph*, 11 April 2000.
16. Arnot *et al.*, 1999, p. 121 (emphasis added).
17. Ofsted and EOC, 1996, pp. 13, 4.
18. AAUW, 1995, pp. 44–5, 76–7.
19. AAUW Educational Foundation Report, 1998.
20. *Raising the Grade – A Title IX Curriculum*, www.edc.org/WomensEquity/title9/raising/index.html
21. Report Card on Title IX at 25, Math and science: C+, www.edc.org/WomensEquity/title9/math.html
22. National Center for Education Statistics, 2000.
23. Greer, 2000, pp. 52, 3.
24. Paechter, 1998.
25. Kenway *et al.*, 1998.
26. Ibid., pp. 38, xx, 50, 2–4, 4, 38.
27. Ibid., pp. 42, 66, 73.
28. Paechter, 1998, pp. 8, 20, 15, 20.
29. See Hoff Sommers 2000, pp. 106ff.
30. Quoting Tannen 1991 in Paechter (1998, p. 75).
31. Paechter, 1998, pp. 75, 78, 117.
32. Kenway *et al.*, 1998, p. 90.
33. Harriet Harman, 1978, quoted p. 6.

34. Quoted Weiner, 1994, p. 36.

35. Phillips, 1987, p. 2.

36. Greer, 2000, pp. 2, 5–6.

37. Middleton, 1992, pp. 16, 84.

38. Greer, 2000, p. 14.

39. Johnson, 2001.

40. EOC, 2000, pp. 26, 14–15.

41. AAUW, 1995, pp. 147, 148–50 (caps in original), pp. 150–1, 149, 152, 148.

42. Equal Opportunities Commission, 1985, p. 14.

43. Ibid., pp. 2–3.

44. EOC, 2000, p. 5 (emphasis added), pp. 12, 15.

45. AAUW, 1995, p. 16; quoted p. 16 (from Harway and Moss, 1983, p. 40), p. 51.

46. Wolf, 2001, p. 60.

47. Friedan, 1982, pp. 79, 81, 92, 94 (emphases added).

3 ROMANTIC ILLUSIONS

1. Fielding, 1996, pp. 119, 116, 131, 132, 297.

2. Krauthammer, 2000.

3. DiManno, 2000.

4. Krauthammer, 2000.

5. Quoted in Editorial, the *Washington Times*, 9 September 2000.

6. Brewer, 2000.

7. Title IX: 'A Sea Change in Gender Equity in Education', p. 3, www.ed.gov/pubs/TitleIX/part3.html

8. Riley and Cantú, 1997.

9. Report Card on Title IX, Career Education, www.edc.org/Womens-Equity/title9/career.html

10. Report Card on Title IX: 'A Sea Change in Gender Equity in Education', www.edc.org/WomensEquity/TitleIX/part3.html

11. Riley and Cantú, 1997.

12. Remarks by the President at Title IX Event, 17 June 1997, The White House, Office of the Press Secretary, www.ed.gov/PressReleases/06–1997/9760617a.html

13. Ibid.

14. DfEE and QCA, 1999, p. 11 (emphasis added), pp. 12, 11.

15. EOC, 2000, pp. 34–5.

16. Arnot *et al.*, 1999, pp. 120, 153, quoted p. 114, p. 114, quoted p. 115, pp. 115, 114, 121, 153 (all emphases added).
17. Graglia, 1998, p. 87.
18. De Beauvoir, [1949], 1993.
19. Quoted from de Beauvoir [1949], 1993, in Graglia, (1998, pp. 106–7).
20. Graglia, 1998, pp. 108, 109.
21. Friedan, 1963, pp. 266, 264–5, 265, p. 265 (emphasis added).
22. Graglia, 1998, p. 119.
23. Arnot *et al.*, 1999, p. viii.
24. See Tooley with Darby, 1998, for a discussion of this issue.
25. Friedan, 1982, pp. 52, 53, 46, 105, 124, 120.
26. De Beauvoir, [1949] 1993, pp. 473, 476, 509, 523, 521, 522, 451, 452, 473, 527, 528, quoted p. 528, pp. 533, 538–9, 539 (emphasis added), 550.
27. Leighton, 1975, p. 26.
28. Evans, 1996, p. 64.
29. Ibid., pp. 22, 42.
30. Quoted from de Beauvoir, pp. 685–6, translated by Leighton, 1975, p. 111 (emphasis added).
31. Quoted from de Beauvoir, 1958, p. 331, translated by Leighton, 1975, p. 56.
32. Quoted from de Beauvoir, [1959] 1974, pp. 340–4 in Graglia, 1998, pp. 14–15.
33. Graglia, 1998, p. 15.
34. Evans, 1996, p. 22.
35. Evans, 1985, p. 13.
36. Quoted from Evans, 1985, p. 13.
37. Evans, 1996, p. 56, (emphasis added).
38. Quoted from de Beauvoir, 1962, p. 77, in Evans, 1985, p. 14.
39. Quoted from de Beauvoir, 1962, p. 61, in Evans, 1996, p. 56.
40. Evans, 1985, p. 101.
41. De Beauvoir [1949], 1993, p. 516.
42. Evans, 1985, p. 15.
43. Quoted from de Beauvoir, 1962, p. 77, in Evans, 1985, p. 14.
44. Evans, 1996, p. 30, citing Hoare, 1991.
45. Evans, 1985, p. 40, citing de Beauvoir 1965, p. 126.
46. Evans, 1985, p. 16.
47. De Beauvoir, 1960, p. 27, quoted in, and translated by, Leighton, 1975, p. 58.
48. Evans, 1985, p. 44, quoting de Beauvoir, 1965, p. 127.
49. Evans, 1985, p. 26.
50. Leighton, 1975, p. 73.
51. Ibid., p. 25.

52. De Beauvoir, 1967, p. 109, quoted Leighton, 1975, p. 25.

53. Evans, 1996, pp. 47–8, 79.

54. Evans, 1996, p. 70, quoting de Beauvoir, 1965, p. 645.

55. Ibid., p. 1.

56. Fullbrook and Fullbrook, 1998, p. 1.

57. Evans, 1985, p. viii.

58. Fullbrook and Fullbrook, 1998, p. 117.

59. Carter, 1982, p. 157, quoted Evans, 1985, p. 123.

60. Quoted Graglia p. 274 from 'Sex, society and the female dilemma: a dialogue between Simone de Beauvoir and Betty Friedan', *Saturday Review*, 14 June 1975, p. 18 (emphasis added).

61. De Beauvoir, [1949] 1993, pp. 733, 734 (emphases added).

62. Graglia, 1998, pp. 91, 96, 23, 5.

63. Graglia, 1998 Crittenden, 1999; Phillips, 1999; Elshtain, 1981; McKenna, 1997; Freely, 1995.

64. Phillips, 1999, p. 218.

65. Graglia, 1998, pp. 356, 19–20.

66. De Beauvoir, 1965, p. 189, quoted in Evans, 1985, p. 58.

67. Evans, 1996, p. 4.

68. Graglia, 1998, pp. 18–19, 19.

69. Crittenden, 1999, pp. 120–1.

70. Graglia, 1998, pp. 24, 112, 364, 365.

71. Greer, 2000, pp. 72, 73, 168, 78–9, 79, 249, 250,–1, 251, 260, 415.

4 'WOMANHOOD IS BEAUTIFUL'

1. Wolf, 2001, pp. 60–1.

2. *Daily Telegraph* headline, 12 September 2001.

3. Ingram, 2001, p. 7.

4. From *The Second Sex*, Vol. II, p. 58, quoted and translated in Leighton, 1975, p. 3.

5. Greer, 2000, pp. 193–4, 209 (emphasis added), pp. 211, 420, 9.

6. Friedan, 1982, p. 27 (emphasis added).

7. Mead, [1949], 1950, pp. 85, 92.

8. Graglia, 1998, pp. 40, 154.

9. Greer, 2000, p 18.

10. Graglia, 1998, pp. 113, 369.

11. Leighton, 1975, pp. 37–8.

12. From *The Second Sex*, Vol. II, pp. 588–9, quoted and translated in Leighton, 1975, p. 215.

13. Kenway, 1993, pp. 93, 90.
14. Friedan, 1982, p. 85.
15. Greer, 2000, p. 384 (emphasis added), 423.
16. Graglia, 1998, pp. 75, 76.
17. Pateman, 1987, pp. 103, 105.
18. Clatterbaugh, 1996, p. 302.
19. Moulik, 1996.
20. Fielding, 1999, pp. 119–20.
21. Goldberg, 1992, pp. 226–7.
22. De Beauvoir, [1949], 1993, pp. 476, 479 (emphasis added).
23. Greer, 2000, pp. 272, 413, 13, 222, 223–4, 422, 422–3, 423, 6 (emphasis added), pp. 6, 419–20, 420.
24. Arnot *et al.*, 1999, pp. 128, 111, 112 (emphasis added).
25. Whitehead, 1999.
26. Paechter, 1998, pp. 116, 117.
27. Arnot *et al.*, 1999, pp. 129, 126, 127, quoted p. 128, pp. 127, 128, 129.
28. Greer, 2000, p. 423.
29. Arnot *et al.*, 1999, p. 130.
30. Friedan, 1982, pp. 121, 122, 133, 97 (emphasis added) 98, 101 (original emphasis), 102–3, 103–4.
31. Friedman and Friedman, 1998.
32. Scruton, 1999.
33. Graglia, 1998, p. 152.
34. Phillips, 1999, p. 258.
35. Mead, 1949, p. 160.
36. Blanchflower and Oswald, 2000, p. 13.

5 LET'S HOPE IT'S NOT TRUE

1. Halpern, 1992, p. xi (emphasis added); repeated in Halpern, 2000, p. xvii.
2. Arnot *et al.*, 1998, p. 57 (emphasis added), p. 56.
3. O'Keeffe, 2000.
4. Hoff Sommers, 2000, p. 7.
5. Evans, 1997, p. 8.
6. Scruton, 1986, p. 255.
7. Browne, 1998, p. 18.
8. Martell *et al.*, 1995.
9. Eagly, 1997, p. 29.
10. Buss, 1999, p. 319.
11. Ibid., 1999, pp. 106–7.

12. Ibid., 1999, p. 108.
13. Kenrick *et al.*, 1990, p. 103.
14. Buss, 1999, pp. 108–9. A meta-analysis by Feingold (1994), looking at studies from 1965 to 1986, finds a similar result.
15. Tiger and Sherper, 1975.
16. Ridley, 1993, p. 252.
17. Geary, 1998, p. 101, citing West and Konner, 1976.
18. Buss, 1999, pp. 212–3; Whiting and Whiting, 1975; Whiting and Edwards, 1988.
19. Buss, 1999, p. 315.
20. Daly and Wilson, 1988.
21. Browne, 1998.
22. Hyde, 1996.
23. Browne, 1998 p. 19.
24. Ibid.
25. Maccoby and Jacklin, 1974.
26. Lever, 1976.
27. Alton-Lee and Densem, 1992, p. 212.
28. Jensen, 1998, pp. 531–2.
29. Halpern, 2000, pp. 87, 88.
30. Baker, (1987a), cited in Halpern, 2000, p. 88.
31. Reinisch and Sanders, 1992, cited in Halpern, 2000, p. 88.
32. Halpern, 2000, p. 88.
33. $d = (M_m - M_f)/S$, where M_m is the mean score for males, M_f is the mean score for females, and S is the average within-sex standard deviation.
34. Halpern, 1992, p. 86.
35. Hyde and Linn, 1988, cited in Halpern, 2000, p. 98.
36. Skinner and Shelton, 1985; Bannatyne, 1976; Gordon, 1980; and Sutaria 1985, cited in Halpern, 2000, p. 95.
37. Halpern, 1992 p. 86.
38. Voyer *et al.*, 1995, cited in Halpern, 2000, p. 112.
39. Masters and Sanders 1993, Resnick 1993, cited in Halpern, 2000, p. 112.
40. Hyde, 1996, p. 111.
41. Hyde *et al.*, 1990.
42. Benbow and Lubinski, 1997.
43. Walsh, 1997, p. 277.
44. Gallagher, 1998, cited in Halpern, 2000, p. 117.
45. See Halpern, 2000, p. 88.
46. Paechter, 1998, pp. 42, 47.
47. Clare, 2000, p. 19.
48. Paechter, 1998, p. 47.

49. Clare, 2000, p. 18.
50. Greer, 2000, pp. 417, 417–18.

6 A THEORY OF EDUCATION AS IF DARWIN MATTERED

1. Graglia, 1998, pp. 15, 240, 169.
2. Wolf, 2001, pp. 99, 100, 103, 104 (all emphases added).
3. Cosmides *et al.*, 1992, pp. 3, 5.
4. Tooby and DeVore, 1987.
5. Miller, 2000, p. 180.
6. Cronin, 1991, p. 113.
7. Ridley, 1993, p. 130.
8. Darwin, 1871, Vol. 2, p. 124, quoted in Miller, 2000, p. 41.
9. Fisher, 1915, p. 187, quoted in Miller, 2000, p. 55.
10. Miller, 2000, p. 55.
11. Ibid., p. 3.
12. This section draws heavily on Miller (2000), with quotes from pp. 17, 2, 122, 92, 258, 267, 268, 269, 281, 275, 321, 326, 292, 318, 244, 350, 352, 354, 376, 377.
13. Tobias, 1978, 1993, cited in Walsh, 1997, p. 271.
14. Jacobs and Eccles, 1992, Yee and Eccles, 1988.
15. Eccles, 1989.
16. Silverman and Phillips, 1998.
17. Silverman and Eals, 1992, pp. 534–5.
18. Paechter, 1998, p. 78.
19. Silverman and Eals, 1992, p. 535.
20. Ibid., p. 545.
21. Geary, 1998, pp. 289–90, citing Eals and Silverman, 1994; McBurney *et al.*, 1997, James and Kimura, 1997.
22. Silverman and Eals, 1992, p. 545.
23. Geary, 1998, p. 12, 311, citing Frith and Happé, 1996 and Willingham and Cole, 1997.
24. Trivers, 1972.
25. Buss, 1999, p. 103.
26. Ibid., p. 102.
27. Geary, 1998, p. 26.
28. Buss, 1999, p. 102.
29. Ibid., pp. 124, 125.
30. Ibid., p. 125.

31. Ibid., p. 127.
32. Kenrick *et al.*, 1996b, p. 47.
33. Buss, 1999, pp. 139, 141, 140.
34. Kenrick *et al.*, 1996a, cited in Geary, 1998, p. 150.
35. Buss, 1999, p. 138.
36. Ibid., p. 213, 214.
37. Ibid., p. 189.
38. Geary, 1998, p. 135.
39. Buss, 1999, p. 193.
40. Ibid., pp. 197–200.
41. White, 1981; Buunk *et al.*, 1987.
42. Buss *et al.*, 1992, reported in Buss, 1999, p. 326.
43. Buunk *et al.*, 1996.
44. Bailey, 2000.
45. Fausto-Sterling, 1992.
46. Rose and Rose, 2000b, pp. 5, 6, 8.
47. Fausto-Sterling, 2000, pp. 186, 176.
48. Miller, 2000, pp. 236, 238.
49. Rose, 2000, p. 254.
50. Rose and Rose, 2000b, pp. 1–2.
51. Miller, 2000, p. 180 (emphasis added), p. 277.
52. Rose and Rose, 2000b, p. 8.
53. Gould, 2000, pp. 100, 100–1.
54. Buss, 1999, p. 58.
55. Gould, 2000, p. 101.
56. Malik, 2000, pp. 247, 248, quoted pp. 248–9, p. 249, p. 246, quoted p. 247 (all emphases added).
57. Gould, 2000, p. 101.
58. Malik, 2000, p. 230.
59. Fausto-Sterling, 2000, pp. 184, 181, 185.
60. Buss, 1999, pp. 18, 19.
61. Rose, 2000, p. 263 (emphasis added).
62. Malik, 2000, pp. 253, 256, 257, 261, 262, 262–3, 263.
63. Fausto-Sterling, 2000, pp. 177, 182, 177–8.
64. Gould, 2000, pp. 98, 102.

7 BIG SISTER IS WATCHING YOU

1. Paechter, 1998, pp. 20, 24–5.
2. Harman, 1978, quoted p. 7.

3. American Association of University Women (AAUW), 1995, p. 20.
4. 'Title IX at 25: Learning environment', www.edc.org/WomensEquity/title9/learning.html
5. Hudson, 1969, p. 11.
6. hooks, 1987.
7. Phillips, 1987.
8. Jaggar, 1983, pp. 6, 353, 316.
9. Clatterbaugh, 1996, p. 295.
10. Halpern, 2000, p. xi.
11. Grim, 1996, pp. 8, 10.
12. Buss, 1996, p. 307.
13. Kenway and Willis, 1998, p. 141.
14. Lasch, 1977, p. 84.
15. Greer, 2000, pp. 399, 403, 404.
16. Miller, 2000, p. 430.
17. Lasch, 1977, pp. 168–71.
18. Wright, 1994, p. 123.
19. Graglia, 1998, p. 44.
20. Miller, 2000, pp. 427, 429.

8 CELEBRATING THE GENDER GAP

1. Fielding, 1996, p. 21.
2. French, 1977, pp. 14, 11, 633, 392, 393, 621, 616, 617, 620, 621, 622, 621.
3. Fielding, 1999, p. 421.
4. Wolf, 2001, pp. 214, 179, 180.
5. Greer, 2000, p. 251.
6. Wolf, 2001, pp. 85, 86, 187, 188, 189 (all emphases added).
7. Johnson, 2001.
8. Mead, [1949], 1950, p. 160 (emphasis added).
9. Tooley, 2000.
10. DfES, 2001.
11. Crittenden, 1999, pp. 186–7, 187, 188.
12. Rimm et al., 1999, pp. 337, 338.
13. Fielding 1999, p. 198.

Bibliography

Adelman, C. (1991) *Women at Thirtysomething: Paradoxes of Attainment*. Washington, DC.: US Deptartment of Education.

Alton-Lee, A. and Densem, P. (1992) 'Towards a gender-inclusive school curriculum', in Middleton, S. and Jones, A. (eds) *Women and Education in Aotearoa 2*. Wellington: Bridget Williams Books (Ch. 13).

American Association of University Women (AAUW) (1993) *Hostile Hallways: The AAUW Survey on Sexual Harassment in America's Schools*. Washington, DC: AAUW.

AAUW (1995) *How Schools Shortchange Girls: The AAUW Report: A Study of Major Findings on Girls and Education*. New York: Marlowe & Co.

AAUW Educational Foundation Report (1998) *Gender Gaps: Where Schools Still Fail Our Children*, October, www.aauw.org/2000/modelsbd.html

Arnot, M., Gray, J., James, M., Ruddock, J., with Duveen, G., (1998) *Recent Research on Gender and Educational Performance*. London: Ofsted.

Arnot, M., David, M. and Weiner, G., (1999) *Closing the Gender Gap: Postwar Education and Social Change*. London: Polity Press.

Bailey, R. (2000) *Education in the Open Society: Karl Popper and Schooling*. Aldershot: Ashgate.

Baker, M. A. (1987a) 'Sensory functioning', in Baker, M. A. (ed.) *Sex Differences in Human Performance*. New York: Wiley (pp. 5–36).

Baker, M. A. (ed.) (1987b) *Sex Differences in Human Performance*. New York: Wiley.

Bannatyne, A. (1976) *Language, Reading and Learning Disabilities: Psychology, Neuropsychology, Diagnosis and Remediation*. Springfield, IL: Thomas.

Barkow, J. H., Cosmides, L. and Tooby, J. (1992a) *The Adapted Mind: Evolutionary Psychology and the Generation of Culture*. New York: Oxford University Press.

Barkow, J. H., Cosmides, L. and Tooby, J. (1992b) 'Parental care and children', in Barkow, J. H., Cosmides, L. and Tooby, J. (eds) (1992) *The Adapted Mind: Evolutionary Psychology and the Generation of Culture.* New York: Oxford University Press.

Belenky, M. F., Clinchy, B. M., Goldberger, N. R. and Tarule, J. M. (1986) *Women's Way of Knowing: the Development of Self, Voice and Mind.* New York: Basic Books.

Benbow, C. P. (1988) 'Sex differences in mathematical reasoning ability in intellectually talented preadolescents: their nature, effects, and possible causes', *Behavioral and Brain Sciences,* 11, 169–232.

Benbow, C. P. and Lubinski, D. (1997) 'Psychological profiles of the mathematically talented: some sex differences and evidence supporting their biological basis', in Walsh, M. R. (ed.) *Women, Men and Gender: Ongoing Debates.* New Haven, CT and London: Yale University Press.

Benbow, C. P. and Stanley, J. C. (1980) 'Sex differences in mathematical ability: fact or artifact?', *Science,* 210, 1262.

Bird, L. (1992) 'Girls taking positions of authority at primary school', in Middleton, S. and Jones, A. (eds) *Women and Education in Aotearoa 2.* Wellington: Bridget Williams Books (Ch. 10).

Blanchflower, D. G. and Oswald, A. J. (2000) *Well-being Over Time in Britain and the USA.* NBER Working Paper Series, Working Paper 7487, National Bureau of Economic Research, Cambridge, MA (www.nber.org/papers/w7847).

Bossert, S. (1982) 'Understanding sex differences in children's classroom experiences', in Doyle, W. and Good, T. L. (eds) *Focus on Teaching.* Chicago, IL: University of Chicago Press.

Brewer, H. (2000) 'Gloria gets married', *Skirt Magazine,* www.skirtmag.com/1100/feature6.asp

Brown, L. M. and Gilligan, C. (1992) *Meeting at the Crossroads: Women's Psychology and Girl's Development.* Cambridge, MA: Harvard University Press.

Browne, K. (1998) *Divided Labours: An Evolutionary View of Women at Work.* London: Weidenfeld & Nicolson.

Buss, D. M. (1996) 'Sexual conflict: evolutionary insights into feminism and the "battle of the sexes"', in Buss, D. M. and Malamuth, N. M. (eds) *Sex, Power, Conflict: Evolutionary and Feminist Perspective.* New York and Oxford: Oxford University Press.

Buss, D. M. (1999) *Evolutionary Psychology: The New Science of the Mind.* Boston, MA and London: Allyn & Bacon.

Buss, D. M. and Malamuth, N. M. (eds) (1996) *Sex, Power, Conflict: Evolutionary and Feminist Perspective.* New York and Oxford: Oxford University Press.

Buunk, B. P., Angleitner, A., Oubaid, V. and Buss, D. M. (1996) 'Sex differences in jealousy in evolutionary and cultural perspectives: tests from the Netherlands, Germany and the United States', *Psychological Science*, 7, 359–63.

Carter, A. (1982) 'The intellectual's Darby and Joan', *New Society*, 28 January, 156–7.

Clare, A. (2000) *On Men: Masculinity in Crisis*. London: Chatto & Windus.

Clatterbaugh, K. (1996) 'Are men oppressed?' In May, L., Strikweda, R. and Hopkins, P. D. (eds) *Rethinking Masculinity: Philosophical Explorations in Light of Feminism* (2nd edn). London: Rowman & Littlefield.

Cosmides, L., Tooby, J. and Barkow, J. H. (1992) 'Introduction: evolutionary psycholgoy and conceptual integration', in Barkow, J. H., Cosmides, L. and Tooby, J. (eds) *The Adapted Mind: Evolutionary Psychology and the Generation of Culture*. New York: Oxford University Press.

Court, M. (1992) '"Leading from behind": women in educational adminis-tration', in Middleton, S. and Jones, A. (eds) *Women and Education in Aotearoa 2*. Wellington: Bridget Williams Books.

Coward, R. (1999) *Sacred Cows: Is Feminism Relevant to the New Millennium*. London: HarperCollins.

Coxon, E., Jenkins, K., Marshall, J. and Massey L. (1994) *The Politics of Learning and Teaching in Aotearoa-New Zealand*. Palmerston North: Dunmore Press.

Crawford, C. and Krebs, D. L. (eds) (1998) *Handbook of Evolutionary Psychology*. Mahwah, NJ: Erlbaum (pp. 595–612).

Crawford, M. and Gentry, E. (eds) (1989) *Gender and Thought: Psychological Perspectives*. New York: Springer-Verlag.

Crittenden, D. (1999) *What Our Mothers Didn't Tell Us: Why Happiness Eludes the Modern Woman*. New York: Simon & Schuster.

Cronin, H. (1991) *The Ant and the Peacock: Altruism and Sexual Selection from Darwin to Today*. Cambridge: Cambridge University Press.

Daly, M. and Wilson, M. (1988) *Homicide*. New York: Aldine de Gruyter.

Darwin, C. [1871] *The Descent of Man, and Selection in Relation to Sex* (2 vols). Princeton: Princeton University Press. (Facsimile edition, 1981).

De Beauvoir, S. [1949] (1993) *The Second Sex*. London: Everyman's Library.

De Beauvoir, S. (1958) *Mémoires d'une jeune rangée*. Paris: Gallimard.

De Beauvoir, S. [1959] (1974) *Memoirs of a Dutiful Daughter*. Harmondsworth: Penguin.

De Beauvoir, S. (1960) *La force de l'age*. Paris: Gallimard.

De Beauvoir, S. (1962) *The Prime of Life*. Harmondsworth: Penguin.

De Beauvoir, S. (1963) *La force des choses*. Paris: Gallimard.

De Beauvoir, S. (1965) *Force of Circumstances*. London: André Deutsch.

DfEE and QCA (1999) *The National Curriculum: Handbook for Primary Teachers in England, Key Stages 1 and 2*. London.

Department for Education and Skills (2001) *Schools: Achieving Success*. London: DfES.

DiManno, R. (2000) 'Feminist delivers the mother of all flip-flops: thanks for nothing, Ms Germaine Greer', *The Toronto Star*, 16 June.

Eagly, A. H. (1997) 'Comparing women and men: methods, findings, and politics', in Walsh, M. R. (ed.) *Women, Men and Gender: Ongoing Debates*. New Haven, CT, and London: Yale University Press.

Eals, M. and Silverman, I. (1994) 'The hunter-gatherer theory of spatial sex differences: proximate factors mediating the female advantage in recall of object arrays', *Ethology and Sociobiology*, 15, 95–100.

Eccles, J. S. (1989) 'Bringing young women to math and science', in Crawford, M. and Gentry, M. (eds) *Gender and Thought: Psychological Perspectives*. New York: Springer-Verlag (pp. 36–58).

Elshtain, J. B. (1981) *Public Man, Private Woman: Women in Social and Political Thought*. Oxford: Martin Robertson.

Equal Opportunities Commission (1985) *Do You Provide Equal Educational Opportunities?* (Revised ed.). Manchester: EOC.

Equal Opportunities Commission (2000) *An Equal Opportunities Guide for Parents*, scotland@eoc.org.uk

Evans, M. (1985) *Simone de Beauvoir: A Feminist Mandarin*. London: Tavistock Publications.

Evans, M. (1996) *Simone de Beauvoir*. London: Sage Publications.

Evans, M. (1997) *Introducing Contemporary Feminist Thought*. Cambridge: Polity Press.

Faludi, S. (1991) *Backlash: The Undeclared War Against American Women*. New York: Crown.

Faludi, S. (1999) *Stiffed: The Betrayal of the American Man*. New York: William Morrow.

Faulder, C. and Brown, S. (1982) 'Introduction to the British Edition', in Friedan, B. *The Second Stage*. London: Michael Joseph.

Fausto-Sterling, A. (1992) *Myths of Gender: Biological Theories About Women and Men*. New York: Basic Books.

Fausto-Sterling, A. (2000) 'Beyond difference: feminism and evolutionary psychology', in Rose, R. and Rose, S. (eds) *Alas, Poor Darwin: Arguments Against Evolutionary Psychology*. London: Jonathan Cape.

Feingold, A. (1994), 'Gender differences in personality: a meta-analysis', *Psychological Bulletin*, 116, 429–56.

Fielding, H. (1996) *Bridget Jones's Diary*, London: Picador.

Fielding, H. (1999) *Bridget Jones: The Edge of Reason*. London: Picador.

Fisher, R. A. (1915) 'The evolution of sexual preference', *Eugenics Review*, 7, 184–92.

Freely, M. (1995) *What About Us? An Open Letter to the Mothers Feminism Forgot*. London: Bloomsbury.

French, J. and French, P. (1984) 'Gender imbalances in the primary classroom: an interactional account', *Educational Research*, 26(2), 127–36.

French, M. (1977) *The Women's Room*. London: Sphere Books.

Friedan, B. (1963) *The Feminine Mystique*. Harmondsworth: Penguin Books.

Friedan, B. ([1981] 1982) *The Second Stage*. London: Michael Joseph.

Friedman, M. and Friedman, R. D. (1998) *Two Lucky People: Memoirs*. Chicago and London: University of Chicago Press.

Frith, U. and Happé, F. (1996) 'Mary has more: sex differences, autism, coherence, and theory of mind', *Behavioral and Brain Sciences*, 19, 253–4.

Fullbrook, E. and Fullbrook, K. (1998) *Simone de Beauvoir: A Critical Introduction*. Cambridge: Polity Press.

Gallagher, A. M. (1998) 'Gender and antecedents of performance in mathematics testing', *Teachers College Record*, 100, 297–314.

Geary, D. C. (1998) *Male, Female: The Evolution of Human Sex Differences*. Washington, DC: American Psychological Association.

Gilligan, C. (1982) *In a Different Voice: Psychological Theory and Women's Development*. Cambridge, MA: Harvard Universtiy Press.

Gilligan, C., Lyons, N. and Hanmer, T. (eds) (1990) *Making Connections: The Relational Worlds of Adolescent Girls at Emma Willard School*. Cambridge, MA: Harvard Universtiy Press.

Gilligan, C., Ward, J. W. and Taylor, J. McL. (eds) (1988) *Mapping the Moral Domain: A Contribution of Women's Thinking to Psychological Theory and Education*. Cambridge, MA: Center for the Study of Gender, Education and Human Development, Harvard University Press.

Goldberg, S. (1993) *Why Men Rule: A Theory of Male Dominance*. Chicago, IL: Open Court.

Goldberger, N. R., Tarule, J. M., Clinchy, B. M. and Belenky, M. F. (eds) (1996) *Knowledge, Difference and Power: Essays Inspired by Women's Way of Knowing*. New York: Basic Books.

Gorard, S., Rees, G. and Salisbury, J. (1999) 'Reappraising the apparent underachievement of boys at school', *Gender and Education*, 11(4), 441–54.

Gordon, H. W. (1980) 'Cognitive asymmetry in dyslexic families', *Neuropsychologia*, 18, 645–56.

Gould, S. J. (2000) 'More things in heaven and earth', in Rose, H. and Rose, S. (eds) *Alas, Poor Darwin: Arguments Against Evolutionary Psychology*. London: Jonathan Cape.

Graglia, F. C. (1998) *Domestic Tranquility: A Brief Against Feminism*. Dallas, TX: Spence Publishing.

Greer, G. ([1999] 2000) *The Whole Woman*. London: Transworld.

Grim, P. (1996) 'Sex and social roles: how to deal with the data', in May, L., Strikweda, R. and Hopkins, P. D. *Rethinking Masculinity: Philosophical Explorations in Light of Feminism* (2nd edn). London: Rowman & Littlefield.

Halpern, D. F. (1992) *Sex Differences in Cognitive Abilities* (2nd edn). Hillsdale, NJ, Hove and London: Lawrence Erlbaum.

Halpern, D. F. (1994) 'Stereotypes, science, censorship, and the study of sex differences', *Feminism and Psychology*, 4, 523–30.

Halpern, D. F. (2000) *Sex Differences in Cognitive Abilities* (3rd edn). Mahwah, NJ, and London: Lawrence Erlbaum.

Harman, H. (1978) *Sex Discrimination in Schools and How to Fight It*. London: National Council for Civil Liberties.

Harris, L. J. (1978) 'Sex differences in spatial ability: possible environmental, genetic and neurological factors', in Kinsbourn, M. (ed.) *Asymmetric Function of the Brain*. Cambridge: Cambridge University Press.

Harway, M. and Moss, L. (1983) 'Sex differences: the evidence from biology', in Liss M. (ed.) *Social and Cognitive Skills*. New York: Academic Press.

Head, J. (1999) *Understanding the Boys: Issues of Behaviour and Achievement*. London: Falmer.

Heilbrun, C. G. (1988) *Writing a Woman's Life*. New York: W. W. Norton.

Hoare, Q. (1991) *Letters to Sartre*, trans. and ed. Quintin Hoare. London: Radius.

Hoff Sommers, C. (2000) *The War Against Boys: How Misguided Feminism is Harming Our Young Men*. New York and London: Simon & Schuster.

Holdstock, L. (1998) 'The ratio of male to female undergraduates', in Radford, J. (ed.) *Gender and Choice in Education and Occupation*. London and New York: Routledge.

hooks, b. (1987) 'Feminism: a movement to end sexist oppression', in Phillips, A. (ed.) *Feminism and Equality*. Oxford: Blackwell.

Hudson, W. D. (ed.) (1969) *The Is–Ought Question: A Collection of Papers on the Central Problem in Moral Philosophy*. London: Macmillan.

Hyde, J. S. (1986) 'Gender differences in aggression', in Hyde, J. S. and Linn, M. C. (eds) *The Psychology of Gender: Advances Through Meta-analysis*. Baltimore, MD: The Johns Hopkins University Press.

Hyde, J. S. (1996) 'What are the gender differences? What are the gender similarities?', in Buss, D. M. and Malamuth, N. M. (eds.) *Sex, Power, Conflict: Evolutionary and Feminist Perspective*. New York and Oxford: Oxford University Press.

Hyde, J. S. (1997) 'Gender differences in math performance: not big, not biological', in Walsh, M. R. (ed.) *Women, Men and Gender: Ongoing Debates*. New Haven and London: Yale University Press.

Hyde, J. S. and Linn, M. C. (1988) 'Gender differences in verbal ability: a meta-analysis', *Psychological Bulletin*, 104, 53–69.

Hyde, J. S., Fennema, E. and Lamon, S. J. (1990) 'Gender differences in mathematics performance: a meta-analysis', *Psychological Bulletin*, 107, 139–55.

Ingram, M. (2001) 'Should a mother report on a war? Viewpoint', *The Times 2*, 12 October, p. 7.

Irwin, K. (1992) 'Becoming an academic: contradictions and dilemmas of a Maori feminist', in Middleton, S. and Jones, A. (eds) *Women and Education in Aotearoa 2*. Wellington: Bridget Williams Books (Ch. 4).

Jacklin, C. N. (1989) 'Female and male: issues of gender', *American Psychologist*, 44, 127–33.

Jacobs J. E. and Eccles, J. S. (1992) 'The impact of mothers' gender-role stereotypic beliefs on mothers' and children's ability perceptions', *Journal of Personality and Social Psychology*, 63, 932–44.

Jaggar, A. M. (1983) *Feminist Politics and Human Nature*. Brighton, UK: The Harvester Press.

James, T. W. and Kimura, D. (1997) 'Sex differences in remembering the locations of objects in an array: location-shifts versus local exchanges', *Evolution and Human Behavior*, 18, 155–63.

Jensen, A. (1998) *The G-Factor: The Science of Mental Ability*. New York: Praeger.

Johnson, B. (2001) 'What Islamic terrorists are really afraid of is women', the *Daily Telegraph*, 27 September, The Thursday Column.

Jones, A. and Jacka, S. (1995) 'Discourse of disadvantage: girls' school achievement', *New Zealand Journal of Educational Studies*, 30(2), 165–75.

Kenrick, D. T., Sadalla, E. K., Groth, G. and Trost, M. R. (1990) 'Evolution, traits, and the stages of human courtship: qualifying the parental investment model', *Journal of Personality*, 58, 97–116.

Kenrick, D. T., Keefe, R. C., Gabrielidis, C. and Cornelius, J. S. (1996a) 'Adolescents' age preferences for dating partners: support for an evolutionary model of life-history strategies', *Child Development*, 67, 1499–511.

Kenrick, D. T., Trost, M. R. and Sheets, V. L. (1996b) 'Power, harassment, and trophy mates: the feminist advantages of an evolutionary perspective', in Buss, D. M. and Malamuth, N. M. (eds) *Sex, Power, Conflict: Evolutionary and Feminist Perspective*. New York and Oxford: Oxford University Press.

Kenway, J. (1993) 'Non-traditional pathways: are they the way to the future?', in Blackmore, J. and Kenway, J. (eds) *Gender Matters in Educational Administration and Policy: A Feminist Introduction*. London: Falmer.

Kenway, J. and Willis, S. with Blackmore, J. and Rennie, L. (1998) *Answering Back: Girls, Boys and Feminism in Schools*. London and New York: Routledge.

Krauthammer, C. (2000) *The Washington Post*, 12 May. A47.

Lasch, C. (1977) *Haven in a Heartless World: The Family Besieged*. New York: Basic Books.

Lee, V. E., Croninger, R. G., Linn, E. and Chen, X. (1996) 'The culture of sexual harassment in secondary schools', *American Educational Research Journal*, 33(2) 383–417.

Leighton, J. (1975) *Simone de Beauvoir on Woman*. London: Associated University Press.

Lever, J. (1976) 'Sex differences in the games children play', *Social Problems*, 23 (4), 478–87.

Lyndon, N. (1982) *No More Sex War: The Failures of Feminism*. London: Sinclair-Stevenson.

Lytton, H. and Romney, D. M. (1991) 'Parents' differential socialization of boys and girls: a meta-analysis', *Psychological Bulletin*, 109, 267–96.

McBurney, D. H., Gaulin, S. J. C., Devineni, T. and Adams, C. (1997) 'Superior spatial memory of women: stronger evidence for the gathering hypothesis', *Evolution and Human Behavior*, 18, 165–74.

McDonald, G. (1992) 'Are girls smarter than boys?', in Middleton, S. and Jones, A. (eds) *Women and Education in Aotearoa 2*. Wellington: Bridget Williams Books.

McKenna, E. P. (1997) *When Work Doesn't Work Anymore: Women, Work and Identity*. New York: Delta Books.

Malik, K. (2000) *Man, Beast and Zombie: What Science Can and Cannot Tell Us About Human Nature*. London: Weidenfeld & Nicolson.

Maccoby, E. E. (1996) *The Development of Sex Differences*. Stanford, CA: Stanford University Press.

Maccoby, E. E. and Jacklin, C. N. (1974) *The Psychology of Sex Differences*. Stanford, CA: Stanford University Press.

Marks, J. (2001) *Girls Know Better: Educational Attainment of Boys and Girls*. London: Civitas (The Institute for the Study of Civil Society).

Martell, R. F., Lane D. M. and Willis, C. E. (1995) 'Male–female differences: a computer simulation', *American Pscyhologist*, 51, 157–8.

Masters, M. S. and Sanders, B. (1993) 'Is the gender difference in mental reotation disappearing?', *Behavior Genetics*, 23, 337–41.

May, H. (1992) 'Learning though play: women, progressivism and early childhood education, 1920s-1950s', in Middleton, S. and Jones, A. (eds) *Women and Education in Aotearoa 2*. Wellington: Bridget Williams Books.

May, L., Strikweda, R. and Hopkins, P. D. (eds) (1996) 'Introduction', in *Rethinking Masculinity: Philosophical Explorations in Light of Feminism* (2nd edn). London: Rowman & Littlefield.

Mead, M. ([1949] 1950) *Male and Female: A Study of the Sexes in a Changing World*. London: Victor Gollancz.

Middleton, S. (1990) 'Women, equality and equity in liberal educational policies 1945–1988: a feminist critique', in Middleton, S., Codd, J. and Jones, A. (eds) *New Zealand Education Policy Today*. Wellington, NZ: Allen & Unwin.

Middleton, S. (1992) 'Gender equity and school charters: some theoretical and political questions for the 1990s', in Middleton, S. and Jones, A. (eds) *Women and Education in Aotearoa 2*. Wellington, NZ: Bridget Williams Books (Ch. 1).

Middleton, S. and Jones, A. (eds) (1992) *Women and Education in Aotearoa 2*. Wellington: Bridget Williams Books.

Miller, G. (2000) *The Mating Mind: How Sexual Choice Shaped the Evolution of Human Nature*. London: Heinemann.

Moulik, A. (1996) *The Conquerors*. New Delhi: UBSPD.

National Center for Education Statistics (2000) *Trends in Educational Equity of Girls & Women*. US Department of Education, Office of Educational Research and Improvement, Washington, DC. NCES 2000–30.

Newton, K. (1992) ' "John says a few words, Margaret listens": "Sharing-Time" in the Primary School Classroom?', in Middleton, S. and Jones, A. (eds) *Women and Education in Aotearoa 2*. Wellington, NZ: Bridget Williams Books (Ch. 9).

Oakley, A. (1981) *Subject Women*. Oxford: Martin Robertson.

Ofsted and EOC (1996) *The Gender Divide: Performance Differences Between Boys and Girls at School*. London: HMSO.

O'Keeffe, D. (2000) *Political Correctness and Public Finance*. London: IEA.

O'Neill, A-M. (1990) 'Gender and education: structural inequality for women', in Codd, J., Harker, R. and Nash, R. (eds) *Political Issues in New Zealand Education*. Palmerston North Dunmore Press: (2nd edn).

O'Neill, A-M. (1992) 'The gendered curriculum: homemakers and breadwinners', in McCulloch, G. (ed.) *The School Curriculum in New Zealand: History, Theory, Policy and Practice*. Palmerston North: Dunmore Press.

Paechter, C. (1998) *Educating the Other: Gender, Power and Schooling*. London: Falmer Press.

Pateman, C. (1987) 'Feminist critiques of the public/private dichotomy', in Phillips, A. (ed.) *Feminism and Equality*. Oxford: Blackwell.

Phillips, A. (ed.) (1987) *Feminism and Equality*. Oxford: Blackwell.

Phillips, M. (1999) *The Sex-Change Society: Feminised Britain and the Neutered Male*. London: Social Market Foundation.

Pihama, L. and Mara, D. (1994) 'Gender relations in education', in Coxon, E., Jenkins, K., Marshall, J. and Massey, L. (eds) *The Politics of Learning and Teaching in Aotearoa-New Zealand*. Palmerston North: Dunmore Press.

Pirie, M. (2001) 'How exams are fixed in favour of girls', *The Spectator*, 20 January, 12–14.

Reinisch, J. M. and Sanders, S. A. (1992) 'Prenatal hormonal contributions to sex differences in human cognitive and personality development', in Gerall, A. A., Moltz, H. and Ward, I. I. (eds) *Handbook of Behavioral Neurobiology: Vol. 2: Sexual Differentiation*. New York: Plenum, 221–43.

Reinisch, J. M., Ziemba-Davis, M. and Sanders, S. A. (1991) 'Hormonal contributions to sexually dimorphic behavioural development in humans', *Psychoeneuroendocrinology*, 16, 1-3.

Resnick, S. M. (1993) 'Sex differences in mental rotations: an effect of time limits?', *Brain and Cognition*, 21, 71–9.

Ridley, M. ([1993] 1994) *The Red Queen: Sex and the Evolution of Human Nature*. London: Penguin Books.

Riley, R. W. and and Cantú, N. V., Secretary of Education, US Department of Education and Assistant Secretary, Office for Civil Rights (1997) *Title IX: 25 Years of Progress*, June, www.ed.gov/pubs/TitleIX

Rimm, S. with Rimm Kaufman, S. and Rimm, H. (1999) *See Jane Win: The Rimm Report on How 1,000 Girls Became SUCCESSFUL Women*. New York: Crown.

Rose, H. and Rose, S. (eds) (2000a) *Alas, Poor Darwin: Arguments Against Evolutionary Psychology*. London: Jonathan Cape.

Rose, H. and Rose, S. (2000b) 'Introduction', in Rose, H. and Rose, S. (eds) *Alas, Poor Darwin: Arguments Against Evolutionary Psychology*. London: Jonathan Cape.

Rose, S. (2000) 'Escaping evolutionary psychology', in Rose, H. and Rose, S. (eds) *Alas, Poor Darwin: Arguments Against Evolutionary Psychology*. London: Jonathan Cape.

Scruton, R. (1986) *Sexual Desire*. London: Weidenfeld & Nicolson.

Scruton, R. (1999) 'Modern manhood', *City Journal*, 9(4), 80–8.

Sells, L. W. (1978) 'Mathematics – a critical filter', *Science Teacher*, 45, 28–9.

Silverman, I. and Eals, M. (1992) 'Sex differences in spatial abilities: evolutionary theory and data', in Barkow, H. J., Cosmides, L. and Tooby, J. (eds) *The Adapted Mind: Evolutionary Psychology and the Generation of Culture*. New York: Oxford University Press.

Silverman, I. and Phillips, K. (1998) 'The evolutionary psychology of spatial sex differences', in Crawford, C. and Krebs, D. L. (eds) *Handbook of Evolutionary Psychology*. Mahwah, NJ: Erlbaum (595–612).

Skelton, C. (2001) *Schooling the Boys: Masculinities and Primary Education*. Buckingham and Philadelphia: Open University Press.

Skinner, P. H. and Shelton, R. L. (1985) *Speech, Language and Hearing: Normal Processes and Disorders* (2nd edn). New York: Wiley.

Sober, E. and Wilson, D. S. (1998) *Unto Others: The Evolution and Psychology of Unselfish Behaviour*. Cambridge, MA: Harvard University Press.

Stern, M. and Karraker, M. K. (1989) 'Sex stereotyping of infants: a review of gender labeling studies', *Sex Roles*, 20, 501–22.

Stufflebeam, R. (1996) 'Behavior, biology, and the brain: addressing feminist worries about research into sex differences', in May, L., Strikweda, R. and Hopkins, P. D. (eds) *Rethinking Masculinity: Philosophical Explorations in Light of Feminism* (2nd edn). London: Rowman & Littlefield.

Sutaria, S. D. (1985) *Specific Learning Disabilities: Nature and Needs*. Springfield, IL: Thomas.

Symons, D. (1979) *The Evolution of Human Sexuality*. New York: Oxford University Press.

Symons, D. (1992) 'On the use and misuses of Darwinism in the study of human behaviour', in Barkow, J. H., Cosmides, L. and Tooby, J. (eds) *The Adapted Mind: Evolutionary Psychology and the Generation of Culture*. New York: Oxford University Press.

Tannen, D. (1991) *You Just Don't Understand: Women and Men in Conversation*. London: Virago Press.

Tiger, L. and Shepher, J. (1975) *Women in the Kibbutz*. New York: Harcourt Brace.

Tobias, S. (1978, 1993) *Overcoming Math Anxiety*. New York: Norton.

Tooby, J. and Cosmides, L. (1992) 'The psychological foundations of culture', in Barkow, J. H., Cosmides, L. and Tooby, J. (eds) *The Adapted Mind: Evolutionary Pychology and the Generation of Culture*. New York: Oxford University Press.

Tooby J. and DeVore, I. (1987) 'The reconstruction of hominid behavioural evolution through strategic modelling', in Kinzey, W. G. (ed.) *The Evolution of Human Behaviour*. New York: State University of New York Press (183–237).

Tooley, J. (2000) *Reclaiming Education*. London: Continuum.

Tooley, J. with Darby, D. (1998) *Educational Research: A Critique*. London: Ofsted.

Trivers, R. L. (1972) 'Parental investment and sexual selection', in Campbell, B. (ed.) *Sexual Selection and the Descent of Man*. Chicago, IL: Aldine-Atherton, (136–79).

Unger, R. and Crawford, M. (1996) *Women and Gender: A Feminist Psychology*. New York: McGraw-Hill.

Voyer, D., Voyer, S. and Bryden, M. P. (1995) 'Magnitude of sex differences in spatial abilities: a meta-analysis and consideration of critical variables', *Psychological Bulletin*, 117, 250–70.

Walsh, M. R. (ed.) (1997) *Women, Men and Gender: Ongoing Debates*. New Haven, CT, and London: Yale University Press.

Weiner, G. (1994) *Feminisms in Education: An Introduction*. Buckingham and Philadelphia: Open University Press.

West, M. M. and Konner, M. J. (1976) 'The role of father: an anthropological perspective', in Lamb, M. E. (ed.) *The Role of the Father in Child Development*. New York: Wiley (185–217).

Whitehead, B. D. (1999) 'The plight of the high-status woman: recent fiction, essays, and self-help books suggest that a harsh new mating system is emerging', *Atlantic Monthly*, 284(6), 284–90.

Whiting, B. B. and Edwards, C. P. (1988) *Children of Different Worlds: The Formation of Social Behavior*. Cambridge, MA: Harvard University Press.

Whiting, B. B. and Whiting, J. W. M. (1975) *Children of Six Cultures: a Psychocultural Analysis*. Cambridge MA: Harvard University Press.

Whyte, J., Deem, R., Kant, L. and Cruickshank, M. (1985) *Girl-friendly Schooling*. London: Routledge (reprinted 1989, 1992).

Willingham, W. V. and Cole, N. S. (1997) *Gender and Fair Assessment*. Hillsdale, NJ: Erlbaum.

Wolf, N. (1990) *The Beauty Myth*. London: Vintage.

Wolf, N. (2001) *Misconceptions: Truth, Lies and the Unexpected on the Journey to Motherhood*. London: Chatto & Windus.

Wright, R. (1994) *The Moral Animal: Evolutionary Psychology and Everyday Life*. New York: Pantheon Books.

Yee, D. K. and Eccles, J. S. (1988) 'Parent perceptions and attributions for children's math achievement', *Sex Roles*, 19, 317–33.

Index

INDEX

INDEX

INDEX

INDEX

INDEX

James Tooley is professor of education policy at

the University of Newcastle upon Tyne, and

author of *Reclaiming Education* and *The Global*

Education Industry. He writes frequently for the

London *Times*, the *Guardian*, the *New Statesman*,

and other newspapers and periodicals.

He lives in England.